Rothschild Buildings

History Workshop Series

General Editor
Raphael Samuel, *Ruskin College, Oxford*

Already published
Village Life and Labour
Miners, Quarrymen and Saltworkers

In the press
Childhood (2 vols)

Routledge & Kegan Paul
London, Boston and Henley

Jerry White

Rothschild Buildings

*Life in an
East End tenement block
1887–1920*

Foreword by
Raphael Samuel

First published in 1980
by Routledge & Kegan Paul Ltd
39 Store Street, London WC1E 7DD,
Broadway House, Newtown Road,
Henley-on-Thames, Oxon RG9 1EN and
9 Park Street, Boston, Mass. 02108, USA
Set in Photoset Bembo 11 on 12pt by
Rowland Phototypesetting Ltd, Bury St Edmunds, Suffolk
and printed in Great Britain by
St Edmundsbury Press, Bury St Edmunds, Suffolk

British Library Cataloguing in Publication Data

White, Jerry

Rothschild Buildings. – (History workshop).
1. Jews in London – Social life and customs
2. London. Rothschild Buildings
3. Spitalfields, London
I. Title   II. Series
942.1'5   DS135.E55L6   80-40495

ISBN 0 7100 0429 X
ISBN 0 7100 0603 9 Pbk

Contents

Illustrations

Plates

between pages 142 and 143

Maps

Figures

Foreword
by Raphael Samuel

London is peopled by minorities, and though the property developers and the comprehensive clearance schemes are rapidly dispersing them, their residues can still be identified by the wide-awake. 'Little Italy' may have migrated from the narrow, sloping streets of Clerkenwell, but 'San Pietro', 'the Italian Church' still stands as a Neapolitan landmark in Clerkenwell Rd; the 'Garibaldi' restaurant in Laystall St has long since been converted into a barber's, but a fading bas-relief to 'Joseph Mazzini, the Liberator' still testifies to its convivial past when, in an atmosphere thick with the fumes of soup and tobacco, and under walls lined with prints of the Risorgimento, it served as a second home for the more republican of the local inhabitants. The High Germans have long since departed from Whitechapel, and so have the Prussian sailors who had their haunt in Bluegate Fields, but there is still a German cemetery in Whitechapel to commemorate them.

The Jews, who are still, arguably, the largest of the London minorities, appear on the face of it to have retained more of their original character than other ethnic groups. Yet, as Jerry White's study shows, they have been transformed almost out of recognition. The people who are the subject of this book were artisans and proletarians, speaking a foreign tongue, and crammed into a ghetto. They carried vivid memories of the persecutions from which many of them had fled, yet they were passionately attached to Russia, and followed the progress of the Revolution in 1905 with enthusiasm. Today, Jews in London characteristically follow businesses and professions rather than trades. They live in the outer suburbs. Their theatre and their literature has vanished, along with the speaking of Yiddish. Their politics are no longer typically anarchist, Bundist or socialist, but as

Liberal or Conservative as their neighbours'. Jewish gang-
sters, like 'Darky the Coon', have disappeared, along with
Jewish boxers, such as Kid Lewis or Cockney Cohen, Jewish
gaming houses, such as the 'spielers' of Whitechapel Rd. . . .
Only the Wentworth St market remains as a token of this
community's former vitality, but it is largely supported by
Sunday morning immigrants; the people themselves have
gone away. . . .

Jewish history in Britain, in so far as it exists, is heavily
institutional in bias, and entirely celebratory in tone, recording the progress of the 'community' in terms of political
status and professional and commercial success. Jerry
White's book is written from a rather different vantage point.
For one thing he writes as a committed socialist – he sees his
subjects in the first place as artisans and proletarians – or
grown ups and children – husbands and wives – rather than
as Jews. He is also writing as an Englishman rather than as a
Jew writing about his co-religionists, and this gives him very
different perspectives, though, interestingly enough, he has
produced a much more vivid account of Jewish life than
Anglo-Jewry's recognised historical chroniclers.

His book is an important contribution to Anglo-Jewish
history, indeed it is the first systematic account of community life focusing not on the synagogue but on the workplace, the street and the home. But it is also of great importance for English social history as a whole. Historians have
long since recognised that in the city every stone can tell a
story, just as in the countryside there is a history in every
hedge. What Jerry White has shown is that every street – if
historians were able imaginatively to reconstitute it – could
be the subject of a book. Using both oral testimony and a
wide range of printed and manuscript sources he has been able
to produce a full-length study of one block of buildings in a
single epoch of its life (roughly from 1890 to 1925). In the
process he does not only bring the past to life, he also
subjects it to critical, if sympathetic, understanding, showing
the very contradictory pressures to which neighbourly relations were subjected, and exposing the notion of 'community' to critical appraisal.

Jerry White is a self-made historian. His only professional

qualifications for writing this book are a failure to get 'A' level history. The book is a labour of love. It was conceived, some five years ago, when as a housing officer he saw Charlotte de Rothschild Buildings just before they were demolished. He was seized with the barrack-like severity of the courtyards, the cliffs of landings with iron railings, and set about systematically peopling them with faces from the past, in the first place by tracing the earliest inhabitants – those who survived – then by following the newspaper and manuscript record of the Buildings. This was work which he conceived alone, with neither publication nor academic preferment in mind. He has now carried it through to a fine conclusion.

Introduction

Rothschild Buildings first seized hold of my imagination one Sunday morning in November 1971. I had been walking round Spitalfields when I wandered into the courtyard of the Buildings through one of the Flower and Dean St staircases. At that time they were approaching the end of a long decline and were partly empty. I had never seen tenements so oppressive, so starkly repulsive, so much without one redeeming feature. The view from the inside of the courtyard gave me an almost physical sense of shock.

The image of that courtyard has stayed with me ever since. It was there when I decided, more than a year later, that I had to find out why they had been built. That was easy. There were plenty of books about the period, about the pressures which led to buildings like that being put up, about Jewish immigration to the East End of London, about the history of housing (or one part of it). The courtyard was there, haunting me, when I discovered these easy answers were so unsatisfying. Surely the most important questions were not who had built them but who had lived in them and how; not to see them as 'housing' but as homes; not to look at the Buildings as I had that morning but to look at them through the eyes of the first tenants.

So I set out to find the people who had lived there. I wrote to the local press and the *Jewish Chronicle* (my reading had told me that the first tenants were Jewish immigrants) and later I visited old people's clubs. There was a good response and I made my first forays with a tape recorder.

But somehow the courtyard, at the same time as the people I was talking to were throwing light into its half-hidden corners, seemed less important. The books had not written about this sort of thing and for me 'history' was embalmed in and defined by these books. My respect for them grew at the expense of Rothschild Buildings. I think it was the footnotes, those meticulous certificates of learning, which most corrupted me and hid the courtyard below a crazy paving of 'op. cit.' and 'ibid.' and 'PP 1871, XXVII, p. 10'. When I found a book on Jewish immigration with 215 pages of text and 70 of notes my admiration knew no bounds. And so I set out to gather footnotes, not interviews, and turned my attention to the Victorian social policies which had laid waste those parts of Flower and Dean St, Keate St and the rest to make way for tenement blocks like Rothschild Buildings.

It was on another Sunday morning, in June 1975, that the crazy paving was rudely hacked up by someone, himself no mean deployer of footnotes, who showed me that my original instincts had been right and that the most important questions I'd asked could not be answered by looking in books or even among dusty files. I set out again with my tape recorder and newly liberated convictions. This is the result.

It will be apparent that my respect for footnotes, representing the use of documentary sources, has not been wholly overcome, and I think rightly. This may be primarily a work of oral history but documents have played a large part in its conception. Written sources and oral sources interact throughout: finding a new document has led me to ask different questions of the people I interviewed, and the oral testimony has thrown fresh light on the documents. The rules printed on the first tenants' rentbooks led me to ask if they were obeyed and how; finding the original plans of the Buildings made me wonder what was kept in the fitted cupboard behind the living-room door; people's memories of shopping led me to take street directories with a large pinch of salt; autobiographical details cast doubts on census classifications, sociologists' assumptions and standard historical reference works, and so on.

But in a study like this, documents at best can play only a subsidiary role, a skeleton perhaps, but even then a skeleton itself partly shaped by the material it has to support. To have written *Rothschild Buildings* using only documents would have revealed insights but no answers, led up many blind alleys and left every other paragraph ending in a question-mark. The records of the dwellings company which put the Buildings up are certainly not worthless by themselves: they record the building process, the rules made, rents charged, even the occupations of tenants. The school log books, unfortunately incomplete for the local County Council school, give insights into the way the school was run which oral evidence cannot systematically provide. Official reports and statistics are invaluable in providing the quantitative evidence beyond the ken of individual memory. Books and newspapers, although rarely referring specifically to the people of Rothschild Buildings, are instrumental in placing them within a historical context.

Yet at the end of it all the people would be missing. Bricks and mortar, rules and regulations, employment classifications, classrooms and streets – and no one to put in them. The courtyard of Rothschild Buildings would have still appeared to me as it had done on that November morning, through the eyes of a half-seeing outsider, as empty and grey. By talking to people who had lived there the canvas was filled and the palette rich with colour.

Between November 1973 and May 1977 I interviewed twenty-two people who had lived in Rothschild Buildings. I have drawn most extensively on the oral testimony of sixteen of these, and a note of their backgrounds is given in Appendix 1. The secondary oral sources are taken from the remaining six people who lived there before the Second World War but after the period which is the main concern of the text, along with some other interviews with people who lived in Flower and Dean St before the First World War but not in the Buildings, the leader of a Jewish girls' club from the same period, and a discussion group in a Stepney old people's club. References to oral sources identify the person interviewed by a code letter (which refers to Appendix 1), the tape number and page of the transcript. Tapes and transcripts will be lodged at the Tower Hamlets Local History Library for future reference.

I have tried to recapture all aspects of life in Rothschild Buildings but, inevitably, the oral and documentary material has been shaped in a way which reflects my preoccupations as a historian. I hope that this has not been at the expense of the material itself as, indeed, many of those preoccupations arose during the course of its collection. Where it led I was happy to follow. But in the course of writing up and moulding it into a

form fit for public consumption certain decisions have been
taken or assumptions made. The most important of these has
been for me to look at Rothschild Buildings as a working-class
community which happened to be Jewish. This, some will
think, has turned the thing on its head. It has meant that, for
example, religious life has received briefer treatment than in
any of the existing histories of Jewish immigrants in England
– this is not by way of apology as I think it fairly reflects the
concerns of the people I interviewed – whereas I have paid
greater attention than others to class control and class tensions
in home and school and workplace.

Second, I have chosen to concentrate on the period from the
opening of the Buildings to the end of the First World War.
This has enabled me to draw in detail the life of the Buildings
during their formative years – from the arrival of new immigrants to the first working years of their English-speaking
children. To have projected the study forward in time, into the
political anxieties of the 1930s, the war and eventual dislocation would have been to have written two books, or to
forego the indulgence of the inch-by-inch reconstruction I
found so fascinating.

The structure of the book is simple, but even this choice has
its disadvantages. The first chapter briefly answers the first
question I asked myself about the Buildings – why were they
built? Life in the Buildings is then divided into five large
sections, separated by subject rather than time, a technique
which tends to understate change or makes it difficult to
discern. The first is on home life, how the Buildings were used
by the people who lived there and how the people who built
them wanted them to be used. The second examines the
community in terms of the pressures which held it together
and simultaneously threatened to pull it apart. The third
analyses relationships between the respectable Jewish artisan
class of the Buildings and the decidedly unrespectable Gentile
casual labouring poor at the other end of Flower and Dean St.
The next describes growing up in the Buildings and the lives
and culture of children – who consistently outnumbered
adults there in the early years. This leads into the fifth section
on work, examining individual work experience around the
time of the First World War.

Finally, there is a chapter on politics and class in the Buildings leading to a wider and more exploratory discussion of trends within the Jewish proletariat. These six aspects of life in the Buildings are not separate compartments. There is an interaction between all of them, and themes which transcend any convenient structure which I have tried to impose.

Acknowledgments

My thanks must first go to those who have made the whole thing possible, the sixteen ex-residents of Rothschild Buildings whose words and experiences I've drawn on so much: Mrs Jenny Billis, Mr Jack Brahms, Mrs Eva Cohen, Mrs Fay Cohen, Mr Daniel Davis, Miss Jane Judelson, Mrs Annie Kushner, the late Mr Reuben Landsman, Mrs Minnie Lane, the late Mrs Ray Lipson, Mr Mick Mindel, Miss Freda Reuben, Mrs Bessy Ruben, Mrs Silver, Mrs Becky Weinbaum, and one other lady. Mr Lawton and Mr K. D. Rubens of the Industrial Dwellings Society (1885) Ltd kindly gave me access to the company's early records and permission to reproduce the posters and rules. I would like to thank the staff of several institutions for their tolerance and assistance, in particular the Tower Hamlets Local History Library, Jews' College, the Guildhall Library, the British Museum Newspaper Library, the Mocatta Library, the Greater London Record Office, the Jewish Welfare Board, and Dowton & Hurst Ltd (for access to the original plans of the Buildings). Miss May Maccoby has given me constant encouragement and much information concerning her grandfather. One person has influenced the making of this book more than any other and that is Raphael Samuel, to whom I referred obliquely a page or so ago; my debt to him is such that *Rothschild Buildings* would not have been written without him. Three others read the book in draft and made invaluable comments, and I would like to thank Anna Davin, William J. Fishman and Mick Mindel (again) for taking on the burden. I would like to thank all those many other people who have helped me and whom I do not have space to thank in person. Last of all but most of all, thanks are due to Sandra White who has been an indispensable source of ideas and support. Finally, and in case anyone should think otherwise, I will add the customary assurance that the errors and omissions in this book are all my own work.

I would also like to thank the following people who have kindly given their permission to reproduce the illustrations between pp. 142 and 143: Industrial Dwellings Society (1885) (Plates 4, 5 and Appendix 2); William Heinemann (Plates 6 and 10, from Major W. Evans-Gordon, *The Alien Immigrant in England,* 1903); Mick Mindel (Plates 7, 24, 26, 27 and 28); Hutchinson (Plate 8, from W. O. E. Oesterley, *Walks in Jewry,* 1901); Tower Hamlets Libraries (Plate 9); Greater London Council Photograph Library (Plates 11, 15 and 16) and Greater London Council Map Collection (Map III); Cassell (Plates 12, 13, and 14 from George Sims, *Living London,* 1902); Mrs Bessy Ruben (Plates 17 and 19); Mrs Jenny Billis (Plates 18 and 23); Mrs Minnie Lane (Plate 21); Mrs Landsman (Plate 22); Mr Jack Brahms (Plate 25); and Pitman (Map I, from V. D. Lipman, *Social History of the Jews in England 1850–1950,* 1950); Mrs Freda Compton, executrix of the late Isaac Frankenstein (Plate 20).

1 Two beginnings

Impressions

One evening, in the summer of 1902, Jack London went for a walk through the main streets of the East End. It was part of his exploration of this 'under-world of London',[1] an exploration characteristically full of both insight and blindness which found its way into print as *People of the Abyss* a year later.[2]

> Last night I walked along Commercial Street from Spital-fields to Whitechapel, and still continuing south, down Leman Street to the docks. And as I walked I smiled at the East End papers, which, filled with civic pride, boastfully proclaim that there is nothing the matter with the East End as a living place for men and women.

If, at the beginning of his walk, Jack London had turned into any one of three narrow streets running left out of Commercial St he would have come across some living places which were considered more fit than most for East End men and women.

At that time, much of Flower and Dean St, Thrawl St and Wentworth St (east) was quite new. Twenty years of demolition and rebuilding had produced one of those colonies of model working-class dwellings which were to be found tucked away behind many of the capital's commercial thoroughfares, much as the old slum districts had been before them. This area, though, was unusual. The streets were narrower and the tenements more densely packed here than elsewhere. And they were home to a different population from that which peopled the abyss of Jack London's explorations. If he had turned down, for example, Flower and Dean St on that summer evening, what 'living places' would he have seen?

Inside the narrow entrance, like a slit between the high walls of the Commercial St warehouses on either side, the street widens perceptibly but still not enough to temper the oppressive closeness of the tall tenements to right and left. In front of him the street stretches like a deep valley, ending in another slit at the far end where some older houses close in on each other before letting the cobbles escape into Brick Lane. To the left, reaching six storeys into the sky and eight blocks into the distance, are Nathaniel Dwellings, their red-brick fronts already darkened by ten years' exposure to the London soot. On the right, dominating the street, are the seven cliff-like storeys of Rothschild Buildings, five years blacker and unrelieved by any of the attempts at decoration which adorn the newer flats.

Walking down Flower and Dean St and turning right into Lolesworth St, Rothschild Buildings are still towering over our explorer's right shoulder, casting deep shadow over the newer, more fancy buildings on the other side of the street. And on reaching Thrawl St and heading right for Commercial St, they are still there, higher even than the equally oppressive Lolesworth Buildings which glare at them across the narrow cobbled way. Turning at the brick and terracotta arch which announces the Thrawl St entrance of Rothschild Buildings and looking back the way he came, he can see more buildings. As he had walked down Lolesworth St he had seen yet more in front of him, even facing him in Wentworth St. As far as he can see, which in these streets is not far at all, stretch the tenement blocks which are the new homes for the people of proletarian London.

But as striking as the buildings – even more so, because these are unusual only in their intensity – are the people. In four streets live some 5,000 men, women and children. And to a stranger, like our explorer, this is the most remarkable thing of all because the large majority are foreign immigrants from the Jewish settlements of Eastern Europe. For this part of what Jew and Gentile alike call The Ghetto 'is one of the most un-English spots in the British Isles.'[3]

The people here are different. Some of the men wear long

black gaberdines and black hats, have long beards and ringlets of greased hair hanging over their ears. Even the workmen in normal dress coming home from a day at the bench look somehow foreign in appearance. On the landings of the buildings, sitting out on chairs and enjoying the streets, are women young and old with richly coloured shawls round their heads, calling out to children below or other women in balconies across the street; or watching an intense game of cards between men too old to work; or returning the quizzical stares of our explorer. Around him, from above as well as from all sides comes a babel of noise in a foreign language which sounds like German; or mainly so, because the children talk to each other in English, but with an accent, and some adults speak pure cockney. These, not so foreign-looking, are in a minority. Even the smells are different, the cooking smells from 1,000 rooms locked in the narrow streets, 'a blended and suffocating odour, as of fried onions and burnt bones, dirty clothing and stale fish, decaying vegetables and over-ripe fruit' as Robert Blatchford has described 'the Yiddish country'.[4] The shop windows are adorned with inscriptions in a strange lettering which also catches the eye on a discarded newspaper in the stone gutter. Every London backstreet has children but never has our explorer seen so many as in these streets of tenements; and again they look different, foreign, even though they play the same street games as usual, perhaps better dressed than in other poor districts – bare feet are rarer here. And again, the odd word (perhaps addressed to him!) is in a language the stranger does not understand.

Not all the people of the area are like this, because at the bottom ends of both Flower and Dean St and Thrawl St, where the houses are older and grimier, he can see men and women sitting on the pavements or lounging at the open door of the Frying Pan public house. These *are* the people of East End fable, 'a different race of people', as Jack London himself calls them, ironically in this context; 'short of stature, and of wretched or beer-sodden appearance'.[5] They are not of the area although they live on its edge looking in, crowded out by the foreign tenement-dwellers.

Our explorer leaves with his impressions. Impressions are all that any stranger can take away with him from an area as

Map I   The Jewish East End, 1900

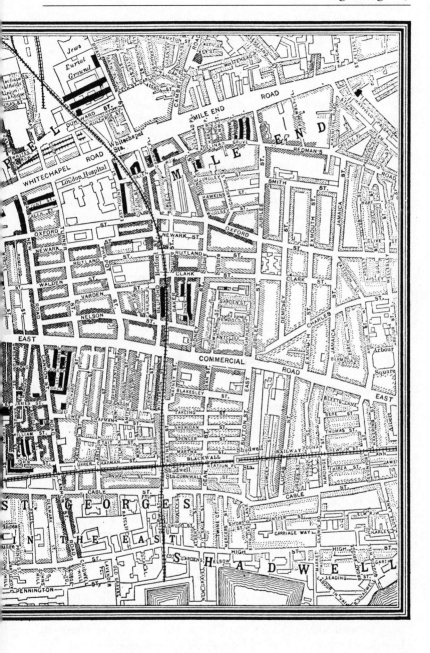

much divorced from his own experience as this. He may record them faithfully, but at the end they are interesting as much for what they tell us about him as about the area he describes. Our task, then, is to enter behind the impressions, behind the walls and landings, shawls and gaberdines which form the outside of Rothschild Buildings and the Flower and Dean St neighbourhood, and which had already, by the time Jack London walked past them, been there for fifteen years.

The story of how Rothschild Buildings came to be as they were in 1902 has not one beginning but two. They are separated by 1,000 miles and cultures a world apart. One begins in the comfortable middle-class drawing rooms of Victorian England; the other in the farms, market towns and cities which housed the Jewish population of Russia in Europe.

The Flower and Dean St rookery

> Within a short distance . . . of the heart and centre of the City of London there has existed for the past fifty years, and still exists and flourishes what is perhaps the foulest and most dangerous street in the whole metropolis.[6]

That was how James Greenwood described Flower and Dean St in one of this journalist's many tirades[7] against the street and its neighbourhood. For in the early 1870s, a decade and a half before Rothschild Buildings were built, that part of Spitalfields was generally recognised as the most menacing working-class area in London. The old Flower and Dean St area was among the last of the London 'rookeries' (see Map II).

The reality of life for the people who lived in the streets laid out by John Flower, Gowen Deane[8] and other local artisans 200 years before need not concern us here. The problems of existence for the unskilled casual labouring class of the Flower and Dean St area and others like it has been fully described elsewhere.[9] But for the middle classes who waged a tireless war against the twenty-seven courts, streets and alleys packed into the 'square quarter of a mile'[10] of the Flower and Dean St neighbourhood, realities of life in the ranks of Victorian London's reserve army of labour were both unimportant and inconvenient. For it was not the reality but the image which provoked church and state into doing battle with sledge-hammers and pick-axes. The real Flower and Dean St problem revolved around casual or seasonal employment, starvation wages, a heartless system of poor relief and brutalising living conditions, but these were far less threatening than the symptoms they spawned. What concerned the middle classes were street crime, prostitution, the threat of revolt, expensive pauperism, infectious disease spreading to respectable London – the whole panoply of shame of this 'boldest blotch on the face'[11] of the capital of the civilised world.

More than anything it was the area's common lodging houses and their roving population which were responsible for its notoriety. There were more common lodging house beds here than in any other quarter in London. Flower and Dean St's thirty-one lodging houses in 1871 housed no fewer than 902 people (the total population of the street was 1,078). One person in three was a young man between 15 and 30 years old. Of the 308 women, 200 were aged between 15 and 40.[12]

The relationship between common lodging houses and crime and prostitution had long been established.[13] Their large shifting populations gave some anonymity to the man or woman wanting to escape the attention of the police. It was said that they were the recruiting places for 'gangs'; they trained children in the skills of crime and vice; they played an important role in the economy of crime, for their keepers were often receivers of stolen property.[14]

Although the area was known as a 'thief-preserve'[15] where pickpockets and thieves of all descriptions could find shelter, it was most notorious for its relationship with street crime.[16]

Flower and Dean Street, Spitalfields, is associated in most people's minds with vice, immorality and crime in their most hideous shapes, and rightly so, for . . . there is no street in any other part of this great Metropolis that has for its inhabitants a like number of the dangerous class. Other streets there are even in its neighbourhood that vie with it in poverty, squalor and vice, but Flower and Dean Street has a character all its own. For to its tenements resort mostly that class of criminals the most daring and the most to be feared

– the men who commit robberies accompanied with acts of violence.

It was largely because of this area that Whitechapel had the highest number of assaults on police in London;[17] and again, Flower and Dean St itself was the most dangerous,[18]

it being useless for the police to follow beyond a certain point, even when they happen to appear on the scene, as the houses communicate with one another, and a man pursued can run in and out, like a rabbit in a warren. Nor is it always safe for the police to venture here alone. Not long ago a member of the force was attacked with an iron crowbar, and he lay for some time in the London Hospital, seriously injured.

The area's relationship with prostitution was just as well established. John Binny, Mayhew's collaborator, and some friends visited the area three times in 1860 or 1861, accompanied by local police officers for safety.[19]

We called at a house in George Street [Lolesworth St], principally occupied by females from 18 to 30 years of age, all prostitutes. In Thrall Street we entered a lodging-house where we saw about thirty persons of both sexes. . . . Here we saw one prostitute, with a remarkably beautiful child on her knee, seated at her afternoon meal. . . . We next went to a brothel in Wentworth Street, kept by a woman, a notorious character. She has been repeatedly in custody for robbing drunken men, and her husband is now in prison for felony. . . . We passed on to Lower Keate Street, and on going into a low lodging-house there we saw a number of young prostitutes, pickpockets and sneaks.

These women were as tough as the men. They were fighting women, with their favourite weapon the hat-pin or the kitchen knife. They, too, would set upon drunken men in the street, beating them up and robbing them.[20]

October 6th [1885] – Disturbance in Fashion Street. Three

women had been knocking about a drunken man, who had a nasty gash on the left eye and was bleeding profusely.

Or they would lure men into the lodging houses where protectors would assault unsuspecting clients, as when a Swedish sailor was robbed of £4 and his trousers by an 18-year-old Flower and Dean St girl and her companions.[21] Small wonder that the district was considered 'one of the most notorious rookeries for infamous characters in the metropolis'.[22]

Such was the Flower and Dean St area by the early 1870s. The challenge to society which areas like Flower and Dean St embodied was complex and operated on many levels. But on any level it was a challenge which shot fear into the very bowels of the Victorian middle classes.[23]

> We fear them for what they are, – beds of pestilence, where the fever is generated which shall be propagated to distant parts of the town, – rendezvous of vice, whose effects we feel in street robberies and deeds of crime, – blots resting upon our national repute for religion and charity. Still they are dangerous, not so much on account of what they are, as what they may be; – they are not only the haunts where pauperism recruits its strength – not only the lurking places, but the *nurseries* of felons. A future generation of thieves is there hatched from the viper's egg, who shall one day astonish London by their monstrous birth.

It was left to James Greenwood to ask, with Old Testament fervour, one angry question.[24]

> Why should these breeding places of disease and vice and all manner of abomination be permitted to cumber the earth?

The Cross Act and demolition

The destruction of the London rookeries occupied more and better minds than Greenwood's. A half-hearted attempt to destroy the Flower and Dean St area had already been made. In the late 1830s the passion for 'ventilating' the criminal slums of the capital stimulated considerable demolition for the next two decades. Wide new roads would be cut through the slums, letting in air, light and police and, most important of all, disturbing the inhabitants from their old haunts. The Spital-fields rookery did not escape. About 1,300 people[25] were evicted from the line of what is now Commercial St, separat-ing Petticoat Lane and Brick Lane and demolishing many notorious courts and alleys. That the road, when built, was useless as a commercial thoroughfare for nearly twenty years because it was not extended far enough northwards was largely irrelevant. Its main purpose had been to displace 'the dangerous classes' and this in part had been done.

But by the early 1870s it was obvious that Commercial St had failed to destroy the rookery. Nor were any of the agencies responsible for social improvement making sufficient impact. The voluntary societies for combating immorality, the police, the poor law and sanitary authorities – all were ineffective in meeting the challenge posed by the Flower and Dean St area. Charity, ideology, religion and coercion had failed to control the rookery. Only its destruction, the removal of its houses, its secret courts and hidden alleys could do away with this menacing threat to middle-class security.

From the time of the Paris Commune onwards, the pressure for a comprehensive redevelopment policy for slum areas grew to invincible proportions. The radical middle classes were united in the move towards reforms which would enable local authorities to deal with areas like Flower and Dean St. Reports were written and released with much publicity;[26] parliament was lobbied;[27] questions were asked by influential reformers on the floor of the House of Commons;[28] respected philanthropists bombarded weighty journals with copy.[29] Such pressure could not go unheeded by the government for long.

On 8 February 1875, Richard Cross, the new Conservative Home Secretary, presented what was later to be the Artizans' and Labourers' Dwellings Improvement Act to parliament. This was no mere housing reform. It was designed to be an answer to the challenge of the criminal slum districts. In advocating the reform, which contained a potentially con-troversial expansion of the state's powers of compulsory purchase, the effects on crime and prostitution in areas which already had similar powers were stressed with the aid of detailed statistics.[30] With such arguments in its favour the Bill provoked almost no opposition, and the Cross Act received the Royal Assent at the end of June 1875.

It had an immediate effect on the East End of London. Its passage through parliament had been watched with keen interest by members of the Whitechapel Board of Guardians, already notorious among the East End casual poor for their ruthless operation of the Poor Laws.[31] The Guardians were solidly representative of the local bourgeoisie. One of their most influential members was the Rev. Samuel Barnett, Rector of St Jude's, Whitechapel, whose parish shared the Flower and Dean St rookery with Christ Church, Spitalfields. He was a zealous reformer and friend of Octavia Hill, who had been an able and articulate propagandist for the new Act. Samuel Barnett knew the Cross Act and the philosophy behind it well. In particular, he knew that under its powers twelve ratepayers could officially represent an area as 'unhealthy' and so demand that it be destroyed.

Just before Christmas 1875, Barnett gave the Guardians advance notice of his intention to bring up the question of having the Flower and Dean St area demolished under the Cross Act. He met with general concurrence. On 25 January 1876, the Whitechapel Board of Guardians, not content with half-measures, formally resolved to represent the whole of the area from Fashion St to Whitechapel High St as an 'unhealthy area'. Eleven days later, Dr John Liddle, the Whitechapel Medical Officer of Health, received an official representation signed by Barnett and sixteen other Guardians, recommending the destruction of an area at that time home to an estimated 4,354 people. All of them would be made homeless if the Guardians' plea were accepted. The representation gave figures for the area's death and sickness rates, and concluded 'That the said Area is fruitful of sickness, misery, pauperism and crime within the Whitechapel Union.'[32]

Dr Liddle was one of the most respected Medical Officers of Health in London. He had already made other representations under the Act and he had been a member of the Committee which had inaugurated these powers back in 1873, so he knew better than most how far he could legally support the Guardians. But the criteria he had to use were based firmly on legal and public health principles. He could not, under the Cross Act, secure the demolition of an immoral or unsavoury area; only one where the houses were not fit to live in. This was a crucial contradiction between the theory of the Act and its practice. For ironically, the common lodging houses – the morally objectionable part of the area's housing stock – were the least likely to be considered unfit for habitation by Dr Liddle. Since 1851 they had been under supervision by the police and although their control was not all that it might have been they still ensured that cleanliness and repair would have been better in the lodging houses than in many other places. The possibility of prosecution by the police and withdrawal of a keeper's licence was a good incentive to maintain minimum standards. There was no such pressure on the slum landlords of Whitechapel who only had two hard-pressed sanitary inspectors to contend with. So the worst properties – in Liddle's terms at least – were the old seventeenth-century tenement houses and the ramshackle wood and brick one- or two-storey cottages of the area's courts and alleys.

This contradiction was to save two-thirds of the Flower and Dean St rookery, and that the most notorious part, from destruction. Liddle removed Fashion St, Thrawl St, half of George St and Wentworth St, and no less than three-quarters of Flower and Dean St itself (among others) from the Guardians' representation when he forwarded it to the Metropolitan Board of Works (MBW) for action.[33]

The MBW didn't need to consider the matter for long. A severe epidemic of typhus fever (news of which reached the Home Office) broke out in Flower and Dean St and it effectively cut discussion short. The Metropolitan Board soon resolved to make an 'Improvement Scheme' for the demolition of a substantial part of the area.[34] Over 1,800 people were to be made homeless, although working-class dwellings were to be built on the cleared land. To effect this the MBW would sell the vacant sites to private companies who would build in accordance with the Board's byelaws. When combined with the clearances in the Goulston St area across Commercial St, this was to be the grandest and costliest slum clearance scheme ever to be carried out by the Metropolitan Board of Works; only at the end of the century were the London County Council to attempt anything as ambitious – in the Boundary St area of Shoreditch. The Improvement Scheme was approved with minor amendments, published and signed by Cross himself on 14 May 1877. It had taken the Guardians more than a year to get so far.

And then – nothing. Nothing was to happen for the next five years. Evictions were delayed largely because the authorities fought shy of creating homelessness in the midst of a trade depression which was hitting the East End particularly hard. Local Improvement Schemes could have put 13,000 people on the streets of East London within a year and the MBW recoiled from the prospect.[35] It was decided that the Flower and Dean St area was to be dealt with later, after schemes submitted earlier had been completed.

After yet further delays demolition in the Flower and Dean St area eventually took place in the autumn of 1883. A quarter of the most notorious street in London was all that was cleared; with it went other places of similar character – Upper and Lower Keate Streets, Keate Court, Wilson's Place, Sugar Loaf Court, Crown Court, New Court, parts of George St, George Yard and Wentworth St. The rookery had not been destroyed but a vital limb had been torn off. About a third of its population had been removed. Many inaccessible courts and alleys had gone, and policing was now easier in the remaining parts. But much of the worst still remained – including the majority of common lodging houses. In practice, the Cross Act had not been able to satisfy the demands of the shopkeepers, employers and clergymen of the Whitechapel Guardians and the Metropolitan Board of Works.

And now other problems arose. The unhealthy parts of the neighbourhood were no more. Empty sites lay between the narrow old streets of the Flower and Dean St area. But who was going to build homes there for the working classes? And how could the authorities be sure that the new dwellings would not be occupied by the same class as the old slums; would not still perpetuate the rookery? The answers to these questions in fact lay 1,000 miles away in Eastern Europe, where events which shattered the Jewish communities of the

Pale of Settlement were to have momentous repercussions on the streets of the East End of London.

The Four Per Cent Industrial Dwellings Co. Ltd

There had been quite a large Jewish population on the borders of the Flower and Dean St area for some years. The 1860s in particular had seen important encroachments on the territory of the English and Irish casual poor. Inkhorn Court, described as 'a fair sample of an Irish colony'[36] in 1861, was almost entirely occupied by Polish Jews ten years later, as was Commercial Place. Dutch Jews dominated Tewkesbury Buildings and Fashion Court. And about half the population of Fashion St and New Court, Spitalfields were Dutch or Polish Jews by 1871. In total they numbered about 1,000 people.[37]

This colonisation had not had a great effect on the Flower and Dean St rookery, although its boundaries had shrunk in response to the pressure from outside. But in the years following the declaration of the Improvement Scheme, the nature of this pressure underwent an immense change. At the same time as the Metropolitan Board of Works were buying up unfit housing in the area, at the same time as the demolition men's carts and waggons were salvaging timber and sound bricks from the ruins, an unparalleled stream of foreign Jews from Eastern Europe were making their way into Whitechapel and Spitalfields.

The assassination of Tsar Alexander II in March 1881 sparked off an eruption of violence against Russian Jewry. The officially inspired pogroms of that year gave way to the May Laws of 1882 which legalised discrimination in business and personal freedom. Jewish emigration from the Pale of Settlement reached a peak that summer.[38] Out of the hundreds of thousands who left Lithuania and the Ukraine, Galicia, Austria, Volhynia and Poland, several thousand immigrants settled close to the eastern borders of the City among their more established co-religionists. They were the harbingers of an influx which was to change the history of the East End.

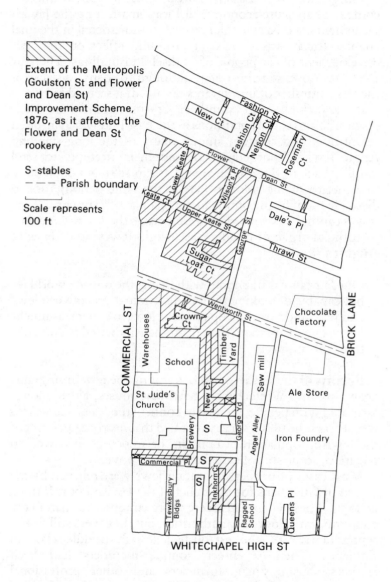

Map II   The Flower and Dean St rookery and the 'unhealthy area', 1876

Emigration from Eastern Europe must be seen within the context of an acute economic dislocation affecting the Jewish settlements, a crisis we shall discuss in more detail in the final chapter for it was to have a profound effect on the later development of the people of Rothschild Buildings. The year 1881 was not a starting-point, although to many, because of the large number of immigrants involved, it seemed to be.

It was these large numbers of immigrants and their economic and social conditions in the East End which inspired resentment and concern among many of the long-standing Anglo-Jewish bourgeoisie. Behind their attempts to send families back to Eastern Europe (2,301 in 1881–5 alone), or on to America or the colonies (881 in the same period),[39] or to dissuade them from coming in the first place,[40] lay a great fear. It was candidly expressed in an editorial in the *Jewish Chronicle,* the official organ of middle-class Anglo-Jewry, as early as 12 August 1881.[41]

> Our fair fame is bound up with theirs; the outside world is not capable of making minute discrimination between Jew and Jew, and forms its opinions of Jews in general as much, *if not more,* from them than from the Anglicised portion of the Community.

Reports of the social conditions among the new immigrants crowding into Whitechapel's tenement houses, already long-saturated with people, seemed to confirm the *Jewish Chronicle's* worst fears. In 1883 a survey revealed that nearly 24 per cent of the Jewish population of London, or 10,000 people, were in receipt of some sort of casual relief from poverty.[42]

Most cases of pauperism among Jews were relieved by the Board of Guardians for the Relief of the Jewish Poor, formed in 1859. These Guardians were more enlightened than many contemporary Poor Law authorities, but they were still firmly representative of the established Jewish middle class in England. Their seventeen founder-members had been lawyers, businessmen, financiers and other professional men.[43] Much of the responsibility for providing for impoverished immigrants would devolve upon them; and indirectly, so would the welfare of middle-class Anglo-Jewry.

To achieve this, the Guardians had to ensure that as far as possible immigrants did not become a charge on the local poor rates but were aided from the 'Community's' own charitable funds. But as the drain on poor relief grew – to the accompaniment of tirades against the immigrants' living conditions – the Guardians were forced to turn their attention to prevention rather than cure.

In early 1884 they set up a Sanitary Committee under the chairmanship of their President. At the Committee's second meeting in May,[44] the head of the 'Royal Family' of Anglo-Jewry[45] accepted an invitation to join them. This was Baron Nathan Mayer Rothschild, soon to be made 1st Lord Rothschild of Tring.

Through 1884 the Sanitary Committee and their full-time sanitary inspector kept up a running battle with the Whitechapel District Board of Works, the local authority for much of the Jewish East End. In October they forwarded a letter – 'a continuous outpour of condemnation and complaint' – to the District Board, inferring incompetence and dereliction of duty. The angered Whitechapel members replied that they had done all in their power but that the local housing problem had 'been greatly intensified by the arrival within the district of a vast number of foreign Jews'. Indeed, the Whitechapel sanitary inspectors were completely occupied in trying to remedy 'the filthy conditions of the rooms, yards and water closets occupied and used by those people'.[46]

With responsibility for the problem passed back firmly to the Jewish community, it appeared that something more was required to achieve a lasting improvement in the dwellings of the immigrant poor, and to ease competition with native workers for house room. Early in 1885 Rothschild was able to reinforce this view when he was appointed Chairman of an East End Enquiry Commission, set up by the influential Council of the United Synagogue.

The Enquiry Commission's Report concluded that the condition of the 'poorer classes of the community' had to be remedied in two ways. First, the immigrants must be Anglicised: 'steps must be taken to cause the foreign poor upon arrival to imbibe notions proper to civilised life in this country.' And second, 'the physical conditions of the poor and their surroundings must be improved.' In fact, as the Report pointed out, the two aims were intimately linked, for new homes 'constitute the greatest of all available means for improving the condition, physical, moral, and social of the Jewish poor.'[47]

> At present, the houses occupied by the Jewish poor . . . are for the most part barely fit, and many utterly unfit, for human habitation. . . . It has become a matter of pressing necessity that healthy homes be provided at such rentals as the poor can pay. It is not suggested or desired that such houses should be erected by eleemosynary aid, but on strictly commercial principles. . . . The Committee believe that if rentals were based on a nett return of 4%, excellent accommodation . . . could be provided at a rental not exceeding five shillings per week.

The Report strongly recommended that a company be at once established to put these policies into effect. The *Jewish Chronicle* carried the Report in full and gave its conclusions unequivocal support.

It was envisaged that any healthy homes for the Jewish poor would be in the form of tenement blocks. They were to become as much a part of working-class life as the slums had been, provided, as the slums before them, by the middle classes – inspired this time by self-interested benevolence rather than vulgar profit.

Large blocks of tenement dwellings had been part of the London street scene since the late 1840s. They were high brick and concrete structures designed to accommodate as many people to the acre as possible in order to utilise fully expensive inner city sites. Generally, they gave accommodation to the skilled worker at rents which could yield a profitable return to the capitalist. Sound commercial principles had to be obeyed and unvarnished philanthropy was frowned upon. And so a reasonable dividend had to be paid to investors but not as much as could be gained from more speculative concerns; the difference between a rack-renting landlord and a 'philanthropist' was perhaps 6 per cent per annum. The boom in dwellings companies in the 1860s and early 1870s was such that by the year of the Cross Act some twenty-eight organisations or individuals had built tenements for nearly 7,000 London families of the artisan class.[48]

The recommendation to establish such a dwellings company for Jewish tenants had been signed by Rothschild, who was its most prestigious supporter in the debate that followed. His interest in housing for the poor perhaps had sentimental (as well as commercial and philanthropic) origins. His mother, Baroness Charlotte de Rothschild, 'a true friend and benefactor to the poor',[49] was reported to have urged on her deathbed in March 1884 that her son devote his energies to improving the housing of Jewish workers.[50] Having made public the aim of a dwellings company to be supported by the whole of the Anglo-Jewish bourgeoisie, he had gone some way to achieving that end. But Rothschild was rich and powerful enough to act alone. And this he did.

On 9 March, six days after the Report had been formally presented to the United Synagogue, there was a meeting at Rothschild's banking house in the City. Rothschild himself was in the chair. Around him were clustered the aristocracy of Anglo-Jewry: Lionel Cohen (President of the Jewish Board of Guardians), F. D. Mocatta (the philanthropic bullion-broker), Claude Montefiore (the wealthy Biblical scholar and philanthropist), Samuel Montagu (later Lord Swaythling, MP for Whitechapel), N. S. Joseph (the future architect of Rothschild Buildings), and fourteen others. After discussing the Report's recommendations they resolved that day to form a building company. It was to be called The Four Per Cent Industrial Dwellings Company. Its capital was to be £40,000 with 1,600 share issues of £25 each producing an annual dividend of 4 per cent. Within four days the *Jewish Chronicle* could report that half that sum had already been privately subscribed.[51]

But this promising financial beginning was to be misleading. Rothschild himself had invested £10,000, a much larger sum than others would risk, and an advertising and fund-raising campaign had soon to be launched. In fact, all the shares were not taken up for another two years, when a loan of £8,000 was granted by the Jews' Free School, another recipient of Rothschild's largesse.[52]

All this was not to distract the Company from its main task.

The first meeting of directors, with Rothschild again in the chair, was held in July 1885. A Memorandum of Association, issued soon after, stated the Company's objectives:[53]

> To provide the industrial classes with more commodious and healthy lodgings and dwellings than those which they now inhabit, giving them the maximum of accommodation for the minimum rent compatible with the yielding of a nett £4 per cent per annum dividend upon the paid-up Capital of the Company.

To achieve this the Company would buy freehold or leasehold land, cleared of buildings or not, and would erect new dwellings. It was thus prepared to take upon itself the role of the Metropolitan Board of Works, if necessary clearing the slums as well as building new homes. This was no idle promise. After Rothschild Buildings had been lived in for five years Flower and Dean St was to feel its effects in a way significant for the history of the rookery.

Charlotte de Rothschild Dwellings

Until the 1890s, philanthropic and semi-philanthropic companies like the Four Per Cent were the sole providers of London's non-speculative working-class housing. The Metropolitan Board of Works were generally forbidden by the Cross Act to build on the sites they had cleared by compulsory powers. Vacant land had to be sold to the dwellings companies, although building control remained in the hands of the Board of Works.

But prospective purchasers were hard to find. The optimism of 1873, when it was believed that clearance would release a fount of goodwill among capitalists and divert funds into dwellings for the poor,[54] had been sadly misplaced. Few companies were in the market at the prices which the MBW, with angry ratepayers at their throats, were forced to charge. Thus it was that one of the largest sites cleared in the Flower and Dean St area remained unsold for nearly two years after clearance, inhabited from time to time by itinerant tinkers and other travellers, much to the vexation of local trades-men.[55]

When the United Synagogue's Commission had recom-mended the formation of a dwellings company they had pointed to this as a suitable site, 'in the heart of the Jewish quarter', and available at that very time for building. It had been previously occupied by the south side of Flower and Dean St (to George St), Wilson's Place, Lower Keate St, the north sides of Keate Court and Upper Keate St, and the east side of George St, and could more truly have been described as being in the heart of the Flower and Dean St rookery. N. S. Joseph, an architect with impeccable Anglo-Jewish connec-tions, had advised the Commission that the site could provide good accommodation for 186 families. When he helped found the Four Per Cent at the meeting of 9 March, it made good sense that the new company should approach the MBW with a view to purchasing the Flower and Dean St site, where a preliminary assessment had already proved satisfactory. If the company were successful in building there, dwellings on this site would significantly expand the boundaries of the Jewish East End.

Again, Rothschild took the first step alone. On 8 May 1885, the MBW agreed to sell the site to him personally,[56] two months before the first formal meeting of the Four Per Cent's directors. The cost was £7,000. Next month Gladstone's dis-solution honours announced that Rothschild was the first professing Jew to be made a Peer of the Realm.

N. S. Joseph worked on his designs for the new dwellings for another five months before they won the approval of the MBW in October. He had submitted plans which originally included provision for workshops in the roof space at attic level. These had been rejected by the MBW but, when the drawings were passed to the Home Office, Joseph was re-quested to reinstate the workshops in January 1886. Other minor amendments were to be made, but eventually the plans received Ministerial consent.[57] Approval of tenders by the Four Per Cent and the Home Office took until June, after which time purchase of the site could actually be completed. To get to the stage where building could commence had taken sixteen months from the beginning of the United Synagogue's enquiry; the Whitechapel Guardians had stimulated clearance of the area ten years before.

The model buildings which N. S. Joseph had designed were to be called Charlotte de Rothschild Dwellings, in memory of Lord Rothschild's mother. The tenants, less grandiose, would know them as Rothschild Buildings. They were two parallel blocks of flats, six storeys high above semi-basements, joined by a narrower block fronting George St (renamed Lolesworth St in 1893). The two main buildings fronted both Flower and Dean St and Thrawl St. Their façades were austere cliffs of yellow brick, relieved at intervals by open staircases; the only attempts at decoration were two courses of red brick between the windows, terracotta keystones to the window arches (their floral patterns soon to be obliterated by grime), and fancy wrought ironwork to staircases and landings. They were built to last. Excavations alone for the reinforced concrete foundations cost £1,000. The superstructure was carefully designed to prevent spread of fire, and so floors were of reinforced concrete on rolled iron joists. External walls and some party walls were one and a half bricks thick. Yet they were also built very much with economy in mind. At each stage of construction costs were kept as low as possible, leading to maintenance problems within the relatively short term.

The parallel buildings were arranged in four blocks each. These blocks were bisected by the open staircase and landings, which also acted as ventilating shaft and light well. From each landing opened four flats, built almost back-to-back but with limited cross-ventilation on to the open staircases. Typically, these were two-roomed dwellings, each with WC and scullery (see Figure 1).

As originally constructed, there were 198 flats arranged as shown in Table 1. Contrary to all previous assurances, it was found that a rent of more than 5s. in most cases was required to give the Company's shareholders their 4 per cent. There were also the thirty workshops in the attics at about 5s. 9d. per week; these, however, proved impossible to let and were soon converted to flats. By 1900 the Buildings could accommodate up to 228 families in 477 rooms, although because of some families renting two flats this figure was rarely if ever

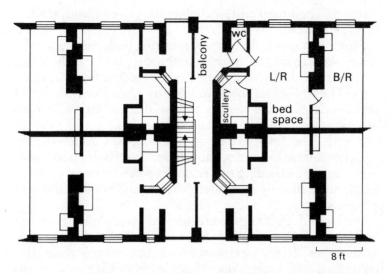

Figure 1   Charlotte de Rothschild Dwellings, 1887. G block, Flower and Dean St, typical floor plan (scale: ½ in. = 8 ft)

TABLE I

Charlotte de Rothschild Dwellings, 1887

No.		Size		Rents
138	of	2 rooms and scullery	@	4s. to 6s. 6d.
17	of	3 rooms and scullery	@	6s. 6d. to 6s. 9d.
5	of	4 rooms and scullery	@	7s. 3d. to 7s. 6d.
10	of	2 rooms and shared scullery	@	5s. 3d.
10	of	3 rooms and shared scullery	@	6s. 3d.
18	of	1 room and shared scullery	@	2s. 3d. to 2s. 6d.
198		415 rooms		

Rent roll: £3,356 12s. p.a.

Source: Four Per Cent Industrial Dwellings Co. Ltd, *First Minute Book,* p. 9.

reached. Their total cost, including the price of land, reached
£40,148 10s. 1d.[58]

From the outside these grim, towering buildings, especially
when seen from the quarter-acre courtyard, starkly stated
their purpose of providing homes for the Victorian working
class. Their function was to provide the maximum number of
sanitary dwellings as cheaply as possible. Ruthless utilitarian-
ism pared away all that was not absolutely necessary to attain
that end. The final results, it appeared, had achieved their
prescribed function and nothing more. But Rothschild Buildings, the ugly offspring of a reluctant paternalism, were to be
much more than their architect, owners and builders had ever
imagined.

Rothschild Buildings were opened on 2 April 1887 and
within a month many flats had been let.[59] The first tenants,
mainly Jewish immigrant workers but among them five
policemen and a clergyman,[60] settled in to their new neighbourhood. As yet, however, there were few real neighbours,
because the area was a mixture of old and new, the new
tenements overlooking the crumbling pantile roofs of the old
lodging houses around them. Events in the first full year of
occupation were to change all that.

Jack the Ripper and the Flower and Dean St neighbourhood

During the autumn of 1888 the first tenants of Rothschild
Buildings were caught up in a world of tense excitement.
During the daytime, the streets around the Buildings were
filled with sightseers, newspapermen and angry locals. Ani-
mated discussion took place in street-corner groups and a
small crowd was often gathered outside the police station in
Commercial St. At night the streets were unnaturally quiet.
Shopkeepers complained that,[61]

Evening business [has] become practically extinct in many
trades, women finding themselves unable to pass through
the streets without an escort.

In their place roamed over fifty vigilante patrols, with men carrying 'police whistles and stout cudgels',[62] and there was a marked increase in the number of police on duty. On the second weekend in September the daytime crowds turned their attention to the local immigrant population. Jews were threatened, abused and assaulted.[63] The authorities feared extensive rioting.

The cause of this anti-Jewish sentiment was the discovery of Jack the Ripper's second victim and the belief that a Jew must be responsible for the outrage – that the murders were 'foreign to the English style in crime'.[64] The people of Whitechapel, 'driven . . . nearly crazy'[65] by these appalling events, gave the East End Jews a difficult time for a few days, after which things returned to normal. But for the first tenants of the Buildings the murders had a special significance. They could not have been closer to the true scene of Jack the Ripper's crimes. For they were near-neighbours of the women who died; some would possibly have known one or more of them, by sight at least. And the murders heralded a period of great change which was to leave its mark on the Flower and Dean St area for the next eighty years.

Jack the Ripper is accredited with the murders of five White-chapel prostitutes in the autumn of 1888. All five were closely acquainted with the Flower and Dean St neighbourhood. Polly Nichols was living at 18 Thrawl St, a registered common lodging house, shortly before she was murdered in Bucks Row (now Durward St) Whitechapel. Immediately prior to her death on 31 August, it was said that she was 'living in Flowery Dean St'.[66] 'Dark Annie' Chapman, murdered in Hanbury St on 8 September, lived at 35 Dorset St but had been well known in lodging houses throughout Spitalfields.[67] Elizabeth Stride, murdered in Berner St on 30 September, was staying in 32 Flower and Dean St (opposite Rothschild Build-ings) where she had lodged 'off and on' for six years. Catherine Eddowes, murdered in Mitre Square on the same night as 'Long Liz' Stride, lived with her common law husband – a market labourer called Kelly – at 55 Flower and Dean St. Eddowes and Kelly had lived in the street for seven years,[68] mainly at Wilkinson's lodging house, and Eddowes's sister lived nearby at 6 Thrawl St. The final victim, Mary Jane Kelly,

was murdered at her home in Miller's Court, Dorset St, on 9
November. For some time before she had lived with a man in
Lolesworth St.[69]

Nothing could have described more eloquently the failure
of slum clearance to destroy the social and moral evils the
Whitechapel Guardians had complained of twelve years before. The existence of such an area, the lifestyle of the five
charwomen-cum-street-sellers-cum-prostitutes, above all the
horrifying mystery surrounding the murders, shook the very
foundations of Victorian middle-class society. 'There is only
one topic today throughout all England',[70] wrote W. T. Stead
in the *Pall Mall Gazette,* and that topic was the Whitechapel
murders. They appeared to crystallise the doubts and fears of
urban society which were beginning to find expression in the
1880s. Reaction ranged through doubt about the social mores
which could produce these awful events; doubt about the
efficacy of religion; fear of revolution and the destruction of
society; an overwhelming feeling of guilt that the conditions
exposed by the victims' inquests should be tolerated 'in what is
boastfully called the capital of the civilised world'.[71] Only a
few conservative journals pleaded that there was little need for
concern as the victims were 'miserable women' who 'preferred
the excess of degradation to entering the workhouse.'[72]

Among the innumerable cures for these ills with which the
leader columns were filled and correspondence pages
bombarded during those few feverish weeks, were practical
solutions for the Spitalfields problem. Besides the pleas for
more clergymen, more policemen, more middle-class 'slum-
mers', more night shelters where poor women could sleep and
laundries where they could work, one theme was consistently
stated. How could housing conditions be improved? And the
most popular means of improvement was not new; the lodging houses must be destroyed and artisans' dwellings put in
their place.

Large-scale redevelopment was Jack the Ripper's most
important legacy to the Flower and Dean St neighbourhood.
In a leading article the *Daily Telegraph* wrung the consciences
of the middle class in a plea for capital to be diverted into
working-class housing. Characteristically, the appeal to
philanthropy was tempered with avarice.[73]

Not only by demolishing slums and rebuilding them should we save all these lives; not only should we protect the community at large from infectious diseases; not only should we go far to extirpate crime and to provide London artisans with plenty of employment; but there is a safe and certain four per cent to be made out of the business – at the very least.

Concurrently with the campaign to clear this 'morally in-sanitary'[74] area aimed specifically at Dwellings Companies like the Four Per Cent – pressure was put on the freeholders themselves to do something about the lodging houses. Their unacceptable profits were seen as disgracing the property-owning class as a whole, and as traitors their feelings were not spared. The campaign culminated in *The Times* calling for their names to be publicly exposed. In November 1888 Canon Barnett commented,[75]

These houses are managed by agents; the landlords are ladies and gentlemen, and the rents ultimately reach their pockets. . . . My hope is that, as they realize that the rents are the profits of vice, they will either themselves take direct action to improve this disgraceful condition of things, or sell their property to those who will undertake its responsibility.

In the face of this considerable pressure, the Henderson family, who had for generations owned much of the freehold land in the Flower and Dean St area, remained silent but probably thoughtful. Certainly, they could have done without the scandal; Kenneth was an army officer, Henry was an active member of the Conservative Club, St James's St, and other members of the family were in the Church.[76] Fortunately for them, the leases and sub-leases with which much of the Flower and Dean St property was encumbered were about to fall in, and as they did so (even before in some cases) the Hendersons offered parcels of their estate for sale.

The bulk of the north side of Flower and Dean St was put on the market probably in 1890. The Four Per Cent, who had by this time completed their second estate of East London dwell-ings in Brady St, Whitechapel, instructed their solicitors to purchase at the negotiated price of £4,500 in January 1891.[77] The site stretched from Tarling's clothing warehouse in Commercial St to 55 Flower and Dean St (where 'Long Liz' Stride had lived), and included some of the tiny houses in Fashion Court. It was to be the future site of Nathaniel Dwellings. To fund this continued expansion, the Company decided to make a further share issue of £40,000, doubling the original subscribed capital of six years before.

At £4,500 the new Flower and Dean St site was the most expensive the Four Per Cent had yet acquired,[78] so that the Henderson family were to the last able to reap a high reward for disposing of the most notorious property in London. Purchase was completed in July 1891 but not without difficulties. When N. S. Joseph sent his assistants to measure the site they were escorted by a Superintendent of Police and two constables to protect them from angry tenants.[79] The 'wretched wanderers of the night'[80] and the casual dock and market labourers with whom they shared the common lodging houses of Flower and Dean St – about 500 people – were evicted in bitterly cold weather around Christmas 1891. As they were being evicted an unknown man died of exposure and starvation on Boxing Day night in Lolesworth St, close to where a few weeks before the lodging houses could have afforded him shelter.[81]

Nathaniel Dwellings (or Nathaniel Buildings as the tenants called them) were completed in 1892. They were six storeys high and eight blocks long – 170 flats in all, accommodating about 800 people. N. S. Joseph had this time wielded his pencil with an eye to a little more decoration than had adorned his first efforts for the Four Per Cent. The façade was less regular than that of Rothschild Buildings, with a mansard roof and shallow bay windows, and the pale red brickwork was broken up by black courses.[82] For the rest of their useful lives, Rothschild and Nathaniel Buildings were to have a special relationship. Kept apart only by mean and narrow Flower and Dean St they were to be close in more ways than one.

Around Rothschild Buildings, the Flower and Dean St neighbourhood continued its transformation in the wake of Jack the Ripper. The only other tenements in the neighbourhood at the time of the murders (excluding the small College

Buildings, built in Wentworth St in 1885 as part of the Toynbee Hall complex) were Lolesworth Buildings. Their 202 flats
faced the Thrawl St blocks of Rothschild Buildings and were
built a little before them by the East End Dwellings Company
Ltd, who had Samuel Barnett as one of their founder-
members. They were poorer flats in terms of the accommodation offered, and the population throughout the early years
had a higher proportion of non-Jewish people than any other
of the neighbourhood's tenements.

Following the murders, the Hendersons immediately
offered for sale a parcel of land on the north side of Wentworth
St, at the rear of Lolesworth Buildings. This, too, was bought
by the East End Dwellings Co. who built Strafford Houses
(four storeys high above shops) there in 1889. But the demo-
litions did not stop with Nathaniel Buildings and Strafford
Houses. In 1893 or 1894, the Henderson family themselves
demolished the houses on a piece of land between Flower and
Dean St and Thrawl St and including the east side of Lolesworth St. The Whitechapel District Board of Works tried to
buy the land and lay it out as a garden but Abraham Davis, a
local speculative builder in philanthropic garb, offered a better
price and erected yet more flats there between 1895 and 1897.[83]
This development of six 'houses', four storeys high over
shops, fronted Flower and Dean St (facing Nathaniel Buildings), Lolesworth St (facing Rothschild Buildings) and
Thrawl St. There were 163 flats in Ruth House, Irene House
and their neighbours, built in red brick with high mansard
roofs.

By the end of 1894 virtually all of the old Flower and Dean
St had been destroyed – all, that is, but three houses on the
north side and five on the south. Three-quarters of Thrawl St
had changed, as had nearly all of Lolesworth St. Wentworth St
was now entirely respectable. The aftermath of the Whitechapel murders thus had major consequences for Rothschild
Buildings. By radically altering the population structure of the
Flower and Dean St neighbourhood, redevelopment gave the
people of the Buildings newer but closer neighbours.

Within six years, then, Jack the Ripper had done more to
destroy the Flower and Dean St rookery than fifty years of
road building, slum clearance and unabated pressure from

police, Poor Law Guardians, vestries and sanitary officers. Yet the response he had provoked varied from those less successful efforts only in its rapidity. It, too, pretended to offer a cure for prostitution and crime by destroying the houses where the 'fallen' and the 'vicious' lived.

Further small-scale redevelopment was carried out in Lolesworth St, facing the severe five-storey façades of Lolesworth Buildings, where Keate House, Spencer House and (round the corner in Wentworth St) Henderson House were built in 1908 by local entrepreneurs. And if not all of the old rookery had been swept away – we shall meet it again! – then it is true to say that by 1897 the area was entirely dominated by the tenement blocks which had leapt up in the previous decade. They *were* the Flower and Dean St neighbourhood for eighty years. And dominating them all in bulk, height, and density of population, sat the 200 or so homes of Rothschild Buildings.

'More like warehouses than homes'[1]

Model dwellings like Rothschild Buildings sharply divided middle-class opinion. At best they were thought to be a necessary evil – the only way of housing a large number in healthy conditions on a small site.[2] Even their greatest advocates, except perhaps Charles Dickens,[3] were defensive about the merits of tenement blocks at a time when they were daily changing the skyline of late Victorian London. When they *were* defended, by the philanthropists and architects who built them, and by the sanitary reformers who campaigned against the slums, it was on grounds removed from the central issue. Tenements, it was said, decreased mortality rates, especially from infectious diseases; they discouraged crime and immorality, and enforced orderly living.[4] The perceived benefits of model dwellings, then, showed largely on the middle-class side of the balance sheet. But how far did they go to meet the needs of the working class, the needs of home, family and community?

Not very far at all, answered the radical and liberal fringes of the middle class. They even attacked the champions of block dwellings on their own ground: mortality rates were low because the people who occupied them were of a different class to the slum dweller;[5] they contributed to the spread of infectious diseases rather than controlled them;[6] disgusting sights were to be seen on the staircases; the blocks were terrorised by roughs.[7] But the main allegation against blocks like Rothschild Buildings was that they were destructive of home life.

'These are not HOMES', spluttered the architect, Robert Williams; 'they entirely rob the beautiful English word of its wonderful charm.'[8] And when George Haw stated unequivocally that, 'Tenements in block dwellings can never be homes',[9] few would have bothered to contradict him. Jack London, who did not have to spend his life in block dwellings, could only imagine what it was like to be so unlucky.[10]

> I stood yesterday in a room in one of the 'Municipal Dwellings'. . . . If I looked into a dreary future and saw that I would have to live in such a room until I died, I should immediately go down, plump into the Thames, and cut the tenancy short. . . .

The monolithic ugliness of these 'towers of Babel'[11] provoked a profound reaction in the minds of many contemporaries. Buildings so large, housing so many people in flats of identical design, hemmed in by rules and wrought-iron railings, would surely destroy one of the very cornerstones of Victorian society. They would become the 'burial-place of the individual man'.[12] The block-dweller had already lost his identity; 'his children are part of a flock, there is no more distinction among them than in a flock of sheep.' This would have frightening repercussions on society as a whole.[13]

> There are great dangers attending the loss of the individual; it tends to destroy ambition, to weaken the power of free thought, to injure the responsibility of self-government. . . .

Thus it was that,[14]

> The cottage has produced great men and women, but forty years of block dwellings have produced no single character of note.

We have still not escaped from such environmental determinism which (as well as mistaking symptoms for causes) conceives of people as unthinking victims of circumstance. Reality, of course, was much more complicated; to approach an understanding we need to find out what the 'victims' themselves made of these 'towers of Babel'.

'We had it very nice'

Home life most commonly had as its framework the two rooms and a kitchen which formed the standard unit of accommodation in Rothschild Buildings. How would such a home have looked to and been used by the families of the immigrant tailors, cabinet makers and other workers who lived there before the end of the First World War? How were these cramped brick and concrete cells actually lived in? The appearance and use of a flat in Rothschild Buildings of course varied from family to family. But there were certain aids or hindrances common to all; and the binding constraints, primarily of space, imposed by the working-class housing problem and the architect of the Four Per Cent affected all 200 or so tenants.

The majority opened the front door of their flat into a tiny entrance lobby. To one side was the door to the lavatory. Directly ahead was the door to the living-room. This main room, or 'parlour' as it was sometimes called, was the centre of home and family life in the buildings. It was of a good size for that period – 17 ft by 12 ft – but it was designed to double as a bedroom at night and this, in almost every case, it did. At one end of the wide room was a rather mean window which overlooked the courtyard of the Buildings or one of the adjacent streets. Only in the upper storeys could daylight reach the other end of the room but this, in many cases, was not of critical importance for that far end formed an alcove designed to take a bed. Otherwise, lighting before the turn of the century was by candle or paraffin lamp, supplemented by the glow from the fireplace which faced the door into the room.

Gas was taken into the flats some time around 1900 and thereafter provided the lighting supply until the mid 1930s. There was one central light in the living room, suspended from the ceiling; its incandescent mantle spluttered through the long winter evenings which drew in unnaturally early in the lower flats.

Light from the gas mantle fell unsteadily on a room furnished according to the means of the family whose home it was. There were certain fixtures which all families had. There was the 'strong Kitchen-range'[15] which faced you as you entered the living-room. It shone black with Zebra Black-lead – 'Make your hands terribly black; there was no gloves then.'[16] To the side of the fire was an oven – used mainly by those too poor to run a gas cooker – and some would even cook on the fire itself, toasting bread of course but also putting smoked herrings 'on top of the coal, without a pan. Come up beautifully.' In front of the range was a brass or iron fender and, if there were toddlers, a large fireguard, always useful for drying 'all the teacloths and towels' constantly in use. Cinders from the fire would be collected, put in a cleaning cloth and used to clean knives and forks as a cheap substitute for a twopenny block of brickdust. But apart from all these uses the fire could be a nuisance; dirty or broken flues let smoke into the rooms, a real problem when ventilation was at the best of times inadequate. The better-off families began to have these ranges taken out at the end of our period. One of the first gas fires went in at No. 101, when the coalman refused to carry coal up to the top floors during the early years of the First World War, leaving women and children to drag the heavy sacks upstairs.[17]

As well as the range, the Four Per Cent provided another fixture in the living-room – a dresser, fitted into an alcove by the window.[18]

'We used to decorate this dresser with that crinkly paper, paste, and make fans all round. It looked so pretty. . . . And that was done before Passover every year.'

China was kept on and in the dresser, with cups hanging on hooks from the shelves and glasses kept in the cupboard below.

Exactly which articles of furniture cluttered the floor of this main room depended entirely on the earning power of the bread winner. In the home economy of the ordinary household, furniture ranked relatively low in priority with so much of the wages taken up in buying food, clothing and warmth. Furniture did not make a home. You bought it slowly, as you could afford it, and in the meantime you made do with what you could. Pleasure would be taken in small things, like the possessions brought from Russia or Austria and prominently displayed in the room, rather than a new suite from Venables'.

Within the Buildings there was a wide range of inequalities; with it went a wide range of possessions and furnishings. At one extreme were the very poor – people like the Kaplans★ at No. 83 (whose sufferings we shall meet with again) who had virtually nothing except each other.[19]

> 'Furniture? . . . One orange box – it was covered with a nice piece of material. We had orange boxes for to eat on. . . . We had three chairs. My younger sister: a boy wanted to take her home, wanted to take her back, so she said, "I can't bring a boy home. We've only got three legs on one chair, where's he gonna sit?" '

The orange-box table, the three chairs, a put-u-up and two beds were all the furniture they had until the children started earning, around 1913.

At the other end of the scale – but only a couple of staircases away – lived a master box-maker and his family at No. 101. Their living room boasted a fine inlaid cabinet for displaying china, photographs, and candlesticks. They also had a piano, the ultimate in status symbols.[20]

> 'Now, we were not rich, but according to some of them we were. I remember, we had a piano. Yes, we had a piano, yes. In the front room we had it very nice.'

Unfortunately, no one in the family played, so one of the daughters was given piano lessons and she practised at home.

> 'Very badly. I was the only one; my parents didn't play. I don't remember how it came about that we got the piano, but it was a *very* great event.'

A more typical home would perhaps have been like that of Mrs Zwart,† one of the Buildings' first tenants, at No. 170, where a widow and her children were saved from the pauper-

★ This is a pseudonym.
† Pronounced Swort.

ism that would normally have been their lot by the personal
benevolence of a wealthy family. They attained a standard of
living which can be accepted as average in most aspects for the
working-class families of Rothschild Buildings, around the
turn of the century.

As well as the black-leaded fireplace and the fussed-over
dresser, they had a chest-of-drawers near the door from the
lobby.[21]

> 'And mother used to put a little bit of lace on the top and put
> all glass and knick-knacks on it . . . you know, cheap glass
> she valued. . . . It used to get cluttered up with it.'

By the side of this chest-of-drawers, which normally would
have done service in a bedroom, was the recess or 'bed-
space'.[22] During the day this was curtained off – 'two screws
put in the wall and a curtain pulled across . . . on a bit of
string'.[23] Behind the curtain was a double bed, which was kept
up during the day; other families, perhaps more commonly,
used one of several forms of put-u-ups which could be folded
away during daylight hours.

In the middle of the room was a plain deal table, scrubbed
white and covered with oilcloth – 'it was very pretty, it was all
flowers.' Around the table and around the walls were plain,
wooden chairs that had to be scrubbed. Everything had to be
scrubbed.[24]

> 'Mother had a lot of chairs. . . . There was one real wooden
> chair with the slats in it . . . and mother was – had
> rheumatism at the time. My brother had the legs cut short
> so that she could sit in it.'

For only in comfortably-off families were there any armchairs
or easychairs.

The remaining pieces of furniture in the living-room at No.
170 were a fancy overmantel above the fireplace and 'a couch
that opened up into a bed. That was underneath the window.'
And a what-not in one corner, which again was a colourful
home to 'all little glasses, you know, pieces of things that
mother wanted.'[25]

A similar inventory of furniture, give or take a piece, would have been common to many a home in Rothschild Buildings. Such possessions as 'sideboards or fancy furniture' came to families, if at all, when children had left school and begun to earn. Next door to the Kaplans at No. 82,[26]

'we had the big sideboard – that's when we grew up and everybody had sideboards so we managed to get one after I went to work, my brother went to work.'

That was some time in the closing years of the First World War.

But at No. 170 there was one notable absence to what most would have considered an attainable standard of comfort. There was no floor covering whatsoever. The 300 square feet of deal boarding in the flat would be scrubbed white so that the grain made beautiful patterns. But that was hard labour which many tried to avoid. And even if, like the Russian baigel-seller next door, you 'didn't trust the bank' and buried your money under the floorboards,[27] that was still no reason to go without lino. Many families just could not afford the expense, like that at No. 82, who had 'Nothing till we started work, till my brother and I started'; but as soon as they *were* working, 'then I remember we bought red lino.'[28]

Yet although this family, the Katchinskys, whose father died just after they moved into Rothschild Buildings, were very poor, they still had possessions which they had brought with them from Russia. Many families brightened their white-washed walls – only the better off could afford wallpaper – with photographs and paintings, and the Katchinskys were no exception. They had photographs of grandparents, aunts, uncles and cousins on the mantelpiece and hanging from nails on every living-room and bedroom wall. They were often large prints, some of them two feet across, in oval, round or square frames, which were enlarged and coloured at a reduced price by a relation who lived near Sidney St.[29] This was not solely a Russian trait. An Austrian presser's family had an equally spectacular exhibition:[30]

'Yeah. Art Gallery! Your grandmother, your grandfather,

hang your father, hang your mother. They had it like an Art
Gallery round the walls.'

Here again the enormous economic differences between
families in the block are evident. For if the Kaplan family had
originally brought with them any of these treasured
mementoes – still kept by some – they would have found
their way to the pawnbroker's – never to be redeemed.

If the attachment to family photographs transcended
national, and to some extent class, differences then so did one
other phenomenon. This was Rothschild Buildings' passion
for window-boxes. Beyond the net curtains, with or without
the Four Per Cent's Venetian blinds which many tenants took
down because they were so difficult to clean,[31] a window-box
gave a coloured border to almost every view. For many Jewish
immigrants, life in England, and tenement block life in particular, was entirely alien to all they had known before. They
had greater difficulties to overcome than problems with space
or washing facilities or beds. From the great farms of the
Ukraine to the closeness of the Edwardian East End was a
shattering change in environment.[32]

'She [my mother-in-law] came from the open villages in
Russia. When she came to the Buildings she thought she was
in Hell after the open life back home.'

As some compensation, this cabinet maker's wife at No. 124
kept window-boxes with extravagant care and affection, and
she spoke to her son of the old ways which had been so
important to her.[33]

'It was so interesting to me, too. Like she showed me a
potato growing – she'd bring it out of the garden box, a
potato, a pea or bean or something – you know, the
growth.'

Nearly everyone had window-boxes. Their tiny splashes of
colour relieved the quickly blackening walls of the bleak
tenements. A photograph of Rothschild Buildings, taken
around 1900 and reproduced in Jack London's *People of the*

Abyss,[34] shows that almost every window in the block had a window-box on the sill. They needed constant attention. Earth would be found in Christ Church gardens, one of the remaining patches in the district not bricked over, and in the streets 'we used to pick up horse's dung to shove in them.' They were a small remembrance of a past that could not be recaptured.

Window-boxes were one of the symbols of a careful, bright home. It was this facet which, inevitably perhaps, was seized upon and taken over by interfering people from outside the Buildings.[35]

> 'My mother [the same Ukrainian peasant woman who showed her son the potato growing] used to win prizes for her flowers in the window-box. I think it must have been the Flower Box Society or something,[36] used to come down and bring her a dress-length or suit-length of cloth as a present because of the nice windows she kept down in the basement'

– as if she would not have kept them nice without the incentive of an organised competition with prizes.

Another reminder of a peasant way of life were the animals which a few families managed to find room for in their flats.[37]

> 'Had a rabbit, chickens. What about the chickens! We had chickens in the flat! I still remember that cockerel standing on the edge of the bed [and crowing]. And a few pullets, she had. When she thought it was time she used to get hold of one of the pullets and put it in the tin bath and cover it up with . . . the scrubbing board until it started clucking, when we knew it had laid.'

This unlikely attachment to husbandry, as well as carrying over a past way of life, helped supplement a poor income by ensuring a small supply of cheap and fresh food. When the chickens stopped laying they would be taken to one of the slaughterhouses off the Lane on Thursday and slaughtered for the Sabbath meal.

Two doors opened out of the living-room. To one side of

the fireplace, nearly facing you as you came in, was the door to the bedroom. In the few cases where there were two or more bedrooms they led directly out of each other. The standard Rothschild Buildings bedroom was a wide but very shallow room, 17 ft by a mere 6 ft 6 in. – 'so narrow that if you put the bed in the width you couldn't go past it.'[38]

At No. 170 the bedroom slept mother and three children. Again, at one end was a mean window. A few feet away from this was a small fireplace, used mainly – if at all – when there was illness in the family (a frequent enough event). It was an inefficient appliance at the best of times, but badly situated as it was most of the heat produced went straight out of the window. Sometimes a more profitable use was found for it. The fireplace[39]

'had like a thing to pull down if you didn't want the soot to come through. And one day mother was very ill and she said to me she had to go into hospital,'

leaving her elder daughter in charge of the housekeeping.

'She said, "Minnie, I've got a little bit of money in," she said, "I've put it up the chimney. And if you put your hand up you'll find it." And I thought, "Oh my goodness, I'm gonna have a find here." And I did, and I got a whole handful of soot, and there was a bag; there was 5s. in it! And she says to me, "Save it till I come back!" Oh I was about 10 years old or 11 years old.'

At that end of the room one daughter slept on an iron single bed. By her slept her younger sister.

'My sister slept near the fireplace, really, on the floor, on a mattress or some – I dunno. She roughed it, she did. Wonder she lived as long as she did.'

The other bed in the room was an iron double bed with a slatted wooden base on which was laid a stuffed mattress with a feather bed on top. This was mother's bed and it was at the end of the room away from, and facing, the window. By her side was a cradle for the baby, so close that she could rock it while lying in bed – 'rocking the children and going to sleep'.[40]

The only other piece of furniture in the room was a chest-of-drawers – with yet more pieces of glassware and cheap ornaments covering it – but further storage space was provided in a small cupboard behind the door. Here mother kept her clothes and[41]

> 'all her papers, you know, all her rent receipts on one of them hooks, all the things she valued in that cupboard.'

Bedroom furniture in other families varied again with means. Some were more fortunate than others. Cabinet makers often had the opportunity to bring home pieces they had made at the workshop. Usually, though, they would have to take a piece in lieu of wages, so it again meant financial sacrifice. The collection of two pieces of bedroom furniture for one family could take several years.[42]

> 'For wages he brought home a dressing table. And that was the first bit of furniture I remember him having.'

That would probably have been about 1912.

> 'And it was during the first war, when we were in No. 4 Nathaniel, and he was a master-man, that we had our first wardrobe. And that's as a master-man, on his own!'

And that was after 1916.

No description of a bedroom in Rothschild Buildings is complete which concentrates merely on possessions. If a visitor to the Buildings had entered a bedroom any time during our period he might have noticed a smell reminiscent of almonds. If he had come on a warm summer's evening he may have found that bedroom empty, its occupants preparing to spend the night on the balcony or in the courtyard.[43] The cause of both may have been the same. In the late 1890s, for example,[44]

'Living downstairs in the basement there was a family called
Binstock. They had eleven children, including two sets of
twins. When it was hot in the summer the husband and wife
used to sit on chairs out in the playground, because they
couldn't sleep with all that crowd of children. It was
hot – and perhaps buggy – and so they slept in the playground.'

Bed-bugs were one of the most important problems of
domestic life in Rothschild Buildings. The people there waged
continuous war against them, but the bugs always won in the
end. Tailors and housewives would face a long day's work
after a sleepless night when the bugs were active. Children
would fall asleep at school because the bugs gave them little
peace at night – 'didn't have any sleep, we used to be up all
night. You couldn't *sleep*.'[45]

Assaults against major infestations of bed-bugs were
launched at least once a year and sometimes more often. Few
people could afford regular purchases of insecticides like
Keating's Powder and they were not very successful anyway.
The popular, but largely ineffective, day-to-day treatment
was to stand the beds in tins of paraffin. The available methods
of fumigation were inefficient and inconvenient.

'Now, my mother used to smoke the place out with sulphur
candles – year in and year out, twice a year she used to. . . .
She used to wait for the warm weather. Before April –
before our holiday – and when the summer had finished.
. . . We used to cut the strips [of paper] up and used to
plaster it round [the doors and windows]. Used to sit
outside. She used to take all the food outside in a shopping
bag, and we used to eat, couldn't get in.'

Smaller families would often fumigate overnight, spending
the time with neighbours and relatives.

'But when we went in there was a pile like this. But Gawd
love us! We had thousands of 'em! And my mother was a
clean woman but you couldn't keep 'em away. They was in

the walls. You couldn't help it. They was under the window
sills, in the cracks in the walls.'

Severe infestations were an embarrassment as well as a
nuisance.

'I always remember – I had a friend up there and they were
crawling up the walls. I didn't know where to put my face.'

When families left Rothschild Buildings the fear of taking
the bugs with them to their new home made important sacrifices necessary.

'But when we came here, my mother left everything there
[except the living room furniture like table, chairs and put-
u-up]. She wouldn't take nothing with her 'cos she said, "If I
take we'll start 'em off here." We just left it and walked out.'

The bugs of Rothschild Buildings were no indication of the
cleanliness of a home, and neither were they tolerant of class
differences. They would often be introduced in second-hand
furniture and could easily travel to neighbouring flats on
people's clothes and perhaps through the half-brick party
walls. As we have seen, once they were established it was very
difficult to control them. In fact, they were probably a spur to
cleanliness rather than otherwise. Rooms would be cleaned
and decorated more frequently in an attempt to make life
tolerable. Flats were normally decorated about every three
years by the porters of the Four Per Cent, but some families
would decorate every year to try and keep the bugs at bay.

The standard of cleanliness in most flats seems to have been
very high. There were, of course, families for whom rigorous
standards were not attainable, in that they had larger problems
to contend with:[46]

'I had a aunt in the Rothschild Buildings, Aunt Bessy, my
father's sister, and she was very *froom* [i.e. orthodox]. Her
eldest son was a cripple, and he used to sit there, like on a
settee where he used to sit there and sleep there and eat there
and everything. It was terrible to go into that place because

he used to do his business in the room – terrible. You used to think twice about going up there. Her husband was a machiner but he was ill, ill for years, as long as I knew him, practically, he was ill. He suffered with his lungs.'

Some very large families, perhaps overwhelmed by the lack of space, also relegated cleanliness to a minor position.[47]

'Of course, there were dirty flats but we avoided those. But can you imagine a family with seven children in two rooms and a kitchen – how *can* you be clean?'

Yet many families, and among them the poorest, were almost fanatically clean. Such families as the Kaplans and their neighbours would not have needed the patronising supervision of the people who organised 'tidy home prizes' for the Jewish immigrants.[48] Floors were scrubbed white, curtains would be washed and changed every Friday, mats shaken out over the balcony and brass cleaned ready for the Sabbath. Generally, it is said that 'the places were kept spotless, though, but spotless',[49] and in spite of the bugs, and within the limits imposed by overcrowding, there is no reason to disbelieve it. One way the Buildings actually helped in achieving this was at least to provide most families with their own scullery – deficient in space, perhaps, but a better standard than could have been expected by many families in the Edwardian East End.

'Not much of a kitchen there at all'

The scullery was entered from the living-room, rather than from a hall or passage. It had only some 40 sq. ft of floor area, and much of that was taken up with fitted amenities of one sort or another. These were a small range – quickly usurped by gas stoves – stone sink 'yellow thing, one [cold] tap, and very shallow',[50] a coal bin, a fitted dresser and a copper. All these left only about 5 ft by 4 ft clear floor space in which cooking, preparing food, laundering and personal washing could take place.

For all their inconvenient use of space, some of these amenities played important parts in the domestic life of Rothschild Buildings. Various uses were found for them; time and effort were put into making them as cheap to run and effective as possible. The copper, for example, was filled by saucepans and heated by a small kiln under the metal lining. Coal was expensive and so pieces of packing cases from Spitalfields market and off-cuts from the cabinet making workshops would be carried home to fuel the copper. A walking-stick maker used to carry waste wood and shavings home by the sackful from his workplace in Crispin St for this purpose.[51] The copper's lid would be turned over to serve as an additional table when it was not in use. Some cabinet makers would also make covers for their coal bins, and these too gave additional surfaces.

Other amenities were not so trouble-free. The Four Per Cent's policy of specifying the minimun costs for each part of the construction of Rothschild Buildings had unfortunate consequences. The WC, entered from the entrance lobby inside the front door to the flat, was fitted (so the second Annual Report proudly announced) 'with the most approved sanitary contrivances'. Yet in 1897 every pan had to be replaced,[52] to the great inconvenience of tenants. And in 1902 most of the sink waste pipes were renewed by order of the Sanitary Inspector, probably because smells from the drains were finding their way into the kitchens;[53] added to their other problems this would have made working there intolerable.

These tiny sculleries were always packed from concrete floor to white-washed ceiling. Their cold, unplastered brick walls were wet with condensation from continuous washing and cooking. The window was small and badly placed in one corner so that it provided little light and air, adding to the closeness of the crowded room. There were buckets, mops and brooms in every corner; in the sink, too shallow for washing-up, stood an enamel bowl filled with crockery from a recent meal; under the sink was a galvanised pail of refuse waiting to be tipped down the dust-chute;[54] next to that was a bowl of cold water with a cloth over it, containing milk in jugs and butter in glass dishes to keep them fresh;[55] in pride of place on the dresser was the samovar for Russian tea used only on high days and holidays, most families preferring perhaps a 'blue enamel teapot',[56] or making the tea in the strainer over the cup;[57] saucepans, plates and cutlery, cups and glasses for perhaps ten people were stacked or hanging on the dresser and shelves round the walls; on the coal bin were sacks of wood and paper, perhaps with the scrubbing-board balanced on top; across the scullery were lines of washing which seemed never to dry – 'there was always clothes hanging, take one lot off and put one lot on';[58] there was fresh fish or chicken on the lid of the copper, waiting to be prepared for the evening meal; the midday meal was already boiling on the gas stove; and in between it all the children, too hungry to wait for dinner time, clamoured for a piece of bread or biscuit to keep them going till father came home.

There was never any space to spare in the kitchen. Kitchen utensils spilled over into the living-room, and even in the little lobby there was a shelf over the front door where many an orthodox family kept their enamelware for Passover.[59] Space was even more cramped from the turn of the century when gas stoves became available to working-class families. They could be bought for £5 – a sum beyond the means of most Rothschild Buildings tenants – or rented for 2s. 6d. a quarter.[60] The Four Per Cent set up a scheme for hiring gas cookers which many took advantage of:[61]

> 'You paid it in your rent. So it was never yours really. . . .
> And then a lot of them used to open the slot meter and
> empty it and spend the money.'

Only the smallest of gas stoves could fit safely in the scullery and this (as we shall see) made special arrangements necessary for the largest dishes.

Laundry was probably the biggest problem. Scrubbing was often done in the living room; pails or pans of water were heated on the stove, and then carried into the main room where elbows had space to move.[62] Whites were boiled in the copper in the scullery; but these may have been carried back into the living room for wringing. In many homes the mangle (if you had one) was kept in the living-room perhaps next to that other common domestic appliance the treadle sewing-machine, solely because there was just no room in the scullery. Ironing too, the heavy iron heated directly on the live coals, was done in the living-room. When finished, it was impossible to hang a large family's wash in the scullery and carry out other jobs at the same time. Things were made more difficult by a rule which attempted to forbid tenants hanging washing outside their flat, yet most families ignored this and, 'Very often we'd hang clothes inside the gate.'[63] 'The gate' opened into the railed-off piece of balcony which provided each flat with its front garden and back yard pushed into one. It gave additional space for keeping inconvenient articles like prams, tin baths, children's carts, and occasionally children themselves, and had an important position in family and community life in Rothschild Buildings.

Problems of space were aggravated when two or more flats had to share a common scullery. Many of these flats were in the attics and in the block fronting on to Lolesworth St. 'Along each corridor there was a tiny little room where the women used to do their washing. They couldn't do it inside, there was no place there for washing.'[64] The scullery had a large but shallow stone sink and copper for laundering and a water supply, but all cooking would be done in the living-room. Sharing the scullery put a strain on neighbourly relations.[65]

'We had more than one argument where washing was concerned. "I want to do the washing today", and my mother said, "Well what about me?" "Well, you'll have to wait till tomorrow." So there was a few words and – .'

In many East End tenements, conflicts like these would have been a common experience, but the people of Rothschild Buildings were generally more fortunate. About 80 per cent of families had access to their own sculleries, and could please themselves when they did the housework. This made things tolerable even when large families in cramped conditions were confronted with the problem of personal washing. There were no baths in the block but then almost no working-class family in the East End had the use of any other than a public bath. And the flats at least had amenities which helped people make do, even when, for the strictly observant, the rigorous Jewish laws made washing in the morning and before meals obligatory.

But they needed ingenuity. Some families used the copper in the scullery to wash the younger children; 'we stood up in it and mother washed us.'[66] For the larger children and adults a tin bath would be filled with water heated in the copper or in saucepans or in galvanised pails on the gas stove. The inconvenience of heating water and emptying the bath made it hard for the larger families. Once a week in the 1890s, the six children of Mrs Zwart, at No. 170 would line up and 'she'd bath us in this big zinc bath, one after the other in the same water; time we was finished it was like ink!'[67]

Some people required more privacy for their washing. A family of nine from Russia in a three-bedroom flat at No. 99 could still afford to give the fussy eldest daughter concessions over use of the kitchen:[68]

'My sister had to have a bath every day, and we had a great big zinc bath. Lucky our kitchen locked up – she used to put the bolt on – and my mother heated pails of water on the gas stove so she could get a bath.'

In the middle of Goulston St – in a part once grandly known as Goulston Square – were the public baths and wash-houses for the Whitechapel District. They had been built for the poor of Whitechapel by private philanthropy and were opened in 1848. Twenty years later they were leased to a local speculator called Pilbrow, who allowed them to decay, closed them and offered them for sale for demolition in 1871. The local squirearchy, including Samuel Barnett and F. D. Mocatta (later to be one of the first Directors of the Four Per Cent), formed a committee to save the baths, and they were modernised and reopened in 1878. There were eighty-nine baths – sixty-eight for men and twenty-one for women – divided scrupulously into first and second class. All modern conveniences were provided, including 'those useful articles, flesh brushes', and charges ranged from 6d. (warm, first class) to 1d. (cold, second class). Three swimming baths – one for women and two for men, first and second class – were added when Rothschild

Buildings were nine years old to make Whitechapel's facilities possibly the best in London.[69]

It was these public baths, then, to which many of the people from the Buildings would go. They were only five minutes' walk away in the heart of Jewish Whitechapel, conveniently close to home, work, and school.[70]

> 'We had to go to Goulston St baths every time. We used to go straight from work, and when we were kids my mother took us. Every Thursday, after school, my mother would take us.'

But public baths or a wash down in front of the fire were not the only alternatives for the people of Rothschild Buildings. For many men would go to the vapour baths which the immigrants had brought with them from Russia as a necessary part of Jewish religious life. The nearest steam bath was just round the corner from the Buildings, in Brick Lane, and it was run by Benjamin Schewzik, 'Shefshick's they called it.' When the religious tailors and cabinet makers and other workers came home early on Friday afternoon they might have a steam bath at Schewzik's before going to synagogue. Women would use full communal baths (the Mikveh) for the ritual cleansing before marriage and for the post-menstrual ritual.

'I don't know where my mother put us'

By 1900, 177 out of 228 flats in Rothschild Buildings were of two rooms with scullery.[71] This proportion of one-bedroom flats was ill-suited to the needs of the community they were designed to serve, for among prospective tenants young married couples with growing families were by far the largest group. This common feature of tenement block life determined that for many years the flats would be overcrowded. Various census reports defined overcrowding as more than two persons per room. By even this low standard, Rothschild Buildings were chronically overcrowded throughout our period; the average density in 1888 was 2.44 persons per room, decreasing to 2.30 by 1900 and continuing at about that figure until the First World War, then falling away to under 1.75 by the early 1930s.[72] This crowding was nearly as severe as in the old rookery, so that slum clearance had not materially reduced over-occupation. Neither had it reduced the population density. Before redevelopment this had been about 600 persons per acre, but it now stood at 1,200, certainly one of the highest in the country.

But what did these dry statistics mean to the people who lived there? Recording the extent of overcrowding is a relatively easy matter, but how did people live with it? At this distance in time the problems seem so immense that it is difficult for some to remember how they and their parents coped. For example, at No. 117 around 1905, in the family of a widowed traveller who had emigrated from Russia some fifteen years before,[73]

> 'My mother had seven children. How we managed is the biggest puzzle I can't answer. I don't know where my mother put us. There were seven children, two adults, making nine; and I think my sister said we had a lodger!'

These very large families did pose extraordinary problems. But for an average family of husband, wife and three or four children a common pattern emerges. The parents slept in a double bed in the bedroom; in their room was also the youngest child in a cot or single bed. The other children slept in the living-room. This arrangement worked very well when all the children, or at least the eldest two, were of the same sex. Typical of many was a Lithuanian bookbinder's family at No. 184 in the early years of the First World War.[74]

> 'I slept with one brother in the front room, as we called it. . . . The two of us slept on – I think it was more of a put-u-up – it used to unfold. My father and mother had their bed. There were actually a double bed and a single bed in the bedroom, in which my younger brother slept.'

The 'more of a put-u-up' was a sofa which could collapse into a bed at night. A frequent supplement to this was a fold-up bed which stood against the living-room wall during the day, or a truckle bed which could be rolled under the double bed when not needed. Whatever the arrangements, the size of family and shortage of space both determined that a child who was one of four or more would rarely have a bed to himself. But such a luxury was not always missed, and sharing had some advantages – advantages which extended through childhood into adolescence. In the Kaplan family, overcrowding does not appear to have been perceived as a major deprivation.[75]

'Oh, I dunno, meself; that's why when people grumble today, I don't know. Child is born today and they must have a room on their own. We slept two, three in a bed like nothing. We never had a hot water bottle or extra blankets – we didn't need it. You all warmed one another.'

Here the sleeping arrangements of mother and six children were complicated by the need to separate boys from girls.[76]

'The two boys in the first room, and the rest of us in the bedroom – one bedroom. . . . We had two beds [in the bedroom] – three and two. Me and me mother used to sleep together. And Yetta and Clara and Becky slept in the other bed.'

Becky slept crossways at the foot of the bed, but in other families the children may have been put head to toe. For example, a Ukrainian cabinet maker and his wife at No. 124, about 1911, had seven children; there the four boys slept head to toe in one bed – 'two at the head and two at the feet'.[77]

When only a year or two separated one young child from another a family could manage without much concern for segregating the sexes. This flexibility, however, was likely to be lost when children approached puberty. Separation of boys and girls then became a worrying problem for many parents. It is impossible to say whether overcrowding contributed to sexual complications like incest, or whether Rothschild Buildings had more than its due proportion of vulnerable families. This is a taboo subject and is only mentioned in hushed tones about a family or two who are never named. Of far greater relevance to most families was the enormous problem of space posed by growing children. The flat only allowed for a certain number of beds and a limited amount of storage space. When the stage was reached where, say, three teenagers had to sleep in one bed, then serious efforts were made to look for larger accommodation.

One quite common way of doing this was to rent two flats in the block. But only in exceptional cases would the two be on the same landing.[78] A walking-stick maker and his family of eight children took an extra flat in the 'Penthouse'. This was the ironic name given later to the attic workshops, converted into living accommodation in the early 1890s. These two-room flats shared a toilet and scullery with their neighbours and so were best suited for use as the Rothschild Buildings version of a second home.[79]

> 'There was my Mum, four sisters and four brothers. Well, even at that time we felt that sexes should be segregated; they were growing up and it wasn't convenient. . . . When my father was alive, he had to sleep somewhere and the girls had to sleep somewhere else, and with the preparatory efforts of making the beds up we were in such a state that everyone felt we had to need two flats.'

And so they rented a Penthouse flat.

> 'Each flat consisted of one large room and one small room, with dormer windows. We had enough room for four beds there.'

The seventeen single-room dwellings were often let in this way, too, rather than to the needy families they were designed for; in about 1905 Mrs Zwart rented one at 2s. 6d. per week for her three teenage sons, giving them each the single bed there had previously been no room to allow.[80] One family in the Buildings who rented two self-contained flats on the same landing used the second kitchen as a bathroom – riches indeed.[81]

There came a time, then, when each family reached its

saturation point in the flat it occupied at present. Not all, of course, were in a position to do anything but put up with it, waiting for the pressure to be relieved by some of the children leaving home when they married or found a job. Alternatively, the family could look out for one of the larger flats in the block becoming empty. The Superintendents knew of the severely overcrowded families and they would almost certainly have been given a flat with the extra rooms in preference to a new applicant. But there were many more large families than flats to match, and the unlucky ones had to move out of the block altogether. The family of nine at No. 117 moved to a house in Pelham St in 1910, happy to accept a 'dirty old cottage' in return for more rooms.[82] The cabinet maker with seven children in No. 124 moved to a two-bedroom flat in Nathaniel Dwellings in 1912 and moved again in 1914.[83] This was a very frequent arrangement. If you could move you did. Thus, particularly among the large families, there was considerable mobility both within and outside the Buildings.

As far as we can tell, these efforts to solve a family's over-crowding crisis were not stimulated by external pressure. Overcrowding theoretically contravened the rules of the Four Per Cent. One of the Superintendent's duties included the prevention of overcrowding;[84] he had the right to enter a flat at any reasonable time to check on its occupancy and to enforce the Company's standards. This was entirely in accordance with contemporary opinion, which rated 'the mischiefs of overcrowding'[85] as possibly the very greatest evil arising from the housing problem. But to the families of Rothschild Buildings, overcrowding was entirely subjective. They knew when they could cope with it and even draw benefits from it: 'You all warmed one another' is a profound insight into the irrelevance of 'statutory overcrowding' as a concept for one family at least. Other families found their own crisis point, above or below another family's tolerance or any statutory definition and reacted to it as best they could. The Four Per Cent accepted the realities of the East End housing problem, particularly among the Jewish immigrants, and saw that eviction of overcrowded families could only deepen the crisis. All those rules, so necessary in theory to protect health and morals, were allowed quietly to remain an empty threat. But there were many rules in Rothschild Buildings, and not all were a dead letter.

Rebuke and repression

The philanthropy which provided Rothschild Buildings was far from unconditional. With it went a detailed programme of class control which stipulated the tenant's duties and obligations to his landlord. In practical terms, the rule book and officers of the Four Per Cent were the means of protecting the interests of the shareholders, ensuring the rents and dividends were paid on time. But safeguarding profits was only one reason for a system of controls which was designed to reach into the very parlours and back-sculleries of the people. In its widest sense it was a tiny part of a bourgeois ideology which depended for its existence on a disciplined and quiescent labour force. In housing terms, the rule book passed blame for the housing problem to the people affected by it, making slum life appear a conscious choice which must be eliminated by restrictions and threats. Without this despotic rule by the middle-class landlord over his working-class tenant, chaos and ruin would inevitably follow. This philosophy was best exploited by Octavia Hill, the doyenne of tenant management. 'The people's homes are bad', she wrote, 'partly because they are badly built and arranged; they are tenfold worse because the tenants' habits and lives are what they are. Transplant them tomorrow to healthy and commodious homes, and they would pollute and destroy them.' The tenants of new buildings had thus to be 'disciplined' by rules and rent-collectors; 'the main tone of action must be severe. There is much of rebuke and repression needed. . . .'[86]

The organ of rebuke and repression in Rothschild Buildings was the Superintendent. If his title was intended to put the fear of the Four Per Cent up the tenants it failed, for it was quickly reduced to the less impressive 'Super'. The Super lived with his family in the ground floor flat on the corner of Thrawl St and Lolesworth St, and if his family were large he would also take another flat in the Buildings. After 1892 he and his staff of porters were also made responsible for the management of

Nathaniel Dwellings, on the other side of Flower and Dean St.

The first Super was a Mr W. H. Smith, an ex-NCO 'with excellent testimonials'.[87] The tradition of a military (or police) background for the Supers was continued throughout the long life of Rothschild Buildings, underlining their almost imperialist role, reminiscent of an army of occupation billeted on the people. Certainly, the Super had considerable power. All the seventeen rules of the Company were his to enforce as he saw fit. He could choose tenants and he could also deprive them of their homes. He had a duty to 'enquire into the respectability'[88] of each applicant for a flat, so that the mechanics of class control in theory operated from the very beginning of the landlord-tenant relationship. It was he who gave each tenant a copy of the Four Per Cent's Rules (see Appendix 2) on entering the block as well as their new rentbook. And it was his job, too, to adorn the walls of the Buildings with the threatening posters which the Four Per Cent had printed from time to time.

According to contemporary observers, the rules of Rothschild Buildings worked well. The flats were described by the Rector of Spitalfields – 'a mild anti-Alien'[89] – as 'one of our best buildings'.[90] When the debate over Jewish immigration reached a crisis in 1903, and the leaders of Anglo-Jewry were on the defensive, they extolled Rothschild Buildings as model 'model dwellings'. In particular, they were singled out as the very opposite of the notorious Booth St Buildings, a tenement block just a few minutes from Flower and Dean St, and occupied by Polish Jews. It was asked why Booth St Buildings were so appalling and yet Rothschild Buildings, occupied by a similar immigrant community, so ordered and healthy. There was only one answer. 'The thing which differs very much . . . is the amount of control which is kept to see that people live decently there.'[91] This was supported and amplified by the local Anglican clergyman:[92]

> 'in the great buildings, such as Rothschild Buildings, Nathaniel Buildings, and all those, there is always a most competent man as caretaker, and he is constantly on the watch to see that the people are cleanly in their habits, and any defect is at once put right.'

But how accurate is this picture of effective repression? It has certainly been accepted by historians since.[93] But how much *were* these controls actually thrust into the lives of the people of Rothschild Buildings?

Some of them undoubtedly were important in shaping the character of the block in those early years. The lettings policy, with its emphasis on respectability and ability to pay the rent in advance, discriminated against workers with irregular earnings, and this largely determined the class structure of the block. But this did not create the uniformity which was hoped for, and law enforcement was no easy matter. Even the most fundamental laws could be ignored or challenged; others were so unreasonable that they could not be enforced; and others still were so much common sense as to be unnecessary.

Of the more unrealistic regulations, Rule 6[94] which demanded in part that 'neither shall any clothes or unsightly objects be exposed to view' has already been mentioned. Rule 7 required that 'Children are not to play or make a noise on the Stairs, or in the Passages', but it would have needed more than one ex-NCO to keep over 600 kids quiet. Rule 10 tried to enforce a common standard of morality, threatening that drunken or disorderly tenants would be evicted forthwith. Drink was not an especial problem associated with the Jewish immigrant working class so that the rule was not of much importance; but near the Kaplans, for example, there was an English family whose head – 'drunken swine!' – was raucous and threatening from time to time but who lived there many years.[95] Likewise, Rule 16, in an attempt to keep out people of the casual labouring class, reminded tenants that the scullery copper was for their use only and must not be used for carrying on business as a laundress. But, as we shall see, many of the poorest women had to do just that.

Even where a rule was effectively kept, it was done so for a number of reasons, and not only the Superintendent was involved in its enforcement. Perhaps the best remembered of all was Rule 5, which demanded that passages and stairs were to be washed and whitened every Friday or Saturday by the tenants of each landing in rotation. It became a rule important to both tenant and landlord alike. To the Dwellings Companies clean stairs and passages were a public declaration

of a disciplined tenantry. They announced to all who could see
that here the people were clean and orderly.

'*There* you had to have it done. Not like now. I remember –
I was a little girl – and we had Mr Barker; he was a military
man. I've never seen anybody like that, there'll never be
another Super like him. Used to come up every Friday
evening and knock at one of the doors . . . and see who's
turn it was, why the steps wasn't cleaned. When my mother
first moved in they were very fussy!'

Even if you had a good excuse Mr Barker would not be
moved.[96]

'You had to clean them stairs; if you was ill or not ill, you
had to clean them. More than once my mother had to come
out while she was ill, she couldn't bend at all, with a mop.'

Henry Barker, as we shall see, was a particularly awesome
Super and it is likely that his successors were a little more
tolerant. But cleaning the steps once a week entered firmly
into the routine of domestic life in Rothschild Buildings,
perhaps because there were other pressures than those applied
by the Four Per Cent.

Frequently you had to do it for your own convenience. On
each landing there was an opening into the communal dust-
chute, 'what they called the dustbin. It went from floor to the
top, like in a box shape in the wall.'[97] Unfortunately the cast
iron door on each landing was not effective in preventing the
occasional accident; 'many times a load of dust used to come
down through there and push the door open and a whole cloud
of dirt would come out.'

But, for the regular weekly cleaning, the people on your
landing would exercise a large amount of social control by
exerting pressure on a family which failed in its duty to neighbours.

'Sometimes there was many quarrels. When you used to
wash your balcony and you noticed the other tenant didn't,
well there was a row! They used to row terrible, murders
sometimes; you could hear it a mile away sometimes.'

Indeed, many families accepted the burden willingly, almost zealously. First, because the regular duty fitted in well with preparations for the Sabbath. On Friday special efforts were made for the Eve of Sabbath celebrations; perhaps the curtains were changed, the flat was cleaned, a fresh white table-cloth would be laid ready for the evening meal. Whitening the steps on Friday morning quickly became part of this religious ritual. Second, and arising out of this, a freshly whitened approach to your flat was a visible declaration of the pride you felt in your home, and the effort you put into it.

Enforcement of some other rules was less effective, probably because it was difficult to check, or the culprits were less easily identifiable. Rule 11 demanded that tenants sweep their chimneys at least once every three months. The Four Per Cent had been concerned from the outset about the risk of fire in the Buildings and so Rule 11 was for them an important safeguard. It was not often heeded. Flues were cleaned when smoke came back into the room, and sometimes not until there was a fire in the chimney.[98]

> 'There was many a fire there because some of them
> wouldn't have the chimney swept. Yes, the firemen was
> about three or four times a week. But you were fined, you
> got into trouble with the Rothschild Buildings if you
> didn't – you must keep that chimney clean. . . . Oh,
> they'd be fined about 5s., something like that, you know.'

The tenants may not have been the only ones not to keep the rules. On the front of each rentbook was printed in English and Yiddish, 'It is strictly forbidden to offer gratuities to the Superintendent.' It is possible, however, that such gratuities may not have been merely offered but expected. Certainly, at an anti-rackrenting meeting in 1898 it was publicly alleged that the Superintendents of the Four Per Cent 'demand tips ranging from 5s. to £1 from poor people who desire to become tenants.'[99] So that the very apparatus of class control was probably corrupt, demanding, as it were, its own 4 per cent, and again at the tenants' expense.

The most important rules, of course, related to the payment of rent. Rule 2 stipulated that rents were to be paid one week in

advance and that no arrears would be tolerated 'on any
account'. This rule, combined with the general stricture as to
respectability, was designed to ensure that tenants would be in
regular employment and able to pay the rent charged. But not
all tenants were so fortunate, and there were people in the
Buildings who had to borrow or pawn, almost as a matter of
course, to pay the rent.[100]

> 'My mother used to go into her [a neighbour] every
> Monday to borrow rent, 5s. rent. And my mother used to
> give her – when she got to the Board of Guardians, Thurs-
> day – give it to her back. . . . And Monday it started
> again.'

But if Rule 2 had not produced a tenantry always capable of
paying the rent as demanded, fear of eviction kept rent arrears
small throughout our period – a tenth of 1 per cent in 1897, for
example, and about the same in 1911.[101] It is impossible to say
how frequent evictions were. By all accounts they were rare.
But if there were problems over the rent then an officious
Super would make his presence quickly felt. Henry Barker
was just such a Super. He took up his job in 1907, and
remained at his post until he died in 1917. Henry Barker, too,
had a disciplined background. 'He was a naval man; 'cos he
had a big naval funeral. I remember as a little girl when he died;
he had a big Union Jack over his coffin. We all went out to see
it. He was very strict. After that there wasn't many strict
Superintendents.'[102] During his reign, Mr Barker, a dedicated
church worker, was responsible for one of the few evictions
from Rothschild Buildings, some time around 1912.

A recently widowed mother from Russia with three young
children had run up substantial rent arrears. Perhaps this
woman was less apologetic than many and with Rule 2 de-
claring that no arrears were to be tolerated 'on any account',
the 'loving, yet stern and determined Mr Barker'[103] and the
Four Per Cent put the bailiffs in. A neighbour's daughter
watched them dispose of the family's goods: 'they absolutely
threw them over the landing they threw it; threw 'em out, all
things went out.' That night the mother and her family moved
in with a neighbour on the same landing and 'another neigh-

bour took a few of my mother's things in.' Mr Barker, however, attempted to break the tenants' solidarity.

> 'She stayed with us a few nights. Stayed with us and then Mr Barker, he says to my mother, "If you keep her, you'll go out with her." My mother had a dead fright!'

The eviction lasted for a few days – perhaps a week – during all of which time the mother and her children stayed with neighbours in the block. And in the end Mr Barker was effectively defied. Pressure was exerted on the Company. 'Somebody or other from a synagogue where my brother used to go to say his prayers for my father, kicked up a row and they let my mother come back again.' Someone, perhaps the same man, paid the outstanding rent and the Company were shamed into accepting her back into the same flat from which she had been evicted. The man who paid the rent also lived in the block: 'Mr Oster done it. *I* knew who done it. They were downstairs.' And in order to prevent a recurrence, the Jewish Board of Guardians were persuaded to pay 3s. a week towards the family's rent.

In this case, at least, solidarity among the tenants had kept a family in the Buildings when they could not be relied upon to pay their rent. Even when tested at their most fundamental level, the mechanics of class control were not infallible. This is not to understate their importance. The tenants had to learn to live with them as with the other disabilities of Rothschild Buildings. But in doing so they forced a compromise where none was originally intended.

The reason given by the middle class for the success of Rothschild Buildings does not stand up to close scrutiny. Even where rules were obeyed, as in the case of a cleaning routine for stairs and passages, the motives for this were mixed, and by no means entirely due to supervision. After that first crucial decision about who could have a flat and who could not, the people of Rothschild Buildings were largely on their own. The myth of an all-powerful rooting system of 'rebuke and repression' which kept the people orderly owed more to bourgeois prejudice than to reality.

'Rothschilds was luxury'

Rothschild Buildings were born out of the housing crisis of the 1870s and 1880s, a crisis which relapsed into a chronic malaise for the next two generations. From the time of their construction until the end of the First World War there was a slow improvement in living conditions but the bulk of working people in the East End were still appallingly housed. The Buildings must be seen in the context of this overwhelming problem – a context of high rents, extortionate key money, universal overcrowding, slum housing and fearful death rates.

The turn of the century saw a resurgence of the housing crisis among the East End's Jewish population. The pressure on house room which in other inner London areas was tending to relax, in Whitechapel continued unabated. The immigrant population in ever-increasing numbers attempted to squeeze into an area which had long since reached saturation point. In the ten years after Rothschild Buildings were first occupied, it was said that rents in the Jewish quarter had nearly doubled – at a time when wage rates were rising only slowly. Tenants 'are paying now 14s. per week, with a premium of £5 for the key for houses that, two years ago, they were paying 7s. for.' Sometimes the key money could rise to £20, or ten weeks' wages for a tailor.[104] In the whole of London it was only in Whitechapel and St George's-in-the-East that these alarming rent rises were widespread,[105] in other words within the boundaries of the Jewish East End.

Such an increase in the cost of living space reflected the growth of demand for a static or declining amount of housing accommodation. High rents forced families to cut their living standards by reducing 'the number of rooms they can afford to occupy from three to two and from two to one – a single room being even shared by more than one family.'[106] Wage earners who were not poor in terms of income were still overcrowded because there was nowhere else for them to go. There was little correlation between overcrowding and poverty.[107] This can be seen in the Buildings, where an employer, his wife and four children crowded into two rooms and a kitchen: 'we were considered pretty comfortable at the time', but even so the housing shortage gave them no opportunity to rent more rooms.[108]

For a Jewish family, needing to live within walking distance of a synagogue, a kosher butcher and the ritual baths, there was no alternative to living in the 'ghetto' and thus no alternative to overcrowding. Freedom of choice was further restricted by the blatant discrimination of some landlords who refused to let to Jews, including some Dwellings Companies. No Jew had access to the model flats in Albert Buildings and Metropolitan Buildings in Mile End New Town, for example.[109] Advertisements like the following of 1906 were commonplace in the East End press.[110]

> Rooms to let, every convenience, quiet house, Jews and children objected to.

This not only aggravated overcrowding among the Jewish population, but it reduced even further a family's chance of obtaining sanitary housing near their work and cultural centre. Large families, or in other words a typical immigrant family, were further disadvantaged by other companies who refused to let dwellings to that category.[111] And the LCC was even reported to have evicted tenants who became overcrowded due to the natural increase of their families.[112]

The housing alternatives for immigrant large families in the East End of that time were thus severely limited, at least for twenty years after the Buildings were opened.[113] There were the courts, alleys and tenement houses of the old Whitechapel, which formed about 80 per cent of the housing stock in 1900.[114] Or there were the model dwellings, dating largely from the early 1880s and later.

The quality of housing which Whitechapel and the adjacent districts could offer was freqently very poor indeed. The advantages of the Buildings over neighbouring houses in terms of comfort was immediately apparent. A little girl would visit a schoolfriend 'I think in Heneage St. . . . They had to go outside to the toilet and that was bad. At least we shut our door, we had a toilet inside. There was go outside to wash, outside in the yard – what they called the yard.'[115] The courts and alleys were, if anything, worse than the tenement houses. Crown Court, Stepney, for example, was closed as unfit for human habitation and the tenants evicted in 1911; five of the houses had no back yards and were of a back-to-back type. 'There is no water supply to any of the houses, but water is supplied by a tap which is close to the w.c. . . . There are two w.c.'s to five houses containing sixteen families. The w.c.'s are situated in the yard. The roofs of the w.c.'s are defective and the seats are very wet and dirty.'[116]

As far as comparable housing conditions went, then, the 20 per cent of families who lived in the model dwellings could count themselves lucky. But even among this one in five, some were more fortunate than others, and few were more fortunate than the people of Rothschild Buildings. For these flats were, in terms of amenity and comfort, well advanced for their time.

Compare them, for example, with Booth St Buildings – 'the most insanitary property in the Borough of Stepney'.[117] These tenements were notorious for their filth and poor management, a state of affairs which lasted for about twenty-five years.[118] Booth St Buildings, it will be remembered, were pointed out as the very antithesis of Rothschild Buildings. The main charges levelled against them were that the drains were frequently choked and overflowing, and that the WCs were always in a filthy state. The responsibility for this lay, so the Medical Officer of Health publicly announced,[119] with the tenants themselves, who obstructed the drains by putting refuse down them and who were not used to sophisticated sanitary equipment like water closets. This could only be remedied by proper management, perhaps by more effective rebuke and repression.

In reality, responsibility for the admittedly appalling state of Booth St Buildings lay firmly at the door of the owner, Mr Gershon Harris. For roughly the same rents as those charged for flats in Rothschild Buildings and perhaps a little more,[120] Gershon Harris provided his fellow Jews with incomparably inferior accommodation. This exploitation left over 600 people sharing a mere thirty WCs, whereas in Rothschild Buildings there was one to every five people. Small wonder that these closets used in common were permanently fouled, yet at no time was this lack of facilities commented upon. Between 1900 and 1907 no fewer than 1,566 notices had been served on Mr Harris by the local Sanitary Inspectors, requiring the buildings to be cleansed or repaired. He had been prosecuted eighty-four times.[121] When the drains were eventually exposed they were found to fall the wrong way and were infested with rats. Yet for many years the tenants had been publicly blamed for these conditions! If there was a debate over responsibility for the condition of Booth St Buildings there is no doubt who took the consequences. Their death rate was about 20 per cent higher than the Whitechapel average and about 40 per cent higher than that for Rothschild Buildings.

Booth St Buildings (which still live on in East End folklore, though long demolished) were exceptionally poor 'model dwellings', but even compared with the prestigious London County Council Boundary St Scheme of the 1890s, Rothschild Buildings stand up well. As late as 1895, the LCC were building family flats with shared sculleries, whereas Rothschild Buildings were largely self-contained.[122] In these terms, at least, they were some ten years ahead of their time in the context of East End housing. The lull in building working-class housing in the area after the Boundary St Scheme meant that Rothschild Buildings were very acceptable accommodation indeed for at least the thirty years up to the end of the Great War. Many East Enders clamoured to get into the flats and out of the conditions in which they were otherwise forced to bring up their children, so that there was in these early years tremendous competition for even a basement flat in Rothschild Buildings. As early as July 1888 the Four Per Cent had decided that, 'in consequence of the large number of applications for tenements in the Dwellings, which were entirely full, the Architect was instructed to look out for a suitable site for the erection of another block of buildings.'[123] Demand for a flat continued to grow for the next twenty years as the Jewish immigrants streamed into the East End. Typical of many was an Austrian cabinet maker, his wife and three small children who emigrated in 1897.[124]

'At first my father and my uncles fixed up a room in Old Montague St . . . above a grocery shop. And we had one large room and a door opened into a sort of a – I presume it was a sort of kitchen where there was a tap.'

Why did they move to Rothschild Buildings?

'Well, because it was a much better dwelling, you know, than to live above a grocery shop. Two of my mother's brothers were there and after a while they tried to get a flat for us, which they did. . . . And, oh my mother was very pleased to get it because it was fairly new at that time.'

There was at least one other reason for trying to get a flat in Rothschild Buildings. This was the reputation of the Four Per Cent as good landlords. Their tenants did not need to worry about the sort of exploitation received at the hands of Gershon Harris. But not even all semi-philanthropic landlords could be relied on to keep their tenements in good repair, and the owner of Irene House, Flower and Dean St was prosecuted for nine offences in 1905, for example.[125] The Four Per Cent, on the other hand, carried out repairs as requested and quickly achieved a good name among the East End working class, some of whom have spent all their lives in the Company's flats. Even their rules were not as repressive as those of other charitable landlords.[126] 'Somebody said, "Why don't you go up to the Four Per Cent? They're very very nice there." '[127] And when a family moved in they found that the effort they put into their homes was not destroyed by damp seeping through walls and ceilings, spoiling decorations and making cleanliness impossible. In the slums, people gave up against uneven odds; in Rothschild Buildings those odds were reduced to tolerable proportions. Compared with everything else that a family could find at that time, 'Rothschilds was luxury.'[128]

But if we acknowledge that the Buildings gave good value for their time, we cannot ignore a strongly expressed feeling of hostility towards them by many local outsiders. To those working-class East Enders who did not live in buildings, life in tenement blocks often had deeply unpleasant associations. This controversy, which seems to resolve itself into a houses versus buildings debate, affected all tenements, not just Rothschild Buildings. To people who lived in houses, buildings were (and still are in the East End) often known as 'Barracks'; to the people of Rothschild Buildings the flats were sometimes, ironically, 'houses'. We know that the Buildings offered better accommodation than the typical Whitechapel house could ever offer; we know, too, that demand for flats in Rothschild Buildings never abated throughout our period. And yet, even the people who lived there could recognise a feeling among those friends, relatives and acquaintances who lived in the East End's streets and alleys. 'Yes, I think so, yes; there was a stigma, sort of, you know.'[129]

The existence of a stigma is not always accepted by the people of Rothschild Buildings. A husband who spent his childhood there will vigorously defend them against the taunts of his wife who spent *her* childhood in an alley off Cable St.[130]

'Oh, well, we had better, we had a house. We were better off than them, we wasn't – I've never lived in flats in my life.'
    'Yes, they had a whole house. But you wanted water you had to go out into the yard. There was nowhere a basin. But you turned on the tap and washed under the tap, in the freezing cold.'

The argument will revolve around convenience, the state of repair, the number of rooms, on all of which points Rothschild Buildings will win. But at the end of it all there is still a feeling that somehow it was just that bit better to have lived in a house.

To these other East Enders it was the inhuman scale of the Buildings which was most repellent. This, of course, was exaggerated in the Flower and Dean St neighbourhood, where the tall buildings seemed to engulf the narrow streets. A little boy from a house in Chicksand St would pass through Thrawl St on his way to the Jews' Free School:[131]

'Now, honestly, honestly, talking honestly, it was never liked. It was daytime but it was always dark, because [of] the overhanging buildings and the closeness of one on top of the other.'

Israel Zangwill expressed the same physical reaction against the Buildings when he complained in 1892 of the area's 'appalling series of artisan's dwellings, monotonous brick barracks, whose dead, dull pose weighed upon the spirits.'[132]

Model dwellings, then, stirred deep misgivings in outsiders of all classes. Perhaps this was a transient reaction, apparent only at the beginning of the relationship between the British working class and cheap high-rise housing.[133] Yet, for the people who lived there, these drawbacks were less important than the real advances which Rothschild Buildings offered. Such problems were something else to struggle against and eventually overcome.

This struggle was helped by coming together and sharing the common burdens. Self-contained tenements quickly dissolved in a wider consciousness. They became cells in an organic unity – the block – which in its turn merged into a greater unity – the Jewish East End.

Introduction

A community is a complex structure. It has many layers and projections to the foundations which underpin it. Its super-structure has many facets, with awkward additions and half-hidden details which somehow unite to produce the visible edifice. Even its boundaries are rarely defined. They overlap from one dimension to another, so that a small community will often merge at certain points into a larger, which in its turn will blend into a still greater unity.

In this way the people of Rothschild Buildings were part of three definable communities. There was the community life of the Buildings themselves. There was the wider community of the streets, buildings and shops immediately around them. And there was the Jewish East End itself, within which the first two interacted.

Only the first two dimensions will concern us here, for in writing of the 'ghetto', or the 'Jewish quarter', or the 'East End', the component parts of the whole have been lost to sight. This apparently homogeneous 'community' was composed of many parts like Rothschild Buildings with their own identity and consciousness and divisions.

Community consciousness in Rothschild Buildings was just as complex as the way it impinged on its surroundings. Rothschild Buildings were a high density community, an immigrant community, a religious community, a community of class. Sometimes they were more one than the other – after the Kishenev pogroms for instance, or during the 1912 tailors' strike. And yet all of those factors which tended to draw people together tended also, but to a lesser extent, to push them apart. The stimulants to community sentiment contained their own internal contradictions. Generally, this was contained by the community and emerged, if at all, as grounds for petty conflict. Yet in the divisions masked by these uniting influences were the seeds which were eventually to destroy the community in Rothschild Buildings.

Although this chapter is labelled 'Community' it is, of course, impossible to separate community life from home life (with its problems common to all), from life outside the community (which helped to define its boundaries), from childhood, or from work, politics and class. All of these areas impinged on the people of Rothschild Buildings and all contributed to the evolution of their common way of life.

1. IN THE BUILDINGS

The playground and the gate

Place is one determinant factor in the evolution of a community. A particular environment will lend itself to the creation of community feeling; another will make it difficult or impossible. Size, design and amenity are important characteristics which shape this role. At first sight it would appear that Rothschild Buildings must be failed irrevocably on all of these counts. Yet unwittingly a Victorian architect of 4 per cent philanthropy had designed a form of housing which, in one respect at least, could have served as a model for progressive urban planners and architects nearly a century later.[1]

The most important feature of the Buildings – more important even than those stark and awesome walls – was the courtyard. It was designed[2] as a playground for the children, and so it was called by the people who lived there. In fact, the quarter-acre playground became much more than this. It was an open space set aside for the use of the residents and their use only. It could only be entered via the staircases which divided the several blocks or the main gate in Thrawl St; it was thus not suitable for use as a right of way or short cut from Thrawl St to

Flower and Dean St. Those entering the playground lived in the Buildings or had business there; anyone else was an intruder. Security was further strengthened by most bedroom and living-room windows overlooking the playground. This produced a two-fold benefit. Any outsider met with a sense of being watched. And any member of the community was given a sense of being protected.

This was especially so for children. The playground offered total security for kids. Half the flats looked on to the courtyard, and mothers in flats fronting the street needed only to step out on the open landing to have it in full view. For this reason, careful mothers liked their children to play in the Buildings, and youngsters felt secure there.

Important as its role as playground was, the courtyard was much more. It became the focal point of life in the block. It provided the community with its meeting place, its entertainment, its medium for all communication. Later, when the community was more Anglicised, celebrations of public events like coronations and royal weddings were held there. It was Rothschild Buildings' village green. There tailors would exchange news about piece-rates in the local workshops; Miriam Gertner would ignore admiring glances from aspiring apprentices; Mrs Davis would use imaginative Yiddish on poor Morrie, caught fighting again; and the old people would sit on white kitchen chairs in little groups, talking of days back home. After supper, the almost ceaseless activity of the Playground would flare up once more before bedtime.[3]

> 'The community was very close. During the summer months people used to be out to all hours, even the children. You had that sense of warmth, of friendliness among the people. . . . They used to stay outside. There used to be talking, the kids used to have singsongs. Even though you were sitting on the cold stone the kids used to enjoy it.'

But the playground was not the only open space provided for the people of Rothschild Buildings. Apart from this communal territory nearly every flat had a piece of open space set aside for its own use. This was the tiny fenced-off area outside the front door and entered by a small gate. It gave additional security to mothers with toddlers, for the scullery window[4]

'looked on to this gate. So the mother was cooking . . . and she could look through the gate at her child and she could make sure that the kid was safe. . . .'

In the summer months the gate would be used for sitting out in by the majority of families too high up to take chairs down to the playground.[5]

'That gate was worth more than money to me when I got married, because I used to take a table out there and play cards. Neighbours, friends used to come down, we used to play Solo – on a Saturday night they used to come down. . . . We used to sit out there the whole evening, have tea out there. They used to knit out there or sew.'

But if the design of Rothschild Buildings conspired – almost in spite of itself – to generate community feeling, it also provided a breeding-ground for minor disputes. The development of Rothschild Buildings was to an almost unprecedentedly high density. People were very much forced upon one another's attention. Through floors, walls and ceilings, across landing and courtyard were heard people all day long, every day of the week. There was a certain amount of privacy behind closed doors, but it was inevitable that even the best of neighbours would get on each other's nerves.[6]

'She'd always make an excuse, the neighbour next door, to look around to see if anybody was there – "Can you tell me the time, please?" – just to have a look around.'

Neighbours would probably know a disproportionate amount about each other's business. 'You'd really wash your linen in public.' It would be difficult indeed to keep a matrimonial dispute or good or ill fortune a secret in Rothschild Buildings.

Frequently children would be the cause of an inter-family dispute, one mother perhaps dispensing summary punishment on another's child. Or there would be arguments, as we have seen, over the care of the steps or sharing arrangements, watering window-boxes which splashed windows below and shaking dusty mats.

Rarely, though, did this sort of dispute turn into a long and bitter family feud. And when it did, the kids would take no notice.[7]

'We never spoke to a person for years. They were living facing me. . . . My mother and her mother were very thick and then – I dunno what they quarrelled over. We were children; we didn't bother.'

If high-density tenement block living had its pros and cons, it is still likely that the inward-lookingness of Rothschild Buildings drew people together and provided a strong template for the growth of community interest. But in those early years the people there had much more in common than the mere accident of living close to each other.

The immigrant community

Between 1887 and 1920 the population of Rothschild Buildings was almost exclusively Jewish. In the first year of occupation probably nine out of ten families were Jews, and in the decades following this proportion if anything increased. Russell and Lewis estimated in 1900 that the block was 95–100 per cent Jewish,[8] forcefully contradicting Lord Rothschild's assertion that 'more than one third of the tenants are Christians and Englishmen.'[9] In fact, after 1900 it is likely that only the Super's and porters' families and perhaps a handful more were without at least one Jewish parent.[10]

The bulk of this population – it is impossible to talk in more precise terms – were immigrants to this country, or the English-born children of foreign parents. It is this second generation which provides most of our oral testimony; only four out of sixteen people interviewed were born abroad, and only one was of long-established Dutch origin (see Appendix 1).

As we have seen, the immigration crisis of the early 1880s was stimulated by the East European pogroms of 1881–4. But this peak of unrest was set against a background of declining industry and unemployment among Jews, a chronic condition which produced a high level of emigration during the next decade. In 1903–6 a further wave of pogroms was officially inspired in Russia as part of the Tsarist counter-revolutionary struggles, and this again added momentum to emigration.

All of this affected Rothschild Buildings in some way. Many of the immigrants of the early 1880s moved into the new flats to escape the worst excesses of East End slum housing. After the pogroms came immigrants escaping from unemployment and poverty; they moved straight into the Buildings, or more usually went through the same filtering process before finding a flat there. The crisis of 1903 and after brought in new people, all eager for a home in one of the 'Rothschild houses'. By that time, the families of the first tenants had grown up, many flats had become too small and were vacated in favour of the new immigrants.

Sadly, the oral testimony of that first influx is now lost to us. Our evidence comes from the children of parents escaping from unemployment, the Russo-Japanese War and the revolutionary disturbances, rather than the wrath of Alexander III. Yet their experiences were not dissimilar to those of the generation before them. Their parents, too, came from White Russia, the Ukraine, Lithuania, Galicia (Austria-Hungary), Germany, Poland, Rumania – separated by immense distances yet moved by a common aim. They had undergone the common struggle to escape from a Jew-hating population or loss of status and lack of opportunity, relinquishing home, possessions, and in many cases families. They had shared the trauma of tearing up all roots and attempting to transplant them in a strange city. And many had to share these common burdens, for part of their lives at least, in Rothschild Buildings.

When the experience of just one of these families is examined, it is small wonder that the people of the Buildings stuck together and faced their new life with sympathy and solidarity. Take the case of a military tailor in Kiev at the time of the 1905 Revolution, whose family moved into No. 82 Rothschild Buildings in 1911. Mr Katchinsky was a relatively favoured member of Russian Jewry: 'we had a plaque on our door which gave us the right to live in a large town.'[11] He and his wife had a married son, and then 'years later' in 1896 another boy (born partially blind), in 1900 a girl, and in 1904 the youngest son. Five other children had died during infancy.

The students and workers of Kiev were in the very vanguard of the 1905 Revolution.[12] The tailor and his family were inevitably caught up in those rushing events of October and after. Public meetings were held where could be heard, among other things, promises of Jewish emancipation. In November, or so the daughter was later told, her married brother came to take her and her 9-year-old brother to see one such meeting and listen to the speeches.

> 'So I was put on my brother's shoulder, and we led my blind brother by hand, and off we went. I heard that in the middle of the speeches and shouts, officers and soldiers and large families and students were also listening. Suddenly pandemonium started. The order went out that the Jews were to be got rid of, and shooting was started.'

That month, martial law was declared in Kiev.[13]

The officially inspired pogroms of the revolutionary period hit this family for the first time soon after.

> 'Then, after a rather quiet and unhappy night we woke up to the cries and screams of the Jews being pulled out of their houses and beds, and the pogroms started. We hid with our friends. Some were non-Jewish Polish people who hid us in a loft. And for three or four days it went on. . . . I was a noisy kid, and the people who were in the loft with us said that if I didn't stop making a noise . . . they would have to do something about it, as if they heard a noise it would be all up with us. My parents said they would stop me, as there were about forty of us. . . . Our neighbour brought us up whatever food or drink they'd got late at night.'

Self-defence groups and vigilante patrols were organised among the Jews. 'The men in our community . . . walked about all night with whistles . . . and life was sad. There was not much work and not much food.'

'Suddenly, most of the Jews in the three towns where the pogroms were, started thinking of emigrating. And somehow it happened that my family, and many more, got started. Funnily enough, they let us go. It was hard and heart-breaking. No matter what happens there is still a feeling of loss and homesickness. But the first thought was survival. We got to London some time in 1905, and settled in one room.'

But there was little consolation for the family during those first miserable months in London, and soon the pull of home became too hard to resist.

'I won't talk about my loneliness, missing my brother and other relatives. Also, work for my father was hard to get. He was a good military tailor who put epaulettes, braids, etc. on officers' coats, but there wasn't that kind of work here for him. So he broke down, and went back after nearly a year.'

Back in Kiev, however, little had changed during the family's absence. The plight of the partly blind son, who as a Jew had little chance of a decent life in Russia, probably convinced the tailor and his wife of the need to emigrate for a second time.

'Now we heard that my brother, who was gradually losing his sight more and more, had a good chance in England of going to a school and learning a trade. One fine day in 1907 or 1908 my father left a note to say he was going away to England once more to try his luck, and when things got OK he would send for us. . . . When a man is a mechanic of some sort and had a plaque on his door, he and his family can stay. But should the man go away or die the family are not allowed to stay in the town. They must go back where his wife was born – some poor little village. That was what happened to us. One day, gendarmes called and said they

heard my father was not at home. My mother tried to say
she didn't know where he was, because we were not
allowed to say that he had left Russia for another country.
But they didn't care. They gave my mother a couple of
months to remove the plaque and get out.'

The tailor's wife decided to try and follow her husband to
London by illegally crossing the German border, where she
could get a ship from Hamburg or Bremen. But the family
were arrested by Russian soldiers just inside the border.

'We were all herded together and taken to prison, where we
got treated like criminals: bad food, little walk in the garden
for a few minutes a day, no baths, etc.. . . . . It was a transit
prison, and we were to stay one week in each on our way
back to Russia – to the village where my mother and father
were born, where they said they would see if my mother
was telling the truth.' [She had told the Tsarists that her
husband was living in Germany.]

The journey to her mother's home village took about six
weeks, with brief stays in transit prisons between travelling.
Children and adults quickly became infested with lice. From
Warsaw, the family was taken to Minsk, back in Russia's Pale
of Settlement. Here, they had to stay in a criminal prison
where there were no washing facilities. The mother 'used to
take off our underwear, shake them out, turn them inside out.
So that was our cleansing process!' Eventually the mother and
her three young children reached her home village where they
were welcomed by relatives and had their first good food and
real wash in over six weeks.

From the Russian officials in this village the family at last
obtained a passport which enabled them to join their father in
England. This they did in October 1909, after at least a year of
separation, hardship and fear.

Although this family's experiences were perhaps more
rigorous than most, many others had similar stories to relate
when finally they reached the safety of the East End. Certainly, all had to undergo the harrowing three-day journey
from Germany to London in dirty and overcrowded ships.[14]

'She [my mother] said it was dreadful, the whole journey [from Bremen in 1897]. And she was sick, and during the whole time she didn't eat anything at all – not anything – because she was ill.'

Solidarity among the immigrants expressed itself in co-operative aid. Although organisations like the Poor Jews' Temporary Shelter, opened at 82 Leman St in 1885, provided accommodation for up to a fortnight after arrival, as often as not established immigrants (especially relatives or *landsleit*★) would find a home for new arrivals. Mr Katchinsky's wife and children, for example, were met off the boat by an uncle who 'lived in Ship Alley, funny little turning, a little courtway' off St George's St. 'They took us to them for a couple of days.'[15]
Reception into the Jewish East End was normally effected in this way, rather than through any official avenue. This worried the opponents of immigration because it naturally tended to exacerbate overcrowding. Rumours were publicly voiced in 1903 that immigrant families 'with all their belongings' squatted by day in the courtyard of Rothschild Buildings and at night were 'absorbed into somewhere or other'.[16] As similar problems had confronted many who now rented flats in the Buildings it would have been extraordinary if some of these families had not been absorbed into Charlotte de Rothschild Dwellings. This was especially so in the case of relatives, whose arrival was greeted with joy, excitement and not a little sacrifice:[17]

'As with all immigrants – I think that's what's happening now – the family lived as close together as possible. I can well understand – people say how crowded the immigrants' houses are. Of course they crowd their houses! Because if you escape from a place . . . as soon as you're settled you send for a relative to come over. And so, even though you only had the two rooms, you'd certainly crowd your place. You always had visitors and for the kids it was lovely . . . the emotional wealth was very high – it was

★ Fellow countrymen from the same village, town or district.

very rich that way – and children did feel wanted because
their relatives would always make a fuss of them. . . . At
one time there were nine people in the flat. We used to use
the doors which had been taken off the cupboards, laid on
chairs and made up as beds. Nobody complained. The
Superintendent didn't mind because everybody was doing
the same. You all wanted your relatives.'

Many families had experience of taking in lodgers,[18]
another contravention of Rule 2, but usually it was only for a
short time, until some more permanent and satisfactory
arrangement could be arrived at. Often, the father or eldest
brother would emigrate and stay with relatives, meanwhile
earning money and seeking an adequate home, so that his
family could join him. Occasionally, however, a crisis would
affect many families in the East End, stimulating compassion
and co-operation throughout the wider community.

Just such a crisis occurred in Kishenev, Bessarabia, during
Passover 1903. Some forty-five Jews were killed in a pogrom
inspired by a local monarchist newspaper. Many hundreds fled
westwards as a result, and the repercussions rippled out to
Rothschild Buildings and beyond.[19]

'These people came in with nothing. Who should they come
to but their fellow Jews in the East End? All the synagogues
were open, and people slept on the floor. In Rothschild
Buildings a lot of people took in children. Nobody had
money, everyone was poor. Now the grocery shops in the
East End were allowed to stay open until 12 o'clock at night.
We children were told by our father to go to the grocery
shops and ask them to fill up this bag with the bread they'd
got over, the herring they'd got over, the milk and so on.
And they used to feed them with this in the synagogues.'

Many of the Kishenev immigrants would merely have used
the East End as a brief resting-place on the journey to another
promised land, and if Rothschild Buildings were a point of
arrival and settlement, they were a point of departure also.[20]

'A lot of 'em went away, a lot of 'em emigrated. And when
we were living in Flower and Dean St [about 1903 to 1912]

there was a lot of emigration going on there, mostly to
America. And there was always every day great big boxes in
the Playground there, they'd put some of their bedding in
and got all their precious things that they took out the flat.
There was people crying and wishing them good luck
where they went, and all the little children. . . . Oh, it was
terrible, it was.'

Periods like the pogroms at Kishenev united the immigrant
community to a degree which transcended any barriers
thrown up by national differences. But it must not be for-
gotten that there were important dissimilarities between a Jew
from Kiev and one from a Ukrainian farming village, or
between the small towns of 'Austria' (usually Galicia) and the
bustling ghettoes of Poland.
Just what these divisions were, however, and how far they
manifested themselves, it is not easy to say. Minor prejudices
there certainly were.[21]

'There were divisions. The Austrian Jews were looked upon
as not necessarily haughty – but bad tempered. The
Rumanians – they were selfish. The Polish – I suppose
there was some differences because the accent was very
different. . . . And the *Litvaks*★ were looked upon as the
intellectuals.'

That, at least, was a *Litvak*'s view of national differences in
Rothschild Buildings. To a Ukrainian girl, however, 'The
Russians were more intelligent', and the Poles 'were a bit more
selfish.'[22] One of the most reiterated beliefs about national
differences in the East End was that *Litvaks* 'would never mix
with Austrians. They hated each other',[23] and Willy Goldman
wrote that 'Rumanian and Polish Jews mutually regard each
other as God's lowest creation.'[24]
Beyond this sort of generalisation it is difficult to delve.
Some national differences were more noticeable than others.
There were recognisable regional accents when people spoke,
'we used to mock each other, the way we used to pronounce

★ Lithuanians.

the Yiddish',[25] and there would be many who spoke Russian
or German as a second language. Clothes, it was said, were
little different. Food, however, was important to the people of
Rothschild Buildings and here differences were more recognisable. A Lithuanian family shared a landing with Russians,
Poles and Anglo-Jews. One of the *Litvak* sons was friendly
with the Grodzinsky family from Poland, and he would often
be invited in for meals.

> 'We used a great deal of pepper and seasoning. The Polish
> used sugar. The essential test was when you had boiled fish.
> Ours was peppery and theirs was sweet. And you were so
> sensitive to all the cooking, the changes in the cooking, that
> some of the dishes were completely unpalatable. . . .
> [Once] I went into Grodzinsky's family and they were
> having black bread with cream cheese, and they sprinkled
> sugar on it. And I thought what on earth were they doing
> that for?'

Differences in national foods occasionally gave rise to nick-
names:[26]

> 'The Rumanians were called the *Mummaligge* Merchants –
> it's a kind of dish, a kind of porridge, really, or some mash
> thing.'

A new immigrant to the East End had all these differences
and more etched deeply into his consciousness. The feelings
associated with his lost homeland were desperately important
to him. Relatives – especially parents – had been left behind
to an uncertain fate. A Galician visited the Buildings every
year until the First World War to stay a month with his
children and grandchildren.[27] One Russian girl promised that
she would take her first child home to his grandparents, and
this – at considerable cost – she did.[28] *Landsleit* shared this
deep attachment to the homeland with each other.[29]

> 'We used to go and see them and they used to come and see
> us as well. Our parents would talk about all the old times, all

the time. There was still that feeling that we left home. Always was. There was always that feeling.'

It was natural, therefore, that the new immigrant should seek out his fellow countrymen on arriving in a strange city. But in Rothschild Buildings national cliques could not be exclusive. As on that landing with *Litvak*, Polish, Russian and English Jews, Rothschild Buildings flung families together. By the second generation it is probably true to say that these original differences had dissolved, in Rothschild Buildings at least. 'There was a kind of teasing rather than hostility.'[30] *Pollaks* (Poles) would play unconsciously with *Litvaks, Mummaligge* Merchants, Russians and anyone else who would kick a ball around or pick up the other end of a skipping rope. Children did not bother to find out if their playmates and schoolfriends were from this or that side of a border which had no meaning for them.[31]

> 'I didn't mind. Providing they spoke English or Yiddish, I didn't mind. I had Polish friends in the block; . . . we've been friends for years from Rothschild Building.'

As with that Lithuanian boy getting his first taste of Polish food, the most significant fact was that he was invited in for a meal at all.

One factor in particular was of great importance in easing the breakdown of national barriers. This was a shared medium of communication – Yiddish. Yiddish was the language of East European Jewry. It was spoken by Poles, Russians, Rumanians, Austrians and Germans alike, and although words and phrases from each national language would be added, and regional accents were noticeable, the people once separated by thousands of miles who now found themselves sharing a landing in Rothschild Buildings could at least understand each other.

Yiddish was used in shops, at work, at union meetings, among neighbours and friends and in families. National differences would thus not cause a family to be isolated – but failure to understand Yiddish would. Anglo-Jewish families and Sephardic Jews from Holland, the *Chuts*, who did not speak Yiddish, tended to be a disadvantaged minority in Rothschild Buildings in terms of communication (if not in wealth) until children began teaching their East European parents English.

This education was one of the great motors of change in the Buildings during our period, the first prerequisite in transforming the immigrants into English subjects. Yiddish was not just a useful means of communication in the Jewish districts – it was the vehicle of a culture which had been so closely integrated with life in the Pale. Any attempts to keep that culture alive made the survival of Yiddish absolutely essential. Its decay was sometimes fought against with a silent determination.[32]

> 'My mother used Yiddish all the time. She *could* speak English but she didn't want to.'

Collective attempts were made to save the language, for example by the Jewish Workers' Circle who tried to set up a school where all instruction was in Yiddish and to which at least one boy from the Buildings was sent for a time.[33] Even after the First World War, Yiddish was still such a common means of expression, particularly in the workshop, that a *Chut* girl from the Buildings took the opportunity to learn some of it when she found herself working with a newly arrived immigrant,[34]

> 'very foreign, couldn't speak English, and she said to me, "If you teach me how to speak English I'll teach you how to speak Jewish." And I did.'

But all this was a rearguard action, in the face of united and overwhelming pressure from state schools and Jewish schools alike, which had sent their ambassadors, the immigrants' own children, into every flat in Rothschild Buildings by the First World War. Probably in most cases parents were happy to learn English from their children who brought home new words and phrases at the end of every school day. Even if this tuition failed to bring fluency – 'My mother spoke English in twenty-six different languages'[35] – it certainly gave an understanding of English to most immigrant parents. By all accounts this process went far rapidly.[36] And in one Lithuanian family, for example, who had emigrated in the late 1880s and all of whose children were born in England, there had been considerable change by 1914. Most children of immigrant parents were forced to become bilingual – using at least some Yiddish at home – but these second-generation children had no need to acquire that skill:[37]

> 'They [my parents] spoke Yiddish but – we somehow, we became Anglicised quicker – because most of the families were speaking Yiddish to the children, and not in ours. . . . I don't remember speaking Yiddish to *my* parents, *ever*.'

If Yiddish (and, among children, English) helped make national differences – but not the immigrant background – relatively unimportant, one event in these early years made the immigrants' place of birth frighteningly relevant to them. This was the outbreak of the First World War. The Aliens Restriction Act of 1914 immediately made life difficult for Jews born in Germany or Austria. The expense and difficulty of attaining English citizenship had deterred many from applying for naturalisation;[38] consequently, most German or Austrian immigrants were declared Alien Enemies under the Act. Within two weeks of the declaration of war it was reported that German Jews were being arrested and interned.[39]

Internment escalated during the first few months of hostilities, largely due to the spy scare manufactured by a jingoistic press. Men were separated from their families and imprisoned in makeshift transit camps like Olympia, prison hulks, and eventually Alexandra Palace.[40] The prisons were overcrowded, dirty and frequently brutal. For those not interned, or released on licence, petty restrictions bound their every activity throughout the war years. Alien Enemies had to reside in stipulated areas. They had to register under the Aliens Restriction Order and report regularly to the police. Their movements at night were often restricted. They needed a special permit to travel more than five miles from home, or to carry certain articles.[41]

The immigrant's place of birth could make a great difference to his treatment at the hands of the authorities. Some Austrians and Germans came from territory which it was proposed to incorporate within Russian Poland after the war. Immigrants from these areas often escaped internment.[42] But the onus of proving that he was not an Alien Enemy rested on the immigrant himself. This led to a case out of which sprang an organisation of Austrian-Polish Jews in Rothschild Buildings. It concerned a girl born near Brody in Galicia who had immigrated with her parents in 1897, and who was living at No. 51, B Block.[43]

'By the time the First World War broke out I was engaged to be married. Because I was born abroad in Austria I was affected by a decree which came out early in 1915 that an Alien Enemy could not marry. Although I was marrying an Englishman (my husband was born here), when I came to register my marriage I was told that I couldn't get married. . . . Well. I thought, "I'd better go home. My mother will be surprised that I can't get married." So I came home and told my mother. She said, "Go back and tell Mr Baker" – his name was Baker, I still remember the name – "that you are not an Alien Enemy. You were born in Poland; by the time you were born our village was inside the Polish border." '

The girl told all this to Mr Baker, who promptly asked for proof of her Polish nationality. This she could not give. But her case was not unique. 'A society was formed there and then amongst the Austrian people who claimed that they were Polish' and who were therefore not Alien Enemies.

'My elder brother became the Secretary of this Association, and all these people used to meet in our flat. Eventually I got married. I was the first one to be allowed to marry after the passing of the Order. Of course, many people were interned, and this Society gave so much a week to those families who had the breadwinner interned. The internees were allowed to come out once it was proved that they were not Alien Enemies but that they were in fact born in Poland.'

The war also brought new arrivals to Rothschild Buildings. As early as October 1914 it was said that 5,000 Belgian Jewish refugees had come to England 'in a piteous state'. The *Jewish Chronicle* published an appeal for hospitality and asked Jews to take them into their homes.[44] Some Belgian families found flats in Rothschild Buildings, and one moved next door to a Russian family.[45]

'They didn't understand the Russian way of life. They were Jewish, yes, but a lot of things that we did, or they did, we didn't understand. . . . They looked down on us – I dunno why. They weren't rich, because they left everything in Belgium, and they didn't know we were poor. We weren't very communicative. Everything that anybody else did was below them. They only stayed about a year and then they went to America or somewhere.'

To some degree, the war had reopened the old national divides which the people of Rothschild Buildings had largely overcome. But after the crisis, community of interest among immigrants returned to the Buildings. Within it, and playing a part almost as large as the immigrant background, was religious life.

'But they kept a Jewish house'

About religious life, too, it is dangerous to generalise. Religious observance in Rothschild Buildings occurred over the widest possible spectrum – from strict orthodoxy to socialist atheism. Yet within that broad band are discernible traces of ritual which were common to all or nearly all, at least among the immigrant population of the Buildings.

On the first day of Passover 1903, it was estimated that less than a quarter of London Jewry attended synagogue on a very important holiday for the community. The population of adult male Jews who attended once a week or more was considered to be much less.[46] Although it can be expected that the immigrant Jews of Rothschild Buildings were generally more observant than London Jewry as a whole, there can be little doubt that only a minority of men went frequently and regularly to *shul*.* Similarly, it was a minority of families who observed the whole range of Jewish religious ritual.

For that orthodox minority, religious ritual was an exciting and fulfilling part of life in Rothschild Buildings. Typical of many was the family of a stall-holder in the Lane, living at No. 80.[47]

'When I left school early on Friday – you used to leave about 2.30 – I used to go home, wash, change, to go to synagogue. That was a must, that was a thing which you did anyway, if you were a Jewish boy brought up in a religious household, which mine was. We used to either go to the synagogue to which one's father belonged, or one at which you enjoyed the service. I used to go along to one in the City near Bevis Marks, Duke's Place, where I sang in the choir. My father used to come home from the market and he used to go to a local one which didn't have the sort of splendour of this other big synagogue. We used to come home and have our Sabbath meal together. The evening was quiet. . . . Friday night's meal was a sacred meal. Father used to make an evening blessing for the Sabbath. Mother would make a most glorious meal. . . . One could feel the atmosphere.'

For some time the faithful in Rothschild Buildings had their religious life enhanced by the presence in the block of the celebrated Kamenitzer Maggid.† This was Rabbi Hayim Zundel Maccoby, pre-eminent orator of the Lovers of Zion (a pioneer Zionist movement) who fled Russia in 1890 and came to London, where No. 99 Rothschild Buildings, Thrawl St, provided him with his first home. This was one of the few three-bedroom flats in the Buildings and he stayed there for many years. In his day he was the most famous preacher in the Jewish community, attracting large and enthusiastic congregations wherever he spoke.[48] At his sermons, especially in the Machzikei HaDath, extra police had to be drafted into the area to control the crowds.[49]

* Synagogue.
† Lit. 'preacher from Kamenitz'.

'I was a youngster, and I wondered where all the people were going. . . . And I asked somebody and they said, "Don't you know? The Kamenitzer Maggid's coming to the synagogue!" So I went. Of course, they wouldn't let me in: there was no room you see.'

He was strictly vegetarian and would wear nothing that had come from a slaughtered animal – like leather-soled shoes, for example.[50]

'I remember, I was fascinated because he walked so quietly. That fascinated me.'

His fame ensured that a regular stream of visitors would present themselves at his flat for advice and inspiration, including the Chairman of the London County Council, who once came to thank him for his charity work among the Jewish poor.[51]

Rabbi Maccoby was one of many links with the wider religious community outside Rothschild Buildings. The dwellings were within easy walking distance of several synagogues. The believer had a choice of *shuls* in Artillery Lane, Cutler St, Duke's Place, Fournier St (the Machzikei HaDath), Goulston St, Hanbury St, New Court (Fashion St), Old Castle St, Old Montague St, Pelham St, Princelet St, Sandy's Row, Spital Sq, Union St and White's Row. In Thrawl St there was a Rabbinical seminary at the Etz Chaim Yeshiva or Tree of Life College. And at the Great Assembly Hall, Mile End Rd, the tenants of the Four Per Cent could have free tickets for special services held during the High Holidays.[52] All of this was apart from the numberless nameless *stiebels,* local synagogues organised on the old village community basis.

For the observant among the men, synagogue became much more than a place of worship. A garment worker at No. 189 during the First World War had no other social life, using the *shul* as other workers may have used pub or club.[53]

'He never went to entertainment at all. He didn't go anywhere. His entertainment was the synagogue. He used to go to the Machzikei HaDath . . . and he used to go there for services, and he also used to go to meet his cronies. And he mostly discussed religious matters, much more than politics. Talmud – and what this bloke said, what does this chapter mean, and oh no it doesn't, so–and–so says it means something else. That sort of thing.'

For the majority of Jews in Rothschild Buildings who were not strictly orthodox, religious ritual tended to be relevant, but centred round the home rather than the synagogue. A typical Rothschild Buildings family would probably have eaten only kosher food, although even this was said to be on the decline by 1910,[54] and would have kept the Sabbath with varying degrees of observance. They would probably also have observed the rituals associated with the various hurdles of life, like circumcision, redeeming the first-born sons of Yisroel one month after birth, rites of puberty, wedding rituals like the Mikveh, saying mourning prayers in *shul* and at home, and so on. They would probably have gone to *shul* at least on the High Holidays, when even the most casual male believer would put in a token appearance on New Year, or the Day of Atonement or Passover. But just which rules were observed was very much a matter of personal taste and convenience. Take lighting the gas on Shabas. At the Katchinskys' in No. 82,[55]

'Oh, well, we would get somebody to do it. Somebody always did it or else we'd light it Friday and put a metal dish over the light and leave a kettle of water on there all the time, right through the night.'

Observance in a presser's family at No. 77 deteriorated over the years before the First World War.[56]

'When we were kids we used to have a woman come in to light the gas. . . . And then, when she was older she'd make fires Saturday, my mother. . . . My mother rode, Saturday. They weren't like the very fanatic religious. But they kept a Jewish house.'

And in a box-maker's family at No. 101, around 1915,[57]

> 'We were Jewish people – we were practising Jews but not
> orthodox. On Shabas, mother would light the gas herself,
> she'd go out on a Saturday and all that. We weren't that
> orthodox, no.'

This could even happen in homes which kept strictly to the
kosher food rituals.[58]

At the other end of the spectrum came Jews who were
almost entirely non-observant. This was naturally noticed by
the daughter of a religious and learned *shochet* or ritual
slaughterer, who moved into No. 99 about 1911.[59]

> 'Some of the Jews were rank English, you know what I
> mean? They weren't a bit orthodox. . . . You wouldn't
> think they were Jews. We didn't interfere [with them].'

She was probably referring to the Jews of Dutch descent. But
some of this non-observance stemmed from political beliefs.
A socialist bookbinder, Morris Mindel, moved with his wife
and three sons to No. 184 in 1912.[60]

> 'My father was not religious. We were not brought up in a
> religious way. He had been trained, I think, to become
> attached to some job of the synagogue. But his political
> views and his reading [turned him from religion].'

There were other grounds for inter-religious bickering than
political ones[61] although perhaps none was as potentially
violent.[62]

> 'I'll tell you one dispute that I remember very well as a child.
> You know, Yom Kippur we have to fast. Well now, there
> was a family, I think they lived in Lolesworth Building, I
> won't be sure. And they were ostensibly Socialists – didn't
> believe in *anything*[!]. And they'd taunt the people who was
> fasting, and come out with bread. And there was a fight, and
> I remember one young man went over and wrenched the
> morsel out of this other man's hand, and said, "How dare

you?" you know, "desecrate our day". And he didn't
believe in that "rubbish", as he called it. And there was a
fight! I remember that. Yom Kippur day! In Thrawl St.'

Although this sort of thing was rife in the East End during the
early years of the century,[63] militant atheists would have been
a tiny fraction of Rothschild Buildings' population in those
early years, and the large majority of families – no matter how
lax they were about other rules – kept one part of the Jewish
ritual. This was the Friday night supper.[64] For many, this was
what 'keeping a Jewish house' really meant. It was observed
even in the socialist bookbinder's home. It was an integral part
of Jewish identity. Even in those families where men were
willing to work on Saturdays,[65]

> 'I think there was a resentment if they had to work late on a
> Friday. I don't think that the employers pressed that point
> too firmly, because the whole Jewish life was centred
> around the Friday evening meal, whether you were
> religious or not. It was the family gathering.'

Again, the amount of ritual associated with the meal would
vary, but in a typical orthodox home, like that of an Austrian
cabinet maker, about 1900,[66]

> 'Friday night was *the* night, you know, where they ushered
> in the Sabbath. . . . My father would go to *shul* . . . my
> mother put the candles on the table, and a *challa,* a nice
> plaited *challa* [loaf] that she either bought or made herself,
> and cover it with a cloth. And then the man of the house
> would come home from *shul* and bless the *challa*, you know,
> make the blessing of the *challa*, cut off a piece, dip it in salt
> and eat it, and then pass on to his wife a little piece.'

The observance of this one ritual had a communal impact far
beyond the four walls of home. On a dark Friday night there
was a hushed excitement in Rothschild Buildings. 'One could
smell and one could feel the impending Sabbath.'[67] The
children were kept quiet, and the Buildings, which at any
other time rang with children's voices, were in unreal silence.

Candles flickered in nearly every parlour window as the menfolk made their way across the playground, coming home from synagogue or workshop. Over it all, hung a sure and welcoming sense of security in home, family and neighbours. It was on nights like this, perhaps, that the community of Rothschild Buildings was at its closest.

A community of class

The population of Rothschild Buildings throughout these early years was solidly of the artisan class. The Buildings were a colony of skilled labour, with substantial proportions of people engaged in retail sale and other lower middle-class occupations. Perhaps only 9 per cent of wage earners were in unskilled or semi-skilled occupations in 1888 (see Figure 2). Redevelopment had turned the social composition of the Flower and Dean St area upside down, replacing unskilled with skilled labour. The cohesiveness of this class structure was further strengthened by the concentration of the Buildings' workforce in certain industries. In 1900, 60 per cent of working men and women in Rothschild Buildings were engaged in only four trades.[68]

The economic characteristics of the community will be dealt with in more detail later. But important themes associated with the class structure of the Buildings were vital in drawing people together; and in pulling them apart.

The predominance of certain trades and skills gave many men a great deal in common. For example, the sixty-three tailors in the Buildings in 1900 would be affected by the same slack seasons, the same alterations in piece-rates, the same union decisions and often the same strike calls. The tensions and gossip of the workshop would be continued in the playground and on the landings of Rothschild Buildings. Class consciousness was thus to some extent translated into a communal consciousness.[69]

'Her father worked with my father. He was a baster and he worked with my father [who was a presser]. So they used to come home together, used to come into my mother's house

a lot. . . . Any day, they would come in any evening if they
had the time. They came in to one another a lot.'

The immigrant background, too, tended to produce
commonly held class ideals. The people who escaped from
unemployment and declining opportunity were likely to have
been among the most energetic of their community. They
were the most dissatisfied with their prospects and the most
eager to do something about it. Once in England, they were
prepared to work killing hours for low pay because beyond
that lay a material security which their homeland would never
have given them.

In Rothschild Buildings, this class structure of skilled
workers tended to be confirmed by the housing policies of the
landlord. These tended to seek out reliable respectable tenants
in regular employment who could be expected to pay their

BEFORE CLEARANCE

| 69% | Unskilled |

| 9% | Semi-skilled |

| 17% | Skilled |

| 5% Retail sale (from premises) |

AFTER REDEVELOPMENT

| 4% Unskilled |

| 5% Semi-skilled |

| 70% | Skilled |

| 15% | Retail sale (from premises) |

| 6% Lower middle class and others |

Figure 2   Class structure, Rothschild Buildings' site, 1871–88

(Sources: before clearance figures from 1871 census; after redevelopment figures from 3rd Annual Report of the Four Per Cent Industrial
Dwellings Co. Ltd, 1888)

rent on demand. If this picture is a little blurred it is none the less generally true. To a large extent, such a tightly unified working-class structure gave common ideals, with a similar standard of living, similar financial problems, similar ambitions. It appeared as though 'everybody around us was just as poor.'

> 'The people round and about Rothschild Buildings,
> Nathaniel Buildings, the people that I knew, the people that
> I came in contact with, you know, more or less their way of
> life and their living was very similar – very much alike. . . .
> And the same pattern was repeated practically in all houses,
> practically.'[70]

This feeling of being 'very much alike' and 'just as poor' owed much to the insecurity of economic life in the Buildings. For although most bread winners were skilled artisans they worked in low-paid unorganised industries founded on an over-stocked labour market. Many of these trades were affected by seasonal demand so that any family, during the year, could expect a period of hardship or even poverty. The dividing line between poverty and comfort[71] was a constantly shifting one. Even in the same industry it could depend on many variables, like the skill of the worker, the size of his family, the ages of his children, and the ability of his employer to negotiate successful contracts with manufacturer or wholesaler. Even the rule book of the Four Per Cent could not legislate away the vagaries of the East End economy.

Such uncertainty produced sympathy and support when hardship eventually struck – as it did for most families.[72]

> 'My wife's grandfather used to say that if you was to hang a
> rope across the room and everybody should hang their
> packet of trouble on the rope, he said, everybody would
> pick their own. Because if they looked to the next one they'd
> find that the other person's got a bigger trouble than what
> he's got. So he'd be satisfied with his own.'

Class sympathy undoubtedly evoked widespread support and protectiveness within the community in Rothschild

Buildings. But there were cracks in the façade of class consciousness. For the aspirations and independence which in many ways characterised the people of the Buildings – as of the Jewish East End as a whole – spawned their own divisions. The struggle for material security was turned into a struggle of ruthless competition between individuals, in which many were willing to force long hours and starvation wages on their fellow immigrants.

From the 1880s onwards, the Jewish East End was a tense salient of class conflict. The people of Rothschild Buildings were affected by this as much as anyone else. During the great tailors' strikes of 1889, 1906, 1909 and 1912; in the cabinet makers' disputes of 1896, 1900, 1912 and 1913; in the boot-makers' strikes of 1891, 1901 and 1912 or the Jewish bakers' strikes of 1906 and 1913, workers in these trades who had their homes in the Buildings would have talked and thought of little else. But if there were grounds here for solidarity there were grounds also for conflict; like an incident in 1912 – atypical only in the trade involved. It concerned two Jewish tenants of English (or Dutch) descent during the dock strike of 1912. They lived in the same block and one of them was a regular docker who obeyed the strike call; below him lived a youth who was out of work at the time.[73]

> 'And he used to wait on him and he wanted to give him a good hiding one night – the one that worked at the docks – 'cos he was on strike and my brother was doing his job, you know, he got well paid for it. And my brother had to avoid him, you know, 'cos he would have murdered him. As he came home, they used to throw bricks through the train windows because they used to watch these men. They were all blacklegs. Course, my brother was glad of the job.'

Away from these flashpoints, and at a more insidious level, class divisions could at any time cause tension in the block. For even within an ostensibly unified community like Rothschild Buildings there was a whole world of inequality separating an employer's family (like, say the master box-maker's) from that of a widow, or even an under-presser. These inequalities occasionally showed themselves in conflict, as did divisions within the other factors producing community consciousness. But whereas conflicts over national background or religion were likely to decrease as the community grew older, class divisions were likely to widen. Some families rapidly collected possessions and aspirations in their new English environment, and this accentuated differences of status between them and others. This made itself felt, even among the children, as perhaps no other difference could.[74]

'I used to play in the playground. And my father came out – I could have killed him – I was in the middle of my play, and he'd say "Come up!" He was disturbed 'cos he used to think the children were rough; but they were all nice children! He was a bit of a snob, you know. . . . The children were all Jewish.'

Children, perhaps, like those at No. 82:[75]

'There was a family there, there was a couple of families there, they used to say, "Don't play with him. He's a *schnorrer*.* Come up. Look at you and look at him." Something like that.'

Inherent in these class divisions were dissatisfactions and status consciousness which eventually dislocated the community of Rothschild Buildings; and perhaps the Jewish East End as a whole.

'At Rothschild we were like one family'

But, at least in the early years of Rothschild Buildings up to the end of the First World War, these contradictions in communal consciousness were easily contained. If there were divisions they were outweighed during our period by the experiences and attitudes held overwhelmingly in common. What did all this add up to? How did place, the immigrant background, religion and class all combine, and what kind of society did they produce?

* Beggar.

More than anything else, this was a protective society. Out of cares and hardships common to all came a shared resistance and shared help. Few families were so secure that they knew they would never need help, and so mutual assistance seemed not only the right way to live, but the sensible way also.

The nucleus of this protective society in Rothschild Buildings was the staircase block, separate streets turned on end. There were nine blocks in all. On each landing and above and below were your neighbours, other families with many needs and problems similar to your own. These neighbours made the community. If you were unlucky in your neighbours, or if you were isolated because you did not speak Yiddish or for some other reason, then the community of the Buildings did not exist for you. In a close society, it was inevitable that some families were rejected because they did not comply with the rules which that society set itself. We are unlikely to hear of the family rejected because it was dirty, or because of rumours of incest or prostitution, or because of mental illness.

With that caveat, however, the community life which centred on the landings of Rothschild Buildings was friendly and vibrant. 'At Rothschild, we were like one family'[76] is a frequently heard description of the relationship between neighbours.

In Rothschild Buildings there was no shortage of neighbours on hand to assist in almost any domestic situation which called for help, but many of the services rendered did not operate solely in emergencies. Long-standing arrangements were come to. Some, as we have seen, regularly borrowed the rent. Some borrowed money for shopping.[77]

'If anybody was on their own – they want anything for like Sabbath and they didn't have no money, my mother would always borrow 'em. She would never see 'em without.'

A widow was able to go out to work because of the regular child-minding carried out by a neighbour, who 'always used to take my youngest sister in, give her sometimes something to eat.'[78] That neighbour would also look after the other children if they were at home ill, and help in time of sickness was perhaps the most regular service provided by neighbours.

It was given without stinting, even where a new tenant was not yet part of the community. Take an incident in 1908 in C Block, which concerned a Polish presser's family.[79]

> 'When we moved there I was 8. We were only kids, we never knew nobody. Sammy must have been about 3. Well, my mother used to get like cramps, and we had to put hot things on her. And when we come in that night, we were terrible; she was so bad the first week we moved in there. And we were kids. Underneath lived a Mrs Van Guilder, Dutch people – Jewish Dutch people. And she heard us walking about all night, heard us crying – we were kids. She came up – she didn't know us – got me mother something hot. Dressed us, sent us to school and everything. So good they were. "I had to come up", she says, "I heard your little children running about." My father had to go to work. And she came up the next day and made my mother's food and everything. Got us a hot dinner. I thought that was so nice of her.'

In emergencies, neighbours would often combine to effect a complex support system of mutual aid. A good example of such a system in operation is provided by a crisis in B Block during the very early 1900s.[80]

> 'We had a Mrs Morris living in Rothschild Buildings at the time when I was there – I was friendly with the children. She had seven children. This Mrs Morris got on to a chair to put 1d. in the slot for her gas to go on, and she fell and broke her leg. Oh, tragedy! She was taken to the London Hospital. What should she do with her seven children? Well, it was no problem. All the neighbours collected around and said they'd take it in turns each day. One would go in the mornings to give them their breakfast to see that they'd get off to school, and in the evening when the husband comes home he'll take in the pot of whatever it was and they'll all feed together. And this went on until Mrs Morris came home. Now, on the day that she came home from the hospital, the neighbours all around collected together and washed the children, made them all clean, sat them in a row.

There was a baby there, tied to a chair with a towel so he couldn't wriggle out. When her husband brought Mrs Morris home from the hospital she was so overwhelmed by this party, they'd collected some cakes and things and made it all look very nice, that she burst out crying. It was really wonderful to know that her family were being taken care of by her neighbours.'

Where neighbours were chronically sick – even with a dangerous disease – hospitality was often open-handed.[81]

'My mother had a sick girl living next door to her. In fact she was consumptive. Well, we were young kids, so my mother used to say to her, "I don't mind you coming in, but please bring your own knife and fork, your own cup." She used to say to her, "Rain, I've got young children." And the whole family was consumpted; years ago there was consumption, wasn't it? But she used to come in and sit with my mother always. Mother never left her alone. . . . If my mother had anything nice she would say, "Knock next door and say, 'Bring your plate over, Rain, I got something nice for you'." '

The dimensions of this protective society were deepened and perpetuated by kinship. In the first decade or so of Rothschild Buildings, kinship would have been relatively unimportant. But as the community aged, families tended to gather kin tightly around them.

We have seen how, at times of crisis, the population of the block was swollen by an influx of newly arrived friends and relatives. Many of these stayed only until they could find a home elsewhere. But the ideal place to look was the block itself, where the new arrivals could be close to their relatives. Many of these new families were eventually granted separate tenancies in Rothschild Buildings, helped by the recommendation of the existing tenants. It seems to have been a tacit policy that relatives were accorded priority when flats became empty. They would often be the first to hear of vacant flats through their relatives and so were able to approach the Superintendent before anyone else. Existing tenants were able

to influence the choice of their relatives by persuading the
Superintendent of their good character. In some cases it is not
unlikely that money changed hands. Be that as it may, the
degree of kinship was an important feature of Rothschild
Buildings for many decades.

For example, in the 1890s at No. 51,[82]

> 'My father was a cabinet maker, and my mother's three
> brothers were all cabinet makers. One uncle of mine lived in
> Brady Street Buildings, and the other two uncles lived in
> Rothschild Buildings. They too had families, so I had a lot
> of cousins around me.'

About the same time, a widowed Polish mother of four boys
had relations in the Buildings – her dead husband's sister.[83]
Before the First World War, a Russian tailor's son had married
and moved away from home but managed to rent a flat in the
Buildings within a couple of years.[84] And in one of the blocks
fronting Flower and Dean St, a Lithuanian pedlar had both a
married brother and a married sister and their families living in
the Buildings, so his seven children again had lots of cousins to
play with. But here kinship was not always the uniting influence which some might assume it to be.[85]

> 'She seemed to have more money than we had, 'cos I know
> my mother borrowed some money from her and there was a
> bit of a rift. Because I think she asked for it back and mother
> didn't have it to pay.'

A kinship network, then, grew quickly in Rothschild Buildings and was well established within and between generations
by 1914. It helped give the community continuity and helped
resist change, even in later years when housing standards had
changed and the advantages of the Buildings were slipping
away; as in the case of a widowed mother and her married
daughter, sharing a landing in B Block.[86]

> 'I wanted to go out of the area but I couldn't, 'cos if I did my
> mother wouldn't want to go, so I didn't. I stayed behind. I

did have a couple of LCC flats given to me because I was
overcrowded, but my mother wouldn't go. So I stayed.'

So did many others. Of the people interviewed from Rothschild Buildings, the average period of stay there and in
Nathaniel Buildings was twenty-six years, and this does not
take into account the time lived there by parents before the
people interviewed were born. The longest period of stay was
sixty-one years.

Probably for the majority, however, neighbours largely
took the place of family. They gave steady help in terms of care
and finance – roles usually reserved for close relatives. They
were also more important than *landsleit,* usually because the
latter did not live so close to the family in need.[87] This
solidarity among the people of the Buildings – wider even
than neighbours in the block – expressed itself in many ways.
One of the most important was in the relief of poverty. It is not
clear how deep this went, or how its benefits were felt by the
poorest, but collective charity in the Buildings was probably
more welcome than paternalistic handouts from Guardians or
School Managers.

We have seen how an eviction was thwarted by solidarity
among neighbours. But many families were saved from even
the notice to quit by collective action.[88]

'Sometimes, when people had trouble over rent, we had to
make a collection to get their rent. If not, they'd be thrown
out. . . . We always saved them. We always generally
saved each other. When we were kids, I remember my
mother went round and another woman, to make the
money up for the arrears. They were threatened – but they
didn't chuck them out. Oh, we didn't let them go out.'

Poverty was most evident during times of celebration,
when in the comfortable home a great fuss would be made
over special meals. The community reacted accordingly.[89]

'At what we would call the High Holidays – that is the
Jewish New Year and Yom Kippur – if there was no money
available then there would be a little collection to help them

to pay for food. There was nothing more tragic than not
being able to celebrate the New Year. I remember my
mother giving me a few coppers to buy a jar of honey or
something to take to one of these people.'

At other special events, too, this protective society would
try to look after the less fortunate. If a girl from a poor family
in the Buildings was going to be married and her parents could
not afford to hire a hall, then perhaps the neighbours on a
landing would get together.[90]

'And all four gave their rooms for the wedding. And it was
wonderful. And every one of 'em was baking and making
things, you know, for the wedding. Door was open and the
band was playing outside . . . a violin player and a
bugler . . . and anybody and everybody was welcome, the
door open, to come in and drink and have a snack. . . . And
they were dancing, they were dancing out in the veranda
and in the playground.'

Poverty was at its hardest and most bitter when it followed
the death of the bread winner. Death in Rothschild Buildings
was inevitably common knowledge. Most families indulged
in some degree of ritual mourning, and the Shiva could last for
seven days. The whole block would have been affected by the
wailing and chanting mourners, and the Buildings would
mourn with them.[91]

'We'd all rejoice in one another's weddings and all mourned
each other's tragedies. That was a wonderful thing. There's
no such thing any more. If anybody died, everybody
mourned with them, like one big family. A funeral we'd
follow – everybody, like a whole queue, giving their last
respects to the dead person.'

In the early years there were about fifteen funerals a year
in Rothschild Buildings. People would line Flower and Dean
St and Thrawl St as the coffin was carried from the block.
'When Jewish women follow a cortège it's like professional
mourners; very dramatic. If a child died it was a very emotion-

al affair.'[92] After a funeral a collection would often be made, particularly for widows.[93]

Besides this collective response to acute or chronic poverty, the community of the Buildings to a small extent catered for other economic and social needs. People could provide each other with services more cheaply or conveniently than elsewhere. For example, at No. 184,[94]

'My father was looked upon as a local intellectual as far as the street was concerned. And the fact that he could write English – apart from writing in Yiddish – this resulted in many people coming to ask him to read letters or write letters, or forms to be filled in. I have very many vivid recollections of people coming to the house, knocking at all times of the day and night, but mainly in the evening. I have very strong recollections of the neighbours coming together in the house and discussing a particular problem.'

More usually these services would utilise the manual skills of men and women in the Buildings. This subject will be examined more closely in the sections on work, but predominantly this would mean that neighbours and friends would make clothes for families in the Buildings. A hatmaker would make a new hat for a neighbour's eldest daughter when she first started courting. Dressmaking, bootmaking, even cabinet making skills would all be on hand – where, that is, the worker had the spare time and energy.

Services like these, of course, only scratched the surface of the needs of the 1,000 or so people who made Rothschild Buildings their home at any one time. Meeting those needs was the function, to a large extent, of the streets around the Buildings; the wider community of the Flower and Dean St neighbourhood.

2. IN THE FLOWER AND DEAN ST NEIGHBOURHOOD

Stairs and railings

The community of tenement block dwellers in the Flower and Dean St neighbourhood was contained within four narrow streets running between two wide ones. Three of the streets ran parallel with each other between Commercial St and Brick Lane; from north to south they were Flower and Dean St, Thrawl St and Wentworth St. Bisecting them, and completing the gridiron pattern, was Lolesworth St.

Within these four streets were island-like communities centred on the individual tenement block. To a limited degree there was cross-fertilisation between them, particularly marked in the special relationship between Nathaniel and Rothschild Buildings. Many families spent parts of their lives in both these blocks – nearly a quarter of those interviewed. The type of population – Jewish immigrant workers – was common to both. Kinship networks overlapped across Flower and Dean St; for example, Mossy Harris* from No. 142 married a girl living in the Buildings who had grandparents living in Nathaniel.[95] The two buildings shared a lot – the same rules, the same Superintendent and porters (and Henry Barker must have been a good topic of conversation). As in the case of the Ukrainian cabinet maker who moved from Rothschild to Nathaniel Buildings because he was overcrowded, many tenants must have seen the two blocks as one. 'Oh, it was the same, it was all one. . . . You knew everybody.'[96] Although, in fact, neighbouring *between* the two buildings would not have been as close as *within* the blocks themselves, they forged a common identity within the context of the Flower and Dean St neighbourhood.

Relations with other tenements were more tenuous. The East End Dwellings Company's tenants tended to be more diluted with Gentiles than the Four Per Cent's, and according to Russell and Lewis in 1900 the Jewish immigrant population

---

* This is a pseudonym (see chapter 6).

of Lolesworth Buildings formed under 50 per cent of the whole.[97] Strafford Houses, however (perhaps because of the shops beneath them which, in 1901, appear all to have been kept by Jewish people), had a similar population to Rothschild Buildings. But because there were closer shops to the Buildings than these in Wentworth St there appears to have been less contact there than other Jewish tenements, although a bright young lad from the Buildings was to find employment there before the First World War.

The other Jewish tenements in the area, up to 1908, were the buildings put up by Abraham Davis in 1897: Ruth and Irene Houses in Flower and Dean St; Helena, Godfrey, Josephine and Winifred Houses in Lolesworth and Thrawl Streets. From the point of view of the people of Rothschild Buildings, these tenements played a central part in the neighbourhood's community life, for they housed the shops which tenants most commonly used. But this relationship appears not to have extended significantly above ground floor level: if children (like the Austrian presser's daughter at No. 77)[98] or adults had friends in these flats it was more likely to be because they were friends from school, synagogue or workshop rather than because they lived nearby. Ironically, the Jewish immigrant workers of Rothschild Buildings were more likely to see more of those people living within the neighbourhood's geographical boundaries but outside its milieu – the remnants of the casual labouring poor in the lodging houses near Brick Lane (see Chapter 4).

But the neighbourhood was still the nutrient on which Rothschild Buildings thrived. And a remarkably self-sufficient nutrient it was.

'Where the shopping was'

Rothschild Buildings may not have been the most attractive housing in the East End but they were, as the house agent would have said, 'close to all amenities'. In fact, they were remarkably well placed. The Buildings were within a small child's running distance of a variety of shops designed to cater for one and every need of the local community.

The shopping area was divided into two parts by the physical barrier of Commercial St. On the other side of this busy main road – but only two minutes from the Buildings – was the Lane, the paramount marketplace for the whole of the Jewish East End. This was the western half of Wentworth St and the streets off it. On the Rothschild Buildings side of Commercial St were shops which could not be compared to the world-famous Lane but which, for the people of the Buildings, were of equal or greater importance.

In that small criss-cross of streets, entirely dominated by the steep tenements, there were sufficient shops to satisfy nearly all of the local community's needs. Supplemented by street-sellers of a surprising variety of articles and services, the shop-keepers of Flower and Dean St, Lolesworth St, Thrawl St and Wentworth St (east) made the neighbourhood almost self-supporting. And to the east, Brick Lane was itself another varied shopping centre.

It is, perhaps, extraordinary that the shopkeepers of the Flower and Dean St neighbourhood could have survived with the focal point for Jewish buying and selling on their very threshold. Yet they did survive; some even prospered. And in doing so these local shops played a large part in the community life of Rothschild Buildings.

In the struggle for a livelihood which the local shopkeepers unconsciously waged against the Lane and Brick Lane, their readiness to adapt to their customers' needs was critical. Their primary function was to provide goods as cheaply and conveniently as possible. This meant they had to be ready to sell in small quantities. They had to stay open as late as possible, perhaps one or two hours after the statutory closing time of 10 p.m., made law in 1911. They had to be versatile in the range of goods and services they could offer.

The religious needs of the community had also to be understood and met as far as possible. All of the neighbourhood shops, with the memorable exception of Mother Wolff's, observed the Jewish dietary and Sabbath laws. Other shops, in particular Rinkoff the baker, helped the community to observe religious ritual by performing special services.

More important still were the economic needs of the community. Many families in Rothschild Buildings could

Map III   The Flower and Dean St neighbourhood, 1910

hardly have managed if they had not been allowed to buy food and other goods on credit – 'on the book' as it was called. Credit was not given in the Lane so they were forced to turn to the local shopkeepers. Grocers like Israel Garfinkle were forced, in their turn, to give credit in order to attract customers from the Lane and its under-cutting market stalls. But, as we shall see, this symbiotic relationship was rarely free from tension.

The neighbourhood's shopkeepers also had important cultural roles to fulfil. The people of Rothschild Buildings could get to know the local retailers better than their counter-parts in the Lane. They would expect to exchange gossip, and talk (always in Yiddish) of the issues of the day: Mrs Hyams's rent arrears, the drunken Gentile in No. 85, the cap-makers at Arthur Morris's on strike again. There they could meet their neighbours, family and *landsleit* in unhurried conversation.

In all of these ways the local shops made themselves indispensable to the people of Rothschild Buildings and their neighbours. Although they were so close to the Lane, their very position was an asset. Above all they were convenient. The small area they served housed some 5,000 people. They all had to shop somewhere; and because of growing families and restricted budgets, they were always running out of necessities, often at hours when the street markets and more fortunate businessmen had gone home. When this happened, a harassed mother would send out her child on an urgent errand. But the child would not be sent across the busy and dangerous Commercial St, nor past the notorious lodging houses near Brick Lane. She would run down the stairs and along the street to the corner shop. And in doing so she assured Max Salcovitch and Samuel Mindelofsky, Isidore Cohen and Israel Garfinkle, of their own daily bread.

There were thirteen different types of shop in the Flower and Dean St neighbourhood in 1910.[99] Of the twenty-five shops in all, there were seven grocers or chandlers selling groceries, household articles, cleaning materials, even coal; there were two kosher butchers, two greengrocers, two dairies, three bootmakers and repairers, and a variety of others including a Hebrew bookseller, tobacconist, furniture dealer and herbalist. Some of the shopkeepers were of long standing but the merciless competition for custom drove many out of the area. 18A Thrawl St, for example, was changing hands almost annually before Rinkoff set up his bakery there in 1914. Redevelopment in the mid-1890s and again in 1908 meant that by the First World War no shopkeeper in the area would have been there since the first days of Rothschild Buildings. One of the oldest established shops was Jacob Nathan's – 'Jacob the Butcher'[100] – of Flower and Dean St who came in 1899, two years after his shop at 4 Ruth House was built. Most of the others who are recalled by the old people who lived in the Buildings, came to the area in the wake of the second wave of East European pogroms after 1903. Many, like Jacob Nathan and Israel Garfinkle, stayed for the best part of their lives.

Large families and small incomes meant that many people in Rothschild Buildings could afford to buy only for present, rather than future, needs, 'We used to shop every day. . . . Six children, and then my mother was seven – seven people. Every day you'd buy. . . .'[101] This inability to buy in advance made it necessary for the shopkeepers to sell in small quantities, even if it meant considerable inconvenience for them, just to satisfy a family's needs for one meal; if there was no jam at tea-time, for example.[102]

> 'In those years they never sold you a pot of jam. There was a big jar, a 7lb. jar of jam in the grocery shop. And we'd say, oh we want raspberry jam or someat else we'd want – gooseberry jam. Mother would give us a little dish and I would go down and buy a ha'porth of raspberry jam – tea-time that would be.'

That was at Annie Levy's grocery shop in Flower and Dean St.

At other shops they would open tins and divide the contents into portions a poor family could afford. At Garfinkle's[103]

> 'We used to get a big tomato herring for a penny, out of a tin. They used to split up the tin and sell it singly.'

Pickles, too, you would buy by the saucer or cup or dish. But there could be disadvantages, especially when the children ran errands: 'You'd bring your own jar and get a pennorth of pickles. Time you got home, half was finished.'[104]

Milk was another commodity for which you needed your own receptacle. Garfinkle sold milk; he kept it in churns in a small off-room or cupboard just inside the entrance to his shop.[105]

'One grocery shop was there where a funny thing happened. My wife's grandfather used to live in Nathaniel Buildings. He used to go to *shul* every morning, the Machzikei HaDath, and when he used to come back from *shul,* or sometimes before he went to *shul,* he used to stand on the balcony there to get a bit of fresh air. The grocery shop was just facing him. And one morning . . . he sees a man come along from the lodging house with a big jug – they used to get the milk in big urns and the urn was outside the door and shop wasn't open yet. He opens the lid of the milk churn, he puts the jug in and takes out a nice jug of milk, and he goes back to the lodging house. Following that, one morning he sees the man opening his shop; he comes out with a jug of water and pours it into the milk churn – a big jug of water! My grandfather didn't say nothing, but anyway he used to do the shopping because she was rather feeble, so he went down to the shop. So while talking there he says in Yiddish, "You know what I saw yesterday?" The man says, "What?" He says, "I saw a man come up from the lodging house with a jug, and he opened your milk and he took out a jug of milk." So he says, "Did he take much?" So he says, "Not much. He only took as much as you put water in!" He was a very witty man, my grandfather.'

Buying milk in this way was just one method out of three available to the people of Rothschild Buildings. They could have it delivered, and many families were able to pay the extra for the convenience of having the milkman come to the door and leaving the can of milk on the door-handle. And then there was the most exciting way of all, for the children at least. There were three dairies, outside the Flower and Dean St neighbourhood but very near it, where you could buy 'hot milk . . . fresh from the cow' – one of a few surprising reminders of a rural culture in darkest Whitechapel.[106]

'There was one at Black Lion Yard [run by the Jones Brothers and licensed for forty-six cows, which seems to have been the most popular]. In Wentworth St, near the entrance to the Infants' School, there was a passageway near Bell Lane and there was another dairy there. Each cow had its own name and you could go in there and say, "When you going to milk Bessie?" because they liked Bessie's milk.'

Bread was an even more important staple of the working-class diet. After 1914, most of the families in Rothschild Buildings bought their bread from Abraham Rinkoff, the baker in Thrawl St. Rinkoff's 'was really the old-fashioned Russian bakery', and it was famous for two things. First, its bread, especially the black bread – 'coarse, beautiful'[107] – each loaf of which was meticulously stamped with the seal of the Jewish Bakers' Union. Second and even more memorable was the service Rinkoff gave to the neighbourhood as baker of the community's own meals.

Although Rothschild Buildings were provided with a good standard of cooking facilities, the ovens of the living-room range or cheap gas cooker were far too small for the largest dishes needed to satisfy an extensive family. This could have serious implications for the Saturday midday meal when the family would expect a *cholund,* a meat and vegetable casserole. To overcome this problem a complex arrangement was added by many families to the list of Sabbath rituals. The *cholund* was prepared during Thursday or Friday, and before dusk Thrawl St would see a procession of boys and girls carrying their mothers' largest pots and pans to Rinkoff's.[108]

'We used to take it in and they'd give you a sort of ticket [like a tin cloakroom ticket, someone else called it] and God 'elp you if you lost that ticket!'

At noon or thereabouts on the Saturday, the *cholund* was collected by the children, after a tantalising quarter of an hour spent queueing, and carried triumphantly home. There could surely have been no more popular errand. In the very *froom**

* Orthodox.

households, however, no carrying was allowed on the
Sabbath and all cooking would have been completed by dusk
on Friday.

Cooking the *cholund* was the most remembered service of
Rinkoff's, but many families would also have their cakes and
biscuits baked there.

Rinkoff was fortunate in having no competition in the
Flower and Dean St neighbourhood, although there was a
baker nearby in Chicksand St, and his brother had a bakery in
Old Montague St. Perhaps for that reason he was able to avoid
giving credit.

Israel Garfinkle was not so fortunate. He was an Austrian
Jew from Lemberg,[109] and he took over the shop at 3 Ruth
House some time in 1909. He had to compete with six other
grocers in the neighbourhood, one of whom was only a few
doors away in Flower and Dean St. This man with his 'little bit
of a beard' and 'dirty apron'[110] quickly became one of the
street's characters, entering into the life and memories of
Rothschild Buildings.

His shop sold only groceries, but still 'he had everything;
bread, sugar, everything. He was a full-blown grocery shop.'
The shop itself was 'long and narrow. Course, you know, not
fashionable like *now*. Just an ordinary grocery shop what years
ago they had.'[111] Many people from the Buildings used
Garfinkle's always, some only occasionally, and others not at
all. The users and non-users were firm about their allegiances.
Their use of rival groceries was committed, and if they
shopped at Levy's then they would never 'buy by' Garfinkle.

The most likely reason for these exclusive loyalties was a
dispute over credit arrangements. Garfinkle was well known
for giving credit. The better-off families in the block could
afford to avoid any stigma which might attach to them by
shopping there. But those families who needed some sort of
credit – even if only occasionally – knew that Garfinkle
would oblige. It was then that the trouble could start. For it
was a common complaint that Garfinkle overcharged for his
credit.

Most people knew that it was dangerous to go 'on the
book'. There were always rumours that 'many times you used
to find extra money was put on the book – oh yes. . . .

Gradually as the week finished you forgot what you paid for the other articles. So they used to bung on a shilling or two.'[112] Most agreed that Garfinkle did just that. 'If you bought something and told him you'd pay the next day, and it was 1s. 4d., when you came down it was 2s. 4d.'[113] This was an exaggeration, but his haphazard accounting system did seem to err generously in his own favour. One bright schoolgirl watched him at work:[114]

'One shop I used to go into occasionally and I used to see the owner with a book in front of him, and he'd put ½d. here and ½d. there, all the way down. And then when the people came at the end of the week to pay up, their bit of paper didn't tally with his book, but his book was always right!'

This frequently led to arguments in the shop about overcharging and paying twice for goods. Once this happened the aggrieved customer would vow never to shop there again; and never did. Sometimes the bitterness lingered for years after the event.[115]

'My mother didn't use to like Garfinkle because she used to call him horrible names. He was a "rogue", a "villain", a "thief".'

And that was for something that happened before her son, who recalled her anger, was old enough to remember.

Israel Garfinkle was, of course, no worse than any of his rival shopkeepers who were forced to give credit. He had to survive in a society of murderous competition, perhaps paying high rent with key money of £50,[116] and many of his customers recognised this fact. 'He wasn't a bad man. He had to. He had plenty of people that didn't pay him.'[117] In that dog-eat-dog world of unrestrained competitiveness you had to cheat or be cheated.

An incident which illustrates the conflict inherent in credit arrangements and their role in changing allegiance from one shop to another affected the Kaplan family. Mrs Kaplan used to shop at Levy's during the First World War. The Kaplans had been unable to avoid running up a large bill.[118]

'My mother done some washing for her, and she didn't pay
her, and she said she'll take it off the book. My mother said,
"All right." Well, I went down [for some groceries]and she
says to me, "Your mother owes me the money"; and I'll
always remember, she was pulling a cabbage leaf off and
telling me how my mother owes her money. Course, I
don't know. I went back and said to my mother, "You'd
better pay up her money", I said. "She showed me up
terrible." My mother said, "I done all her washing and she
said she'd take it off the book. What does she want?" Well, I
went down and gave her what for. I gave her washing! I was
a kid – and I had the jaw – you'll never believe it but I have.
I did, and I says to her that time, I said, "You're a wicked
woman!" My mother never went back to her no more.'

Significantly, 'after that she went to Garfinkle's.'

Garfinkle's was at the corner of Lolesworth St, on the same
side of Flower and Dean St as Rothschild Buildings. Next to
him, towards Brick Lane, was Jacob Nathan. Many people got
their meat from Jacob the Butcher, but one important item of
the Jewish diet he refused to sell.[119]

'My mother used to buy by him till we moved here [that
was for twenty-four years]. Butchers didn't sell chickens
years ago – they all say chickens have got lice in them. It's
true. You'd never see a butcher selling chickens.'

Two shops away from Garfinkle came Levy's chandler's
shop. The Levys are remembered as martyrs to the tough life
of a Flower and Dean St shopkeeper.

'Oh, they had such hard times; they died young, both of
them. They had a terrible life. They never closed their
shop – you could go in at 12 o'clock midnight[120] and the
shop would be open, honestly, just to get a customer. And
people were owing and owing. I mean, it was getting so
there was nothing in it.'[121]

Next to the Levys came Solomon Finegold, the bootmaker,
at 2 Irene House. He would repair boots and he, too, gave
credit.[122]

'Mother would say, "Go down the *shuster* and tell him to knock the heel in." So I would go down to the *shuster* and when he'd knocked the heel in the shoe, I'd say, "Mummy thanks you very much." And he'd say, in Yiddish, "I don't want your thank you. Tell Mummy I want 2*d.*, please!" That's how it was in those days – on the book.'

In Thrawl St, on the corner of Lolesworth St, was Isidor Cohen's grocery shop. He took it over in 1908, probably from his father who had in turn run it since 1898. He is remembered as 'the *froom* man, Cohen. They were very *froom*. He was particular. He wouldn't stand in the shop without a hat, and things like that.'[123] Two doors away was Israel Landon, a bootmaker and repairer, who moved into his shop at 4 Thrawl St in 1906. The street directory of 'bootmaker' again only tells half the story; for in the front of the shop Mrs Landon sold sweets. 'She had sweets on the counter and he'd sit at the back with a couple of pairs of boots or something. And they were the kindest, the nicest kindest people you could meet. All the children called her Bube Landon* because she was so nice.'

On the Brick Lane side of the Landon's was Benjamin Sidlin's barber's shop, where men would go as much for the conversation as the haircut – 'it was like a club, you know.' The children would probably have preferred Hyman Dekovnik's, just round the corner in Brick Lane, where 'they used to give the kids a whistle when they had a haircut.'[124]

Then next to the pub on the corner of Brick Lane called the Frying Pan, came Joe Harris's chandler's shop. Only the street directory records this as Joe Harris's; to nearly everyone else it was Mother Wolff's.[125] She had run the shop for years, probably since 1902. She was Jewish, possibly of Dutch extraction, although her defiance of the kosher dietary laws created a doubt in many people's minds as to whether she was perhaps only half Jewish. She sold bacon. And it was this fact which marked her out. To the orthodox 'she was a wicked woman because she was Jewish; we could see the terrible thing of a Jewish woman selling pork in those days.' Children from religious homes would walk past this shop holding their breath – 'Mustn't breathe in the bacon.'[126]

* Granny Landon.

But to many people in the area, Mother Wolff 'was a nice person. Everybody liked her. . . . She had a very good name. According to what my mother used to say, she had a very good name.'[127] She was a favourite character in the local children's world.[128]

> 'She was a big fat old woman which we would call very old, but maybe she was only in her forties. She used to have a pinafore on. And murder us kids when we played outside her shop.'

Mother Wolff's shop catered almost exclusively for the Gentile – and very poor – population of the lodging houses in Thrawl St, Flower and Dean St, and Brick Lane. She sold in very small quantities; penny packets of tea wrapped in a screw of paper, small portions of cheese, a slice of ham. The shop – 'long, narrow shop, back parlour, always full of people'[129] – was known as an 'English' shop, although some of the very poor Jews of Rothschild Buildings occasionally found it convenient to buy small quantities there. For Mother Wolff was good to the poor, especially children. Indeed, 'she was good to everybody.'

Just round the corner from her shop, in Osborn St (a continuation of Brick Lane south of Thrawl St), was Dr Turiansky's surgery. Louis Turiansky, physician and surgeon, set up his practice at 10 Osborn St, part of the Victoria Wine Company premises, in 1906. It was probably his first practice after qualifying with his Bachelor of Medicine degree, and he was to stay in that same surgery for nearly forty years. In 1909 the premises were renumbered 24 Osborn St and so they were to remain until destroyed during the Blitz.

It was Dr Turiansky who was most frequently summoned to attend the ailments of the swarming population of Rothschild Buildings. Home visits were more expensive than surgery consultations, about 2s. 6d. including medicine,[130] and because of this the poorest would delay calling him for as long as they could. Visits were attended by some fuss, as the doctor was a conspicuous figure in his 'high hat' and with his pony and trap.

But the area's streets were rarely free from other men of

business who were equally recognisable. For the neighbourhood shops, many and varied as they were, were supplemented by a parade of street-sellers. Most sold food, and some
aimed to fill gaps in the local supply. There was no fishmonger
in the neighbourhood so one vendor at least could be sure of a
welcome.[131]

> 'I remember this man – he was ginger. He had a barrow,
> just an ordinary barrow with a couple of boxes of fish on it,
> and he had a slab, and he had a board across the front of the
> barrow, and he put out plaice, perhaps about a dozen small
> dabs, perhaps about half a dozen small haddocks – 3*d*. a lot!
> I remember my mother buying from him.'

Then there was the muffin man, the winkle man, the
women baigel sellers who would sell hot baigels at 4 o'clock on
a Sunday morning, the platzel sellers whose bread rolls would
often make a boy's breakfast before he left for school, the
watercress man and the toffee-apple man. There was another
who sold pieces of coconut: 'Used to shout "Coconut!" We all
knew already, the kids would all come out.'[132] And then, of
course:[133]

> 'Remember the banana king? He used to stand at a barrow
> with his old mother. . . . He'd say, "Open your pinafore,
> quick, open your pinafore" and bung a lot of loose ones in.
> He used to wheel it round the streets calling "Bananas!"
> Harry the banana man.'

The catsmeat man would call in the morning, carrying his
meat in a box on his barrow and selling it by the skewerful. 'He
was an old man. We used to be frightened of him!'[134] Like the
muffin man, he was not much in demand in Rothschild Buildings, and by about this time it was said that the catsmeat man
was becoming a rare sight in Whitechapel because cats were
not popular pets among Jews,[135] even though there were
plenty of strays around.

Many street vendors performed services for the home.
There was the chair mender who would mend the broken cane
seats on cheap chairs; and there were also travelling knife- and

scissor-grinders, and a glazier, who must have been much in demand in an area with so many windows vulnerable to children's games.

When the people of Rothschild Buildings were unable to satisfy their needs from these local shops and street vendors, they did not have far to go to the commercial nucleus of the Jewish East End. This was the Lane: not the Petticoat Lane of the Sunday morning tourist but the six-day street market in Wentworth St and the narrow turnings off it – mainly Old Castle St, Bell Lane and Goulston St, as well as part of Middlesex St.

It was here that you could buy those goods which were difficult or impossible to get in the Flower and Dean St neighbourhood. For example, the street-seller of fish would not always be there when you wanted him, but there was always fish in the Lane. If you wanted herrings, where better than from the famous Fanny Marks, who has contributed much to the folklore of the Lane. She would stand with her stall on the pavement 'with a sack on her. . . . One barrel of herring she started out with – one barrel of herring! And made all that money.'

But otherwise, when would people shop in the Lane and when in the Flower and Dean St neighbourhood? Generally, a housewife from Rothschild Buildings with a regular income, able to buy in advance and with no need for credit, would use the Lane because it offered variety and cheapness. Shopping in the Lane would be done on a Thursday or Friday morning for the Sabbath. 'Odds and ends' or emergency purchases would be made in the corner shops. For the poor, the Lane would only be used when ready money was available. But for both poor and not so poor the Lane's reputed qualities of variety, low prices and fresh food were great attractions – although the last of these may be yet more folklore, as prosecutions for selling unfit food there were common during the early years.

But there can be no doubting the variety. The housewife who did her shopping in the Lane was confronted by a bewildering choice, for as well as the shops there were over 1,000 stalls licensed to trade in its vicinity.[136] Here, then, you could buy everything: meat from no less than fifteen kosher butchers and poulterers in Wentworth St alone in 1901, of whom

Barnett's is best remembered; a quarter of a chicken from a stall for 8*d.*, if that was all you could afford; second-hand (new if you were lucky) clothes and boots from Jacob Vitsen; children's clothes from Sheletski's in Bell Lane; china from Joseph Palkowski on the corner of Old Castle St; matzos from Bonn's the baker's; splendid cakes, if you could afford them, from Ostwind's or Monickendam's, round the corner in Middlesex St; fresh fruit from any one of a dozen barrows, especially that one near Old Castle St; broken eggs, carried away in your own basin, from another barrow, or 'six pen-north of cracks' from Boxers the egg people on the corner of Commercial St; groceries at Kramer's on the corner of Goulston St; fried fish from Bodger Hart in Middlesex St; gas mantles from a place near Ostwind's; cooking oil from the vats outside Simon Lewis's at 44 Wentworth St; wigs and hair-pieces from Eva Lazarus in Bell Lane. There was nothing which the people of Rothschild Buildings wanted, that the Lane did not provide; and which the Lane provided more cheaply or with more fun in allowing haggling to gain an even better bargain.[137]

Besides its economic importance, the Lane was in many ways the social nucleus of the wider Jewish community. 'The beloved Lane', as Zangwill called it,[138] had wonderful charisma, with its colour, bustle, laughter, the voices of dispute and greeting, all in the universal language of the Jewish working class. It helped unite the Jewish East End, for in the Lane shopped women from Cable St and Mile End, as well as Spitalfields and Whitechapel. Sometimes, when adolescents began courting, their respective parents and relations – some from Cable St and some from Rothschild Buildings – found they knew each other from sharing in the life of the Lane: ' 'cos they used to queue up for meat from Barney the Butcher.'[139] And the Lane's traders helped provide the basis for many of those stories of financial success which play so large a part in the legends of the community – like Fanny Marks and her barrel of herrings, set up as an example to many a Jewish child.

The Lane, the Flower and Dean St neighbourhood, and the added variety (if such were needed) which Brick Lane, too, could offer, produced a unifying adhesive, built of and for the community, and drawing people ever closer to it. They helped keep the community in Rothschild Buildings contented and stable, counteracting those pressures like class aspirations which tended to destroy community feeling.[140]

> 'I suppose it was because he knew everybody there, he wouldn't move away from his own little community. The mother could go down the Lane to do her shopping. There were people there who spoke Yiddish if she spoke Yiddish. The Jews want to be near a synagogue, near a kosher butcher, near where the shopping is. Across the road was the Lane, Wentworth St, where the shopping was. You see, there was all the conveniences there.'

'It was all non-Jewish at the top end'

The new Flower and Dean St neighbourhood which grew up in the wake of the Jack the Ripper murders did not entirely push out the people who had made the old area so notorious. A few common lodging houses still clung on to the sides of the towering tenement blocks which overshadowed all around them. The lodging houses show up as black spots on the poverty maps of the time, in contrast to the pale grey of the respectable artisan dwellings around them. In reality, no scheme of colours or shading could have represented the chasm which separated their respective inhabitants in background and lifestyle. There were differences of class and culture within Rothschild Buildings; but there was nothing to compare with the divisions between the model dwellings and that narrow end of Flower and Dean St.

The people of the Flower and Dean St lodging houses, with their companions in Thrawl St and Wentworth St, were the survivors of a once dominant culture in that neighbourhood. Their way of life – the way of the rookery – now ran in parallel with that of the people of Rothschild Buildings. The two cultures were largely separate; but not entirely so. For there were points of contact which enabled these two widely different groups to come together – sometimes in conflict, but sometimes also in mutual aid.

The lodging houses of Flower and Dean St itself had the greatest impact on the people of Rothschild Buildings. In the early years there were four. Three were on your left as you passed through to Brick Lane, and opposite them was the fourth, at first a lodging house but later divided into small tenements.

At the turn of the century these houses could accommodate

323 people.[1] This number was a legal maximum; because of their special problems common lodging houses had to be registered with the London County Council and were subject to regular inspections. All four were owned by James Smith of Bancroft Rd, Mile End. Jimmy Smith married a girl who had relations in Rothschild Buildings. He made real money from his tenants and as early as the First World War 'he used to drive up in a beautiful car, chauffeur with a chocolate-coloured uniform he used to wear, and the Pomeranian dog with it.'[2] The sixpences which each lodger paid nightly could soon mount up. No. 56 Flower and Dean St was registered for 46 single persons and 29 married couples; No. 57 for 47 persons; and No. 58 for 34 females and 8 married couples. No. 5, opposite, which stretched right into Brick Lane, was registered for 122 men. Some called Nos 56–8 the White House.

They were not the only lodging houses in the area. No. 28 Thrawl St, on the corner of Brick Lane opposite the Frying Pan, was registered for 177 men. It was kept by Mrs Annie McCarthy, the widow of John McCarthy of 27 Dorset St, who had run lodging houses all over the East End. This lodging house survived into the 1920s, as did those in Flower and Dean St, and another in Wentworth St.

What sort of people lived so close to Rothschild Buildings in Smith's and McCarthy's lodging houses? According to Booth, these houses were reservoirs of 'the lowest class of occasional labourers, loafers and semi-criminals'. Economically, they could be classed as very poor, compared with the people of Rothschild Buildings who hovered between comfort and poverty. They survived on a hand-to-mouth existence of casual labour interspersed with out-relief from the workhouse authorities. When in employment the men worked at the docks as labourers, coal whippers and carriers, in the markets as porters, or in the streets as costermongers, hawkers, sandwichmen or anything else they could pick up. Women worked as washerwomen, charwomen, street-sellers or unskilled hands in the clothing industry. When even such employment as this was not available, many would resort to alternative forms of earning like prostitution and petty crime. The women murdered by Jack the Ripper were all, except one, *casual* prostitutes. Usually, they earned by street-selling –

perhaps fruit from Spitalfields market, matchboxes, anti-macassars crocheted in the lodging houses – or as charwomen or washerwomen in nearby homes and offices. But when such work was not to be had then they had to make the choice between starving, the workhouse, or taking their chance on the streets. Annie Chapman had faced such a choice the day she was murdered in Hanbury St.[3]

> She said she felt no better, and she should go into the casual ward for a day or two. I remarked that she looked very pale, and asked if she had had anything to eat. She replied, 'No, I have not had a cup-of-tea today.' I gave her twopence to get some, and told her not to get any rum, of which she was fond. . . . She used to . . . sell flowers. On Fridays she used to go to Stratford to sell anything she had.

There were 100 or so women of the same class as Annie Chapman in Flower and Dean St at the turn of the century. A survey of twenty-three women in the street in 1902 found that their ages ranged from 18 to 48, with an average of 27 years. They were largely single women and it appears that they had each stayed in the lodging houses a matter of weeks rather than over long periods, indicating an unsettled, almost nomadic, existence.[4] Although this may have been so for the majority, some women (like Elizabeth Stride and Catherine Eddowes) lived in the same house for many years, often renting a 'double' with a male partner in a long-term attachment.

This licence for couples to rent beds in the White House was almost certainly withdrawn by 1920. But although its possible use as a brothel had disappeared it was still a resort of casual labouring women (many of whom were prostitutes) right up to the late 1920s.[5] Oral evidence from *within* the lodging houses is necessarily difficult to come by but one case history may be instructive. Clarissa Harriet Knight★ was born the daughter of a Norwich fishmonger in 1899. Perhaps because of a chronic disability (she was born with diabetes) which made schooling irregular, Clarissa left school unable to read or write. When she was 19 she decided to cast herself adrift from

★ The surname is a pseudonym.

her Irish mother and German father and came to London, where she worked as a cleaner in various hospitals in Bloomsbury and the West End. By the early 1920s she had drifted into the lodging houses of the East End, spending a short time at one in Hanbury St and then coming to Flower and Dean St. Clarissa found what work she could as a charwoman: but 'many women used to pick up with men. You understand me, now? *Good* many of 'em.'[6]

The lifestyle of the women of the lodging houses forced itself on the attention of Rothschild Buildings. They were so close to that end of the street that it was impossible to avoid it, although some parents tried to keep their children away from such noisome influences. In at least one family the kids were forbidden to go through that end of Flower and Dean St at all; to get into Brick Lane they were instructed to go via Thrawl St.[7] Although this was an extreme case, many children, perhaps warned off by their parents, viewed the lodging houses with some trepidation.[8]

> 'Oh! Terrified to go past it! There was so much going on down there. We used to run, tear down there.'

Respectable Jewish kids just had to stare at these strange and rough *goyim,* but when they did there could be trouble.

> 'Say if we stopped for a minute, it was "What you lookin' at?" you know, or we thought, oh, we were going to get a whack or something, or they might use some foul language, you know.'

Living so close to the women of the lodging houses, the children of the Buildings could hardly avoid noticing their way of life. The immediate area was to be notorious for its prostitutes for many years to come, and inevitably they affected the people of Rothschild Buildings. It was said that local children would be tipped a penny or two while a client was taken to a dark doorway or a secluded basement.[9]

> 'What was bad down there was the sex life. You saw life in the raw. At the end of the street was a lodging house . . .

for single women. . . . These women were available, prostitutes, old bags, you know. We used to call them Fourpenny Bits. We used to nickname them Woodbine Kates. And they used to come along, drunk as a lord, walk down and meet a man, and sometimes used to do their business in flats up and down the dark staircases. We children, boys and girls, used to see what was going on. Sometimes when you got up early in the morning they'd be lying in a drunken stupor, both of them. They used to mess all over the place. Those who lived on the ground floors always had that trouble of washing down the steps.'

Rough behaviour like this was compounded by another human failing not generally exhibited on the respectable landings of Rothschild Buildings. The odd group of Jewish working men would be regular drinking partners and would frequently arrive home late, singing and quarrelling. But this was nothing to the virtuoso displays put up by some of the lodging house inmates; like one Saturday night before the First World War, just around the corner in Commercial St.[10]

'There was terrible screams. And years ago when they would arrest somebody they used to put them on a sort of barrow or something to take them to the police station. It was like a barrow – if they were drunk they'd put them on this barrow and take them to Leman St Police Station or Commercial St. Now one Saturday night we were all playing, and then there was heard a commotion just opposite our turning. And police and oh such a – And we all ran over and there was a drunken woman laying there using all the language in the world, and all us kids standing there watching. And all of a sudden she picked her head up and said, "I'm not going until you get rid of these so-and-so Jews." So he said, "Come on, children, go home." And we all went home, and then he picked her up and took her away.'

Saturday night brawls and drunkenness at the wrong end of Flower and Dean St were, of course, commonplace. William Mead, an ex-soldier who lived at No. 58, died after a pub brawl in the summer of 1898 outside the George and Guy on the corner of Fashion St and Brick Lane.[11] Another man died five years later after being wounded in[12]

> a quarrel between the women the men were living with in a public-house in Brick Lane, and all were ejected. Outside, the deceased man kicked the woman the prisoner was living with, and later in the night the quarrel was resumed by the two men in Flower and Dean St, where they lived, in the midst of which . . . the prisoner stabbed the deceased man with a pocket knife, which was found a few days later beneath the street grating.

Besides rows which could flare up through drunkenness, there were more vicious feuds of longer standing between the women of the lodging houses themselves. Again, this violence spilled into the streets, in full view of the wide-eyed children of Rothschild Buildings. In March 1908, Cissie Clare, a 19-year-old charwoman, was charged with cutting and wounding the face of a woman street hawker in 'the notorious Flower and Dean St'.[13] Then there was 'Mog the Man', who (some said) was the daughter of a north-country clergyman. When she was sober she was most remarkable for the spotless apron she displayed while standing outside the door of the lodging house she used most often in Flower and Dean St in the late 1890s.[14]

> When she was drunk [a local policeman recalled] she was a 'he-man' and a terror. Stripped bare to the waist, I have seen her fight the worst Amazons of Spitalfields and White-chapel, and despite their inborn knowledge, nearly beat the life out of them, after which she would resist the united efforts of several policemen to remove her to the station, which they were never able to do until they had strapped her to an ambulance.

The police were a normal part of the Flower and Dean St scenery. In the year of the Whitechapel murders five police-men were actually living in Rothschild Buildings, although all had moved out by the end of the 1890s. They were not welcomed by the men and women of the lodging houses.

Their interference in disputes occasionally provoked violent resistance. The autumn of 1906 saw large-scale rioting and window-breaking among striking Jewish bakers in the Spital-fields area. Such heady enterprise infected the people of Flower and Dean St's lodging houses, who came out in force to confront the police.[15]

> The crowd, . . . which was resenting the arrest of the first man, arising out of a sordid domestic broil, was 'mobbing' the police furiously; and the officer originally called on, PC 58H, was kicked many times, and the others were also set upon and handled roughly. [It took one constable] ten minutes' struggle to get through the hostile mob to the assistance of his brother officer.

Ten or twelve years later, an incident involving the police was watched by a small boy from Rothschild Buildings and his friends.[16]

> 'I probably saw one of the most brutal fights of my life there. . . . There was one between a policeman who was challenged to fight with a seaman. It went on for quite a while. We stood there petrified and horrified. The actual fight was in Flower and Dean St, evening, late afternoon. The word soon got around and the police came in force. The seaman was very drunk. All I can vividly recall was this terrific stand up fight. Both were very blooded.'

Another incident which fixed itself in the memory was one which hinted at an equivocal attitude on the part of the police to the prostitutes of the lodging houses.[17]

> 'A woman running after a policeman shouting, "You promised me 1s.!" In tears, because I think she needed 1s. to sleep, and she'd probably gone with him or – And he wouldn't give her 1s.'

The women of the lodging houses and their nefarious habits helped perpetuate the memory of Flower and Dean St's twi-light past and almost obscured its post-redevelopment respectability. Perhaps its reputation would not have remained so indelible if the Four Per Cent and the East End Dwellings Company had been successful in having the name of the street changed, as they had formally petitioned the LCC to do in 1887.[18] As it was, the street's picturesque name evoked many a shudder among residents and outsiders alike for many years to come.[19]

> 'The Flowery's reputation was horrible, horrible. "Flower and Dean Street – you live there?" It had a reputation as regards Nogoodniks, prostitutes, old bags and drunks.'

> 'I used to live near Cable Street, right? And we only lived in one room at that time, of course, see? . . . And a very great friend of mine lived in Flower and Dean Street Buildings. And as far as I can remember, my mother said, "You'd better not go round and see her, 'cos it's terrible round that way." '[20]

'You're not going in that bloomin' churchyard to play!'

In the early years the most frequent point of contact between the immigrant Jews of Spitalfields and their Gentile neighbours was the street. The streets of Spitalfields – and in particular its main artery, Commercial St – had long been notorious for violent crime. Day and night the better-off pedestrian was prone to theft from the person, either by having his pockets picked or by being bludgeoned and his belongings forcibly taken from him. The Flower and Dean St rookery had been home to many of those who lived at least partly by street crime.

Although redevelopment had substantially improved the safety of the streets in Spitalfields, robbery from the person was still commonplace. And as the population of the area grew increasingly dominated by the immigrants, Jews became the victims of the 'thieves and rovers of Flower and Dean St',[21] and their neighbours. Street crime was still so alarming as late as 1898 that the Spitalfields Vestry petitioned the Commis-

sioner of Police for an increased police presence in the area –
just as they had done in the heyday of the rookery, forty years
before.[22]

Anyone, Jew or Gentile, was at risk from the street robbers
of the lodging houses. In August 1896, for example, a Polish
bootmaker was walking through Commercial St early in the
morning, probably to his home in Brushfield St. On the
corner of Flower and Dean St he was attacked by four men of
the lodging-house class:[23]

> They struck him over the head and arms with big sticks and
> tore open his left-hand trouser pocket, but did not get his
> money as it was in another pocket. They threw him down,
> struck him again, and kicked him, but just then a constable
> came up and secured Sullivan, the others escaping.

At the level of the street, then, the relationship between the
indigenous population of the Spitalfields lodging houses and
the immigrant majority was a parasitic one, ironically with the
immigrants performing the role of host. It was acted out in the
wider area around the Flower and Dean St neighbourhood not
only by the men of the lodging houses but by the local women
and children as well.

The people of Rothschild Buildings, like other Jewish
immigrants, were occasionally on the hurting end of this
parasitic relationship.

> 'When I was young – this comes back vivid, you know – in
> the olden days they used to pierce your ears, and I had a pair
> of gold earrings; mother said, "You'll have these in." '

Like many children from the Buildings this young girl played
when she could in the grounds of Christ Church, laid out as
public gardens in the early 1890s. From the earliest days they
were known as a rendezvous for destitute men and women; it
is said that their habit of scratching themselves on the railings
quickly earned the gardens the nickname of Itchy Park. Some
children were accordingly refused permission to play there;
but occasionally parental authority needed reinforcing by
experience.[24]

'My father used to say, "You're not going in that bloomin'
churchyard to play." Well, I used to like to play in the
gardens there 'cos they had swings, and as I came out one of
these rough women, I suppose a prostitute, said, "Oh,
ducky", you know, "let's see your earrings!" And she took
the blooming things out of my ears. She stole them from
me! I didn't know what to do, I was too young. My mother
was very upset. She said, "Where have your earrings got
to?" And after that I never went any more.'

Examples of spontaneous preying on the newcomers
extended to the more wide-awake Gentile kids who lived in
the streets to the north of the Flower and Dean St neighbourhood. By the 1890s few, if any, children lived in the lodging
houses, so the villains of the following scenario would
probably have hailed from the streets beyond the Great
Eastern Railway line into Bishopsgate station.[25]

'My father belonged to a society, and we had to pay the
money in on Sunday. If father couldn't go he would send
my elder brother and myself to pay the dues – it was 2s. for,
I think, a month. He wrapped the 2s. up, so that we
shouldn't lose it, in an envelope or something. We were
walking along Brick Lane towards Bethnal Green and two
little Christian boys came along. They weren't little to us,
they were bigger than we were. My brother had the society
book in his hand. One of the boys said, "Oh, are you going
to the society?", and my brother said, "Yes." The boy said,
"You know, there are a lot of thieves up there. You'd better
give me the money and I'll wrap it up for you." . . . We
didn't have any idea that anybody would steal from us and
these two boys seemed to be our friends. So the boy took the
2s. Needless to say he slipped the 2s. in his pocket, wrapped
the paper up and gave it back to us. The society used to have
their meetings over a public house where we used to pay the
dues. When we came to the society – no 2s.! We were
stunned. What to do? We came home and told our father the
sad story. He lost the payment for that particular period.'

'Do I remember Dosset St? Not 'alf!'

If the streets of Spitalfields were a potential hazard for the immigrants and their children, always at the risk of falling easy prey to the casual poor, there was one street in particular which could boast hazards and threats far worse than any other. This was the notorious Dorset St, across Commercial St from Itchy Park and a mere four or five minutes from Rothschild Buildings. Dorset St was renamed Duval St in 1904 but it was always locally known by the significant corruption of its old name – Dosset St.

As the notoriety of Flower and Dean St waned after re-development, that of Dorset St grew in importance. There was almost certainly a direct causal relationship between the two. Demolition of troublesome working-class areas was designed to secure 'the scattering of the individuals'.[26] But the 'vicious and semi-criminal class' of the old Flower and Dean St would have looked for similar lodging house accommodation in the neighbourhood of their former haunts. Used to a semi-nomadic existence, moving from house to house, the evictions of the 1880s and 1890s may have hurt these people less than any other class. Whitechapel and Spitalfields still offered the greatest concentration of common lodging house beds in London, and nowhere in the district now offered as many as the Dorset St area. When the demolition men came, many lodgers just walked across Commercial St to Dorset St or White's Row,[27] perhaps ousting the inadequate and the incapable, the aged and the mentally ill, in the struggle for living space.

By the turn of the century, 'the hells of Dorset St'[28] could be matched by no other street in the capital. The indefatigable Canon Barnett made it the subject of a letter to *The Times* in 1898; he alleged that the street had grown worse in 'the last four or five years', that is since the last redevelopment of Flower and Dean St.[29]

> Men and women seem to herd as beasts, they feel no restraint for public opinion or a child's innocence, they drink and get drunk as if there was no law, they fight and steal as if there were no neighbours, and they crouch

huddled on the doorsteps as if there was no charity. . . . [The] area is a centre of evil, and, being small, ought not to be beyond the resources of civilisation.

And in 1902, Toynbee Hall was even more explicit in its call for the demolition of the street.[30]

Dorset St was feared and avoided by the people of Rothschild Buildings. Only one person interviewed had ever walked through the street before one side was demolished to make way for the market extension at the end of the 1920s.

'We were told by the children round and about not to go near Dorset St. We heard about Jack the Ripper, but who or what he was we didn't know.'[31]

'Dorset St we used to call Dosset St, and we young Yiddisher boys had an unnatural fear of that street because of the yobbos, yoks.'[32]

'Dosset St was full of prostitutes, case-houses. Never went through there.'[33]

'Do I remember Dosset St? Not 'alf! A Jew didn't, couldn't pass through that street, because there were Christian boys, they used to come in groups, you couldn't go through. I never went through that street. . . . We all fought shy of Dosset St.'[34]

Whatever the truth about Dorset St its local image was certainly bad enough. It had all the characteristics of the wrong end of Flower and Dean St, but in much greater doses. Its domestic disputes were more shocking and violent than elsewhere.[35] There were more fights and stabbings, more talk of 'thieves' dens', than anywhere else.[36]

Gang warfare or less organised fighting among the men of Dorset St, Flower and Dean St and their neighbours frequently impinged on the respectable Jews of Spitalfields. Much of the violence was internecine,[37] but the local Jewish population were often the outraged spectators. Even at the end of the First World War, gang warfare in Spitalfields could still be frightening for those lookers-on like one small boy from Rothschild Buildings. It was[38]

> 'on a Derby Day in Wentworth St, in the market, the Lane. It was with – he used to be known as Darky the Coon, he was dark-skinned. There was a whole series of brothers. Fishermen's knives were used. And I remember the City police coming down; they all appeared to look like giants of men. . . . I'm sure the police finished off what they started in the street.'

Dorset St and its 'ribby riff-raff' were at the centre of such violence. And perhaps the fear that local children had of going near the street was not altogether misplaced. In August 1902, a woman known around Dorset St was found guilty of kidnapping an 8-year-old boy (not Jewish) and forcing him to beg for her in the East End streets. Jane Kelly, alias Steele, alias Kitching, was sentenced to five years' imprisonment; she had been convicted of similar offences several times before.[39]

Yet even with 'the worst street in London', the relationship with the people of the Buildings was not in every case one of shocked remoteness. For from the early 1920s until the north side of Dorset St was cleared to make way for the fruit exchange, the Blue Coat Boy beerhouse was kept by the son of an Austrian presser, brought up in Rothschild Buildings. He and his wife would be visited there regularly by his younger sister. So even at this level there were surprising bridges between Jew and Gentile: and across the almost as powerful division between rough and respectable.[40]

Anti-Semitism

It is difficult to divine the depth of anti-Semitic feeling which confronted the people of Rothschild Buildings in the early years. Many of the incidents which showed the local indigenous population in a questionable light – like the incident with the two 'Christian boys' in Brick Lane who stole the society money – were seen as acts of anti-Semitism rather than ordinary petty crime. So were the fights and name-calling indulged in by groups of children, who battened on the Jewish kids' race and religion rather than their respectability or school or street. But certainly race gave an edge to the conflict, and although that conflict in itself was not on any larger scale than the normal schoolboy dispute it was perhaps more hurtful, giving rise to memories more deep-rooted.

The children from both communities went about in groups. When a group from Rothschild Buildings met one from Hare St or Underwood St – or more especially from Dorset St – they found each other separated by culture, religion, class and territory. It was such a wide and unspannable separation that it inevitably led to hostility.[41]

> 'They used to tease us. I remember when we used to go to Wentworth St School, the non-Jewish boys used to tease the Jewish boys by singing out songs:
>
> > Stick a lump of pork
> > Upon a fork
> > And give it to the Jew boy
> > J-e-w b-o-y-s.
>
> That sort of thing used to frighten us. . . . Amongst the non-Jewish element round there they were poor, ignorant, illiterate. We used to save our schoolboy knickers and suits for Shabas; in the week we used to wear anything. . . .
> So that on Sabbath we used to look nice. We used to buy some grease, vaseline, and smarm our hair down, because we wanted to look smart. We used to go past Dorset St . . . and we used to pass these people who used to call out. We used to retaliate, like boys, and sling things at 'em!'

Although all this tended to look like anti-Semitism to the people of Rothschild Buildings it was no different in scale from the exclusiveness produced by street or school in almost any neighbourhood. Jews' Free School boys would have battles with 'boys from another school, Christian boys' in Bell Lane or the Christ Church National School in Brick Lane, whose pupils would fight with local Jewish kids outside the entrance, just past Fashion St. 'They would have called us Jew Bastards or Jews Killed Christ or something.'[42]

'My brothers were the backward type – they never fought. If they could avoid it, they did. But they used to take their overcoats off and slash the boys, and I'd run away.'[43]

Children had always to be wary of straying into others' territory. This was especially so when they were far from home, south of the river, for example,

'We used to go down the side of the Tower to the Thames and paddle our feet. But when we went across the other side, from Hayes Wharf there used to be warm water coming out and we used to paddle there sometimes, but then there was trouble there with the local boys. So we had to run quick! There was constant fighting between the Jews and the Christians. There was often street fights. . . . And we had to run the gauntlet in those days . . . it was difficult to walk through [some] streets.[44]

The situation probably appeared more threatening than it really was. This was particularly so for these children's parents. To the adult immigrants of the Buildings who had escaped the pogroms of Eastern Europe, the casual poor of the lodging houses may have taken on a significantly sinister look that reminded many of the worst side of the old country. At the height of the pogroms the violence was fuelled by the unemployed and the lumpen-proletariat. At such a time, it was said, 'The doss-house tramp is king.'[45]

In fact, violent incidents in the street affecting the people of Rothschild Buildings solely because of their race appear to have been rare. Some never met with anti-Semitism at all. And it is not unreasonable to assume that statements like, 'It was difficult to walk through some streets', and 'I had to run the gauntlet to get back home', could have been said by any respectable boy finding himself outside his home territory.

Certainly, in the East End as a whole, large-scale riots directed against the Jews were scarce, localised and of short duration. In Whitechapel during the Jack the Ripper murders (1888), in Ernest St, Mile End (1898), and Cornwall St, Shadwell (1901) – the last two sparked off by the housing problem – anti-Jewish sentiment which flared into violence

'failed to ignite the East End.'[46] Although isolated incidents –
with an Irishman picking a fight with a Jew here and Jews
assaulting men who called them names there – were fairly
common during the first decade of life in Rothschild Buildings, they were generally of a trivial nature.[47]

> Mrs. Annie Cohen stated that she had charge of the baths for
> Jewish ladies at Colchester St, Whitechapel. On Wednesday
> evening the defendant rushed into the bath-house, broke
> two windows, a vase and a flower-pot. The defendant
> (Eleanor Gaiger, 32) made use of bad language, and used
> threats respecting Jews. Her conduct was so outrageous that
> many of the ladies there fainted.

After the turn of the century such incidents were if anything
less frequent and equally trivial, although in 1904 a 20-year-old
Dorset St labourer was stabbed in the stomach during what
seems to have been quite a serious clash between 'Englishmen
and a number of foreigners' in Spitalfields.[48]

There was one part of the East End, however, which had a
consistently threatening reputation for the people of Rothschild Buildings. This was Bethnal Green. To those who lived
in Flower and Dean St, Bethnal Green was merely at the top of
Brick Lane, under ten minutes' walking distance away.[49]

> 'Bethnal Green was a Christian area and we avoided it
> because we were afraid of being beaten up. I remember a
> friend of my mother's coming up to us with his hat all
> bashed in. And he had been attacked at the end of Brick Lane
> going towards Bethnal Green. I remember somebody
> saying, "Well, why did you go that way?" He should have
> gone another way to avoid Bethnal Green. It had a very bad
> name.'

Children would not be deterred from going to Victoria Park
or Vallance Rd Recreation Ground, even though these both
lay beyond reputedly hostile territory. But they would expect
trouble in certain streets. Underwood St (now Rd) had a bad
name: 'That street we always avoided going down.'[50] So did
the ill-famed Russia Lane on the way to Victoria Park. And so

did the streets around the animal- and bird-fanciers' market of
the East End, Club Row, like Weaver St and Hare St.[51]

Experience of the area to the north of Rothschild Buildings
was not a happy one and hostility to Jewish people probably
played a part in the insularity of the Flower and Dean St
neighbourhood. The boundaries of the area were clear cut and
some people strayed outside them hardly at all. Knowledge
even of the rest of the East End was sometimes very limited,
with Jewish areas like that between Commercial Rd and Cable
St visited only if you had relatives or *landsleit* there. Otherwise
they were quite separate, and for some people in the Buildings
the attempted fascist march through the Jewish East End in
1936 was the first time that they had ever ventured down to
Cable St.[52]

'It was a funny thing. We were halved. Now, if we came
from Russia, say *suddenly* sort of thing, and there was
nobody to meet you, there was a shelter in Leman St where
the foreign people came and asked for this, that and the
other. Well most of those people – we youngsters used to
call it the other side of the Jordan. Being the Commercial Rd
end most of those people found rooms up there, if you
know what I mean, and remained in that neighbourhood –
clicked round there. But if you had somebody to come and
meet you, like my father came . . . they brought us to
Brick Lane end, 'cos a couple of my cousins lived there. And
we stayed on this side. We never lived on the other side of
the Jordan.'

It is not surprising that Gentile areas like Wapping where,
according to William Goldman, 'Abuse was the very least one
could expect; a bottle across the head was the more likely
penalty',[53] rarely received visitors from Rothschild Buildings.
But some people hardly ever went east of Brick Lane, so that
they were virtual strangers in Old Montague St and Vallance
Rd.[54]

'I mean, I have a friend now, and she used to live over
Chicksand St [directly opposite Flower and Dean St across
Brick Lane]. And d'you know, we never – she sometimes

tells me about streets down there, and I don't even know them. We hardly ever used that end. The only time we used that end when there was a Picture Palace in Brick Lane. And that was the only time we sort of went there, but we didn't go further. No. It's amazing.' [And that was in sixteen years at Rothschild Buildings.]

'The Shabas goy'

The street, with its conflicts and hostility, abhorrence and suspicion, was not the only point of contact between Jew and Gentile, artisan and the casual poor. There was a more positive side to the relationship. For to some degree the two communities needed each other – as employers and providers of labour in the home. This symbiotic relationship, with both sides receiving mutual advantage, extended throughout the Flower and Dean St neighbourhood and beyond, and produced both casual and long-standing alliances. It brings into question the accepted analysis of the Jewish immigrant community as forming 'a society apart', 'a society unto itself';[55] for in Rothschild Buildings, at least, the ghetto walls had gaps in them at the most unfavourable places, affording access even to those lodging house women of the Flowery.

As we have seen, it was necessary for the religious families in Rothschild Buildings to have their gas turned off and on and their fires made up on Friday night and Saturday. These Sabbath requirements had to be met by employing a Gentile to do these things for them. Payment was made after Shabas was out, on Saturday night or Sunday. To the people of the Buildings, this Gentile was known as a *Shabas goy*; to the Gentile himself he was a Jews' Poker.[56]

In Rothschild Buildings this need largely gave employment to the non-Jewish children of Spitalfields, although occasionally, 'We used to get our women to light the fires from the lodging houses.'[57] Boys and girls from Lolesworth Buildings, and Strafford Houses in Wentworth St, would probably have had territorial rights to these gleanings, rather than the children from the other side of Commercial St. They would be

called up by the women of Rothschild Buildings and would
know exactly what to do without complicated explanations in
broken English.[58]

'My mother was very orthodox and we never lit a fire on
Saturday. So we used to get a youngster in on Friday night,
after the Sabbath was in, to put more coal on the fire. And
then the fire would go out and she'd come on a Saturday
morning and light it, and come during the day to put more
coal on, and at the end of the day she'd come along and
you'd give her a couple of coppers. These kids were around,
you know, and they'd come week after week. They might
have been 10 or 11, 12, something like that.'[59]

Sometimes firm arrangements with Gentile families would
be arrived at.[60]

'When we were kids we used to have a woman come in to
light the gas. Used to come from Lolesworth Buildings –
they had a lot of English people living there. . . . She'd send
a kid, her little kid, to light the light. Used to send her up on
Saturday if we want anything done.'

More commonly, however, a family and their *Shabas goy* met
on a purely *ad hoc* basis. The method of hiring proved
embarrassing for at least one mother in Rothschild Buildings.[61]

'My brother lit the gas for a lot of other people 'cos he was
blond and they used to pick him up in the street and give him
a penny and tell him to light the gas. And when he came
home he got a good hiding. He used to come home, he said,
"I got 3*d*.!" Course, my mother said, "Where d'you get it?"
"Somebody took me in to light their fire." But my mother
said, "Didn't you say you were a Jew?" '

A more important economic relationship affected the adult
casual poor of the lodging houses. In 1871, fifty-six women in
Flower and Dean St had described themselves as washer-

woman or charwoman to the census enumerator. Most of these probably worked part-time for local shopkeepers, artisans and publicans, washing and cleaning for a couple of hours a day. After the Jewish influx of the 1880s, many local women found employment among the new arrivals.

In Rothschild Buildings a large number of housewives were financially able to save themselves the drudgery of certain kinds of housework. They were prepared to pay to have the steps and landing whitened, some of the heavy washing for a large family done, and even some domestic cleaning taken off their hands. The women of the lodging houses – and the wives and widows of the local labouring class – were glad to take even the few coppers that could come their way through this heavy work. What they could earn at such employment was not usually enough to enable them to survive and many women from the lodging houses combined it with casual prostitution. Catherine Eddowes from 55 Flower and Dean St was reported as earning some money as a charwoman for Jews in the area; she would almost certainly have worked at Rothschild Buildings.[62] The same went for women from Dorset St, one of whom – the victim of a stabbing in a lodging house – was described as a 'bed-maker in . . . Jews' houses around'.[63] And Clarissa Harriet Knight was doing the same kind of casual labour when she came to the Flower and Dean St lodging houses forty years later. She would knock on doors and ask for work – 'go about and if somebody wanted anybody to do their washing or help 'em – that's how I used to be.' To get work she would have to go 'ev'rywhere, all over the place' so that she could have sufficient weekly contacts to earn enough to live.[64]

Some of the women of the lodging houses, who normally would have been shunned by the respectable families of Rothschild Buildings actually found their way into the model dwellings from which rules and rents barred them.[65]

> 'Mother used to get a woman from there for 3d. or 4d. to come and clean the place out, and she'd give her a meal. One of these strays, you know? And oh, she'd scrub every corner for her, for about 4d. Once a week. Steps and all. . . . And she was glad to sit down and have a meal.'

This particular arrangement, with Mrs Zwart, was longstanding and reliable enough to allow credit to be given to the lodging house woman.[66]

> 'And then she'd give her her money, perhaps 4d. or 6d., and she'd say to her would she mind giving her the money for next week as, you know, she was short of money. Mother used to give it to her.'

More remarkably, a situation very occasionally occurred where the lodging house portals were crossed by one of the residents of Rothschild Buildings.[67]

> 'Susie, an Irish woman, lived in one of the lodging houses in Flower and Dean St and she used to do work for my mother. She used to clean up the flat and go little errands – mother was getting on. This was after I'd got married and left the Buildings [about 1919]. Susie was very trustworthy, although she drank. And I'd go up to the lodging house to ask Susie if she'd come over to the flat to look after my eldest baby while we went out. It was a terrible place. It smelt awful, it was horrible. Her room, which she had to herself, was terrible; very dilapidated, really shocking.'

These relationships, with their regular arrangements and mutual trust, were probably exceptional among the people of Rothschild Buildings and the lodging houses of Flower and Dean St. But there was certainly considerable contact on a less intimate basis, particularly where the rule about cleaning the stairs and landing had to be obeyed.

> 'We used to have a woman used to come and do it, from the lodging house. From the lodging house somebody would come up and do the stairs – give her the water outside.'

The population of Rothschild Buildings probably gave considerable employment to the casual poor of the lodging houses. 'They used to come up from the lodging house and ask us what we wanted done. Young women, usually', perhaps like Bridget, the Irish woman, 'always drunk', who did a

Litvak family's washing for some time around 1910.[68] In 1914, when an unemployment crisis hit the East End clothing industry and there was deep and widespread distress among the Jewish population, its repercussions were felt among the women of the casual labouring class. With husbands out of work, Jewish housewives were unable to pay out even a few coppers for a charwoman or laundress.[69]

The lodging house women were not the only ones to benefit from employment in Rothschild Buildings. In fact, they were possibly not the major group to work there,[70] for domestic help would also have been sought among the more respectable Gentiles of the neighbouring model dwellings or, as we shall see, among the few destitute Jews of the Buildings themselves. It was more likely to be women of this class who did the comfortable family's washing, either in the employer's scullery or in their own homes.[71]

> 'I know we used to have our washing done for us. There was somebody who used to – in those days . . . a woman would do a week's washing for 9*d*. And they were all taken away every Monday morning, washed and ironed, and brought back at the end of the week. . . . There was a woman who lived in Lolesworth Buildings and she used to do it. We always found who'd do our washing. Not Jewish.'

The relationship between the Jews and Gentiles of the Flower and Dean St neighbourhood's model dwellings grew more cordial as time wore on. Certainly, the cash nexus was not the only meeting ground. A young girl, daughter of a presser from C Block, Thrawl St, lived opposite many non-Jewish children in Lolesworth Buildings.

> 'They weren't so bad. I don't know – we mixed very well with them. . . . Well, they used to play with us when we were children – we played with a lot of English children, in the Building, we did.'

Indeed, the children among the returning hop-pickers from Lolesworth Buildings would bring back 'hopping apples' for their Rothschild neighbours.[72]

Plate 1   Rothschild Buildings, c. 1902. This is a photograph taken from the Commercial St end of Thrawl St. The main entrance to the Buildings is on the left, a similar gate in Flower and Dean St was kept locked to stop people from crossing the courtyard as a short-cut between the two streets. The window-boxes which had a special significance in these Buildings are much in evidence and appear in some instances to be of quite luxuriant growth. There is a blatant contravention of Rule 6 on the staircase nearest the camera at first floor level where some washing has been hung over the balcony. If Jack London *did* see the Buildings on that summer evening in 1902 this is how they would have looked: the photograph was taken for an early edition of his book, *People of the Abyss*.

Plate 2 *above* The courtyard of Rothschild Buildings, 1971.

Plate 3 *left* Flower and Dean St, 1971. In its last years Flower and Dean St, crowded for almost all its history, was often as deserted as in this photograph. On the left are Nathaniel Dwellings, half empty by this time, having been classified as slums a year or two before. In the right foreground Rothschild Buildings are visible to attic level and Ruth House faces us where Flower and Dean St narrows and where Lolesworth St begins. The original line of Flower and Dean St can be seen at the far end where the old lodging houses close in on each other before the street reaches Brick Lane.

Plate 4 *above*   Poster, Rothschild
Buildings, 1902.

Plate 5 *right*   Poster, Rothschild
Buildings, 1902.

Plate 6   A Whitechapel court and local Jewish children, c. 1902. More
immigrants lived in houses like this than in the model dwellings. Built in the early
nineteenth century or before, with shared taps and closets, owned by rack-renting
landlords, these courts and their two- or four-roomed houses were inferior in
every way to Rothschild Buildings: yet they avoided the stigma of 'barrack-life'
which the model dwellings still had about them till the 1920s. These would have
been cheap houses to rent, as cheap as anything else Jewish immigrants could have
obtained at the time, yet the children are not particularly poor. All have boots and
all the clothing appears intact, but two boys are (perhaps temporarily) without
the obligatory cap. The girl on the right of the picture, isolated from the group of
comradely looking boys, has a clean pinafore over her smart dress and boots.

Plate 7 *above* The Russian passport used by Mrs Mindel to take her first son back to his grandparents near Vilna for a visit in 1913.

Plate 8 *right* Newly arrived immigrants at the Port of London, c. 1900. Still with the marks of Eastern Europe—Russian caps for men and boys, many-coloured shawls for women and girls—these immigrants wait for permission to leave the port and be absorbed into the Jewish East End. The Katchinsky's were picked up from just such a group by their uncle and taken to a little house in Ship Alley, only a few minutes away, before finding rooms in Rothschild Buildings. Possessions, roughly bundled up or, if too bulky, carried for all the world to see like the boy's pot in the foreground, lie on the cobbles or rest on shoulders. Many would also be clutching scraps of paper with the address of already established friends or relatives with whom they could lodge or who could help them find rooms. Many others, without the good fortune of the Katchinskys, walked to the Poor Jews' Temporary Shelter in Leman Street where they were taken in for a few days before fending on their own.

Plate 9   Schewzik's Vapour Baths in Brick Lane, 1910. Schewzik's was a few minutes' walk from Rothschild Buildings, up Brick Lane towards Bethnal Green. One of the attendants on the women's side lived in the Buildings. The men's vapour baths were the most used in Schewzik's and Friday evening was the busiest time. Orthodox men would go to the vapour baths from their workshops and would come out invigorated and glowing from the treatment (which could involve steaming, rubbing down with loofers and being lightly beaten with birch twigs to get the circulation moving), in a suitable state of mind for prayers in the Spitalfields Great Synagogue across the road. Non-believers, too, would use the baths because they were also a part of the East European culture which the Jews brought with them to the streets of the East End. It's immediately visible in the fancy minarets of the illuminated sign and the wrought iron at the tops of door and window openings. Parts of this large building were let out by Schewzik to a watch-maker (left) and shipping agents, again strengthening the links with the ports of Europe from which the Jews embarked.

Plate 10   A Jewish club in Stepney, c. 1903. An old mission hall in a working-class street has been quickly converted into a club, one of the many which people from the same areas in Eastern Europe set up in the East End, or which had politics as their object (like the Jewish Workers' Circle at 136 Brick Lane). 'Mission Hall' is rudely covered by a plank and posters in Yiddish or Yiddish and English are pasted on the walls and noticeboards. The top poster is advertising a mass meeting of East End Jews at the Wonderland, Whitechapel Rd, perhaps to protest at the pogroms taking place in Kishinev at about this time.

Plate 11 Commercial St, c. 1900. This was the hazard faced by errand-runners between Rothschild Buildings and the 'Lane' on any weekday, although we see the street at its busiest point with waggons being loaded with flowers and vegetables from Spitalfields Market, the gabled building on the left. The first turning on the left is Dorset St, with the Britannia beerhouse on the corner and the office of the *Jewish Express* next door. On the right are the railings of 'Itchy Park' beside Christ Church—like Dorset St a world apart from Flower and Dean St but just 100 yards away.

Plate 12 *above*   Corner of Goulston St, Wentworth St (the Lane) and Bell Lane, c. 1900. The commercial centre of the Jewish East End, this street market catered for every need of the people of Rothschild Buildings and also provided many of them with employment. Most stalls are uncovered on this sunny afternoon at the turn of the century enabling us to pick out the sacks of nuts in the left foreground with the measuring can on top; the vegetable stall in the near centre which appears to have just cauliflowers and bananas; barrels, perhaps of pickled herrings, middle right, other fruit stalls and various unidentifiable commodities on barrows, stalls and just sold from wicker baskets in the roadway. Behind the stalls are the shops— Goodman's the pickle makers across the road in Wentworth St, and next to that Dubowski's prosperous provision dealer's and chandler's shop.

Plate 13 *below*   'Dosset St', c. 1900. This was the most notorious street in London, reminiscent of Flower and Dean St in its heyday. Jewish people were afraid to walk down Dorset St and only one person I talked to from the Buildings ever did so. Lodging house lamps can be seen all the way down the street on the left-hand side and it was these which gave the street its evil reputation. There was a surprising link between the Buildings and Dorset St: from just after the First World War a beerhouse in the street called the Blue Coat Boy was kept by a man of Austrian Jewish descent who had grown up in Rothschild Buildings. Apparently it was a more orderly pub than many he kept after that side of the street was demolished, in the late 1920s.

Plate 14   Women outside a Flower and Dean St lodging house, c. 1900. This is 56 Flower and Dean St, next to Nathaniel Dwellings, the railings of which can be seen on the left. It was one of three lodging houses adjoining each other which mainly accommodated, at the time this photograph was taken, women and 'married couples'. Many of the women earned a living by a combination of casual jobs and prostitution. Some of the women found cleaning jobs in the flats of Rothschild Buildings and some had positions of trust there. These women were among the poorest in Stepney: their landlord was among the richest. The women and two children in this picture, apparently engrossed by something on the ground between them, remind us that a great deal of home life spilled over onto the pavements and did not end at the street door.

Plate 15 *below*   Cabinet making class, Jews' Free School, 1908. Although this is evidently a carefully posed photograph with not a wood shaving in sight, these excellent cabinet making workshops were cleaner and airier than anything the boys would find as 'improvers' in the real world. At about this time there was a tendency among the Anglo-Jewish middle class to find the sons of immigrants work outside the crowded trades of the Jewish East End but this did not inhibit the instruction of traditional skills. Boys like Reuben Landsman, son of a cabinet maker and destined to spend a working lifetime in the trade, picked up their first knowledge of timber and tools at Jews' Free School.

Plate 16 *above*   The sand pit, Victoria Park.
This was just one of the attractions of the park
in its heyday, which made the 40-minute walk
from Rothschild Buildings, through strange
and sometimes hostile streets, worth while.
Trips were often planned with some care, for
the park was by no means an everyday treat,
and older girls would make sure of adequate
provisions for the youngsters before setting out
on the expedition. On the day this photograph
was taken, some time around 1900, the sand pit
was busy with boys and girls, most of them
respectably (and some even well) dressed. The
sturdy child's handcart made an effective
pushchair for one well-swaddled baby.

Plate 17 *right*   Sophie and Betsy Schiffenbaum,
c. 1902. On a half-day holiday from
Commercial St School the two young
Schiffenbaum children went to a photographer's
in Commercial Rd to have an impromptu
portrait taken. They didn't dress up for the
occasion and wore their school clothes, in
Betsy's case (right) a red and white blouse and
pleated skirt, made for her by the dressmaker in
Nathaniel Buildings. It was summer and
the girls wore shoes to school—most
had to make do with boots.

Plate 18   Stepney Jewish Lads' Club
certificate, 1918.

STEPNEY ✶ JEWISH ✶ LADS' ✶ CLUB.

GERALD · G · SAMUEL · MEMORIAL · PRIZE

——AWARDED TO——

——NOAH   AARONS——

"whose conduct, public spirit, unselfish character
"and loyalty to those ideals of our faith and coun
"best conform in the opinion of the managers to the
"aims and aspirations which the Stepney Jewish Lads' c
"was founded to foster and inculcate."

President : REV. J. F. STERN
Chairman : GEORGE H. FAY

JULY 1918

Plate 19   Infants' department classroom, Commercial St School, 1921. Here are the children of the first children of Rothschild Buildings, the second generation brought up in the English or Anglo-Jewish school system. The classroom is more colourful and relaxed than it would have been just ten years before, even though the children have apparently been told to look especially studious and grown-up.

Plate 20   Schneider's clothing factory, Whitechapel, 1916. The trend away from the small workshop and towards large factories employing hundreds of hands affected the tailors and tailoresses of Rothschild Buildings even in the years before the First World War. Schneider's was one of the biggest local firms with premises in Durward Street, a fifteen-minute walk from Flower and Dean Street. At the time this picture was taken they had gone over to war production. The firm had a history of workplace struggles and in October 1916, 500 men and women struck for better conditions and won within a week. The photograph reveals that even factories were cramped and crowded, with the 'khaki' knee-deep in the gangways. The workforce in the machining room is predominantly young foreign men (largely exempt from military service) with a few boys and women.

Plate 21 *above, left* Minnie Zwart at the time she was working 'on the khaki'.
This was for Mr Gershon in Shepherd St, about 1915 when Minnie was 22.

Plate 22 *above, right* Reuben Landsman on a day-trip to Brighton about 1922.
Reuben is the motor-cyclist, glad to be out for a day from his father's workshop.

Plate 23 *below* The Schlom family, dressed for a wedding, c. 1917. The family
are off to the wedding of Mrs Schlom's nephew, the son of a cigarette maker
from Bow. By this time they had left Rothschild Buildings and were living in
Heneage St where Mr Schlom could keep his bananas in a shed at the back.
Nathan Schlom is on leave from the army and stands next to his fiancée. Next to
her is Jenny Schlom, still making cigarettes for the Ardath Tobacco Company.

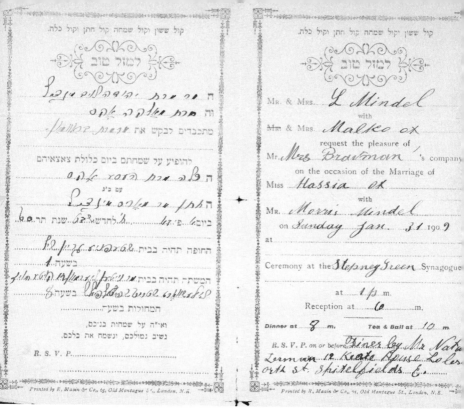

Plate 24 *above* Wedding invitation in Yiddish and English, 1909.

Plate 25 *below* Jack Brahms, Army Cycle Corps, 1916. Jack, the only Jewish boy in his unit, is in the front row on the right. Within a few months of the picture, taken in Reepham, Norfolk, Jack was invalided out of the front-line trenches with severe frost-bite.

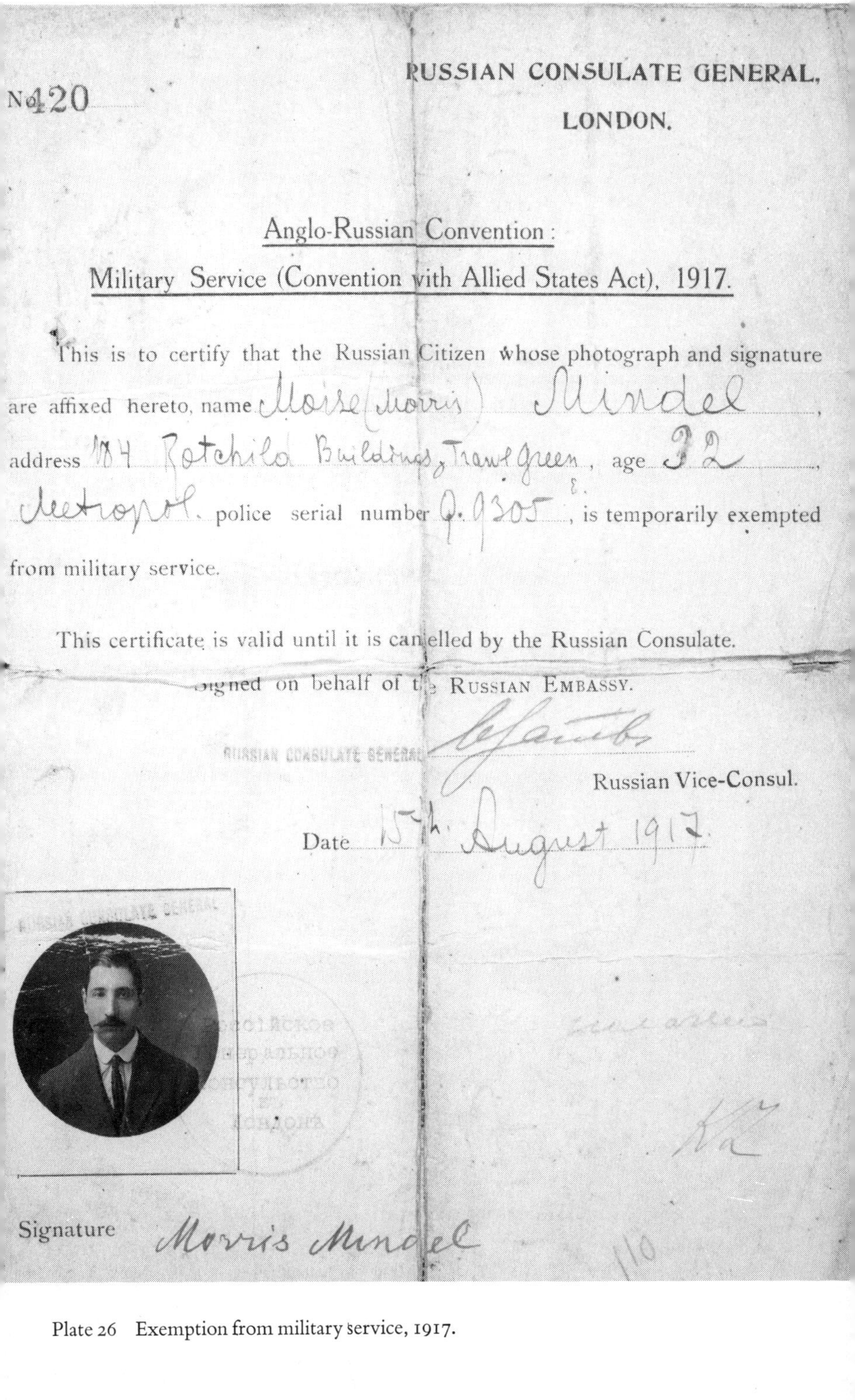

№ 420

RUSSIAN CONSULATE GENERAL,
LONDON.

Anglo-Russian Convention:
Military Service (Convention with Allied States Act), 1917.

This is to certify that the Russian Citizen whose photograph and signature are affixed hereto, name Moise (Morris) Mindel, address 184 Rotchild Buildings, Trawl Green, age 32, Metropol. police serial number Q. 9305 E., is temporarily exempted from military service.

This certificate is valid until it is cancelled by the Russian Consulate.

Signed on behalf of the Russian Embassy.

RUSSIAN CONSULATE GENERAL

Russian Vice-Consul.

Date 15th August 1917

RUSSIAN CONSULATE GENERAL

Signature Morris Mindel

110

Plate 26 Exemption from military service, 1917.

Plate 27 Morris Mindel, c. 1915 (standing, on left). Born in 1885, Morris Mindel emigrated from Vilna, Lithuania, after the post-revolutionary reaction of 1905-6. He was a life-long socialist and a respected community leader in Rothschild Buildings. He was also one of the founder-members of the Jewish Workers' Circle, a non-sectarian organisation of the left which helped keep alive Yiddish culture and socialism among the East End Jewish working class until the Second World War.

Plate 28 The rules, annual reports and balance sheets of the London Ladies' Tailors, Machinists and Pressers Trade Union were printed in Yiddish and English up to its amalgamation in 1939.

Neither were close friendships between Jewish and non-Jewish schoolchildren unheard of. At the Commercial St School there were only a handful of Gentile kids at the turn of the century. An Austrian cabinet maker's daughter from Rothschild Buildings became the close friend of one of them; it led to an incident which for once confounded her mother's religious logic.[73]

> 'We had a girl in my class called Nelly. She was a Christian girl and I liked her very much. She used to come to school without shoes on her feet. I couldn't understand it – no shoes and stockings and it's raining, it's winter. She used to sit next to me, and I said, "Aren't you cold?" – her feet were so cold. No, she didn't feel cold. I used to very often go home to her for tea, and I could smell a very nice welcoming smell. It was bacon. Although her mother offered it to me I had an idea I mustn't eat it. I told my mother what had happened and asked her, "Why mustn't I eat it?" I couldn't have been more than 9 at the time [in about 1901]. And mother said, "Because it's not very healthy." And I said, "But Nelly Conlan walks about with bare feet and she's never had a cold in her life!" But that was all the information my mother gave, and I had to be satisfied with that!'

For many, like that cabinet maker's daughter, contact with the indigenous poor of the East End gave an insight into poverty and hardship far greater even than their own. It evoked a natural sympathy which displayed itself in acts of kindness on various levels. At its most altruistic it could involve a family – itself subject to periods of want – regularly giving to the nameless poor who shuffled past their window.[74]

> 'When we were living in the Buildings, if you ever had any lunch over you'd wrap it in paper and hang it on the railings outside so that somebody would come along and take it. If we had half a loaf left over it would be left out like that for the ultra-poor, the beggars.'

On a more personal level, affection and concern were generated among individuals from widely different backgrounds.

Some charwomen would be employed by many housewives in the Buildings, probably recommended by word of mouth. One of these was Mrs Anderson, remembered by several families.[75]

> 'She was very fond of me – a lovely old dear – I'll always remember her. She had a flat cap and a shawl which she tied with a great big hat pin round her bun, and she used to smoke a clay pipe, with bloody tobacco!'

She found work in enough flats in Rothschild Buildings to make it worth her while to come all the way from Bermondsey, where she lived amongst the deepest poverty in London. She worked in the Buildings for years. But in the early 1920s she suddenly stopped coming. One of her employers was so concerned that she went to Bermondsey to find out what was wrong, and she took her daughter with her.[76]

> 'I tell you what I remember so vividly about it: the poverty. 'Cos when we got there she was lying in bed with old coats over her. The windows were broken and there was coats over the windows. It was so pathetic. Never went again. You know, we just left her some money and came away. . . . I can just remember the inside – the little grate with nothing in the grate, and that, laying in the bed, and oh it was really pathetic. . . . No, she didn't get better. The next we heard she was taken into hospital and she died.'

5 Growing up

'Incubator Row'

Children played a predominant part in the home and community life of Rothschild Buildings in those early years. You might almost have said that children *were* Rothschild Buildings. Certainly, there were usually more children living there than adults. In 1899, for example, there were 665 out of a total population of 1,162, and this numerical balance of power was largely maintained through the 1890s and probably throughout the whole of our period.[1] The young marrieds of Rothschild Buildings were parents to 205 children aged 5 or under in 1894, some one in six of the total population (see Figure 3); there were 37 births in the Buildings that year.

The world of children stamped itself as firmly on the character of Rothschild Buildings as anything the pencil of the Four Per Cent's architect had done. It etched itself in sound. Alongside the cries of new-born babies demanding feeds and attention through every day and night, rang the voices of up to 200 toddlers, more articulate in their demands but equally vociferous. There could never have been a moment when the voices of children were completely silenced throughout those massive Buildings. The brick of walls and concrete of courtyard rang with the sound of laughter or tears; it bounced from one side of the Buildings to the other and filtered from above and below. Now, when there are streets in the East End where the sound of a baby's cry is a rarity, the only modern parallel would be a school playground at break-time. But this was a break-time which lasted the best part of a day and lingered on through the night.

Nor were Rothschild Buildings alone in being home to so many kids. The Flower and Dean St area as a whole was a community of children. In 1896 the model dwellings of

Flower and Dean St and Thrawl St alone thronged with 1,547 of them.[2] Small wonder that to the local sanitary inspectors Flower and Dean St was known as 'Incubator Row'.

The story of childhood in Rothschild Buildings has a special place. For the children of the Buildings had their own community, their own struggles and their own culture. And what's more, it was a majority culture.

Childhood for many in Rothschild Buildings began in the two-roomed flat which was to be its home for many years to come. In the 1890s there was a birth in the Buildings every nine or ten days. For expectant mothers, it was a more than usually difficult time. They had to drag themselves up those unending flights of stairs, perhaps carrying bags of shopping or other young children. 'My mother was pregnant on the fourth floor. Can you imagine? . . . She nearly lost her life having twins.'[3]

The inequalities within late Victorian and Edwardian society expressed themselves immediately in the manner and circumstances of the birth. Probably the majority of women had their babies at home. But compare a birth in the Kaplan family – with the father of the unborn child just buried and the

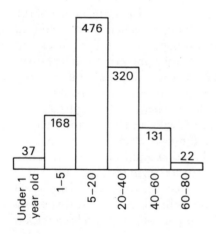

Figure 3   Population of Rothschild Buildings, 1894

(Source: *Annual Report of the MOH for the Whitechapel District*, 1894, p. 13)

mother working to support five youngsters – with one in a family which had money enough for almost middle-class luxuries. Perhaps the following incident meant less to Mrs Kaplan herself – she was a strong woman, experienced in childbirth – than it did to her anxious daughter.[4]

'I remember my mother went to Fashion Street. And my mum done a day's washing and came home and our Morrie was born! I'll *never* forget that. She done a day's washing – and she couldn't – we begged her not to go – she was just waiting for the money. And as she walked in she had my brother at home.'

That was in 1911. Six years later a young wife left her flat at Stamford Hill and came back to Rothschild Buildings to have her first baby at home with her mother. She was married to a qualified engineer earning good money at the Woolwich Arsenal and he had been comfortably brought up in Burdett Rd, Mile End. The wife's parents were renting two flats in the Buildings at the time so that space posed no real problem.[5]

'I had a nurse. I engaged a nurse for a month. She stayed with me six weeks. For which I had to pay her. That was my own, you know, I wanted or my husband wanted and we paid. Her name was Nellie Vaughan. . . . She stayed with me in this flat that I'm talking about, you see. There was my bedroom, and in the front Nurse Vaughan slept.'

Normally the caring duties of Nurse Vaughan were more likely to be performed by one of a choice of women relatives, or a neighbour, or by a 'woman-help' provided with the aid of the Sick Room Helps Society for a small payment.[6] Comprehensive care was particularly important at a time when medical caution prevented a mother rising from her bed for perhaps two weeks after confinement.[7]

The excitement and preparations for a birth must have ignited the landings of Rothschild Buildings. It may have been very much a family affair but as with other dimensions of home life it was all public property in the Buildings. So many mothers were all well aware of the signs of impending birth and neighbours listened for the slammed door and precipitous footsteps down the concrete stairs which told of the summons for the doctor. After the bustle and anxiety of the birth were over someone was dispatched for the triumphant husband, and the cot was delivered. 'I had a cot for Cyril that my mother bought just before he was born and it wasn't delivered until he was born because of the, you know, they're superstitious.'[8] An aunt, perhaps, would provide a bassinet for displaying the baby to best advantage in his smart new dress and petticoats, although those tiring stairs made outings with the pram a trial.

Most mothers breast-fed if they could, a procedure which doctors and social workers heartily applauded.[9] There was no need for 'Back to the Breast' propaganda in Rothschild Buildings. The breast-feeding habit undoubtedly contributed to the low infant mortality rate of the Jewish East End, particularly at a time when alternative feeds were unreliable and medical knowledge sketchy.

The Jewish mother's celebrated care for her children was thus given a firm foundation, helped by the fact that only a very small minority had to go out to work. Those who did would have their youngsters looked after by a neighbour, as we have seen, or by older children, or they could take them to the crèche at 23 New Rd. This modern nursery was opened in 1901 by philanthropic subscription and could accommodate up to fifty young children of working mothers; one of its aims was to 'teach mothers cleanliness and care' and it charged 2d. per day per child.[10]

This combination of charity, thrift and paternalistic interference in the lives of the respectable working class was to steal its way into every pore of the children of Rothschild Buildings before they could reach adulthood. Even before they were born, organised charity for the deserving poor might well have affected them. A substantial number of the women of the Buildings had their children in Mrs Levy's Lying-in Hospital, Underwood St – 'Mother Levy's' as it was known. Mrs L. A. Levy had undertaken charity visiting work for Charlotte de Rothschild herself, and this led her into the work for which she is best remembered in the Jews' Lying-in Charity.[11] Generations of East End Jewish children first saw light in the Lying-in Hospital: 'They were all Mother Levy's children.'[12]

'For midwife's bills they paid Mother Levy. They used to pay a couple of pence a week when they were in the stages of having children. She'd come and see if you had room or convenience in your own house. There was a Mrs Levy and a Lady, a titled Lady, Mocatta. One of them would come and see, "Oh, you've got a nice bedroom, you can have your children at home." But if you couldn't you'd go in there.'

Mother Levy's child or not, babies were a stimulus to pride and competition. There were regular baby contests for which many immigrant mothers were barred by just one of the superstitions they attached to their children's welfare. To weigh a child was apparently to threaten it with death inside a year.[13] Perhaps that year was up when one of the *Litvak* mothers of Rothschild Buildings gave in to temptation and entered her second son in this strange and alien competition, some time in 1912.[14]

'He was a massive child. When my mother entered him for a competition at Spitalfields Church – babies of a year old – there were protests that he was above the age! And he had a beautiful head of blond curls, and he won a prize!'

At least one baby had been successfully launched into that larger world of competition, protest and prizes.

Parents and children

The role of children in the home and the relationship between parents and children varied from flat to flat. So too did the daily routines of individual families. Consequently, it's unwise to talk of 'typical' lifestyles or 'average' households. But into these unique individual patterns were inserted economic influences – common to the large majority in Rothschild Buildings – which maintained a commanding grip on many aspects of family life. The most important of these influences left children without fathers for by far the greatest part of their waking hours. The effect is summed up by the son of a cabinet maker who vacillated irregularly between employer and workman status.[15]

> 'I never used to see my father, as a schoolboy. Never saw him in the daytime. Well, I never saw him till the weekend. The only time I saw him was Saturday. 'Cause he went to work in the dark and came home in the dark.'

Many others, of course, were more fortunate (although in some cases it could be a blessing in disguise) but most families felt the pressures of the workshop penetrate the stout walls of Rothschild Buildings. It began in the mornings when most men had left for work by the time mother called the children. How long a man remained at his bench depended on the trade involved, the time of year, his skill as a worker and his employer's skill in obtaining contracts. But whatever those conditions, for the rest of that day, six days in the week, a child's contact with his father depended on one very simple rule:[16]

> 'If he had more work then we saw less of him; if he had less work we saw more of him.'

It was a bald statement of the subjugation of the needs of family to the needs of workplace.

> This enforced separation meant that moments which some fathers and children (particularly sons) could snatch together were lived as fully as exhaustion and other demands would allow. The socialist bookbinder wasted little of the time he had with his two boys.[17]

> 'I used to see him over the weekends. But then, my father was perhaps a little different, because he would take us on a Saturday or a Sunday to visit museums, so therefore in some ways I probably saw more and was more influenced by him because of that than if I'd seen him continuously. . . . I recall my father singing the Red Flag to me. I was still at school. We would talk about May Day. . . . And one of the most pleasant memories I have [is] of him reading to us the

works of Sholem Aleichem and Peretz, and other Yiddish
writers. . . . Because we very rarely quarrelled.'

Other fathers, too, would take every opportunity to use
their time with the family for special occasions – giving
children things to look forward to and things to remember.
The master box-maker, also,[18]

'was one for going to museums, and the Tower of London
and Kew Gardens and that type of thing – Richmond. We
used to go, I always remember because we used to go to
Broad Street . . . and get the train, about 5*d*., and go all the
way to Richmond or Kew Gardens. . . . Yes, on Saturdays.'

Neither of these men was religious and it may be that time
spent with orthodox fathers was less informal than in these
more liberal homes. Certainly, the synagogue would take the
father away from wives, daughters and even sons as much as
the public house may have done in other circumstances. In
these homes there was little or no time for anything besides
work, *shul* and sleep. Home, for the children of these men, was
sometimes an almost ferociously silent environment where
father and sons would find no common ground for communication outside the Old Testament and the Talmud. In the
home of a widowed Russian tailor, an elderly man whose
youngest son was born when he was in his fifties ('I always
used to think he was my grandfather'),[19] his children's *spiritual*
welfare was preserved at the expense, and to the exclusion, of
any basic material provision. Every evening the son spent his
little spare time having a 'chat-chat' outside the sweetshop in
Lolesworth St, or a 'warm-up' in the kitchen of McCarthy's
lodging house. For meals he depended on the soup kitchen or
Phillip's fish-and-chip shop in Brick Lane.[20]

'He never made any meals or anything like that. Most of my
meals was a ha'porth or pennorth of chips, every night . . .
sitting on the doorstep with it. . . . I didn't know what
home life was when she [my mother] died [in 1911]. . . . I

had to fathom for meself. . . . My father couldn't do much
for *me*. . . . I had to bring myself up.'

Yet at the same time,

> 'my father used to *make* me go to the synagogue every
> morning, 7 o'clock in the morning, and in the evening
> services, every morning and every evening.'

This single-minded relationship which, as we shall see, led
to extraordinary gaps in communication, was mirrored in
another Russian family, a family of cabinet makers. This
father, again, was a very religious man who enforced his rule
at home with an Old Testament in one hand and a cat-o'-nine
tails in the other.[21]

> 'I tell you, I couldn't talk to him. Well, I remember as a kid
> they used to buy the straps, a little stick like this [about nine
> inches long] with four or six bits of leather hanging on it.
> They used to buy it down the Lane. . . . Yes, as kids we had
> it, course we had it.'

In religious and disciplined families like these entertainment
had to be fitted in with the demands of ritual, and so itself
became ritualised. For some children probably the only contact with their father outside home would have been the
weekly promenade in stiff Shabas-best. The 'Saturday Walk',
usually along Whitechapel Rd from Mile End to Aldgate
Pump, was a feature of life in the East End. Alternatively, a
widowed bootmaker would take his son and daughter 'to
Tower Hill, every Saturday afternoon – that was our Saturday walk.'[22] An orthodox cabinet maker would spend the
occasional Saturday afternoon with his wife and four children
in Victoria Park,[23] and so on.

In many cases, these periods of contact were tragically brief.
The immigrant worker was susceptible to a number of debili-
tating chest infections, especially tuberculosis.[24] Cramped
living conditions, ill-ventilated and damp workplaces, the
steam from the pressing cloths, exhausting labour for long
hours, all took their toll. The White Death claimed many

victims among the men of Rothschild Buildings, leaving
widows and children deep in poverty. In 1913 the death rate
from TB in Rothschild Buildings was two and a half times that
of the rate for Stepney as a whole.[25] As treatment improved
and convalescent homes mushroomed, the death rate from the
disease among East End Jewish workers declined; TB was just
as prevalent but it killed fewer people. But one who failed to
escape was that military tailor from Kiev whose family had
struggled so hard to emigrate. Soon after he moved into
Rothschild Buildings in 1911 Mr Katchinsky was taken into
hospital for the last time; his daughter was 11 years old.[26]

'He was in St Peter's Hospital – it used to be in Vallance Rd.
And I used to go to Jewish Free School, and I used to tear my
dinner ticket up instead of going to dinner and run to wave
to my father from the window.'

The plight of widows and their families in the Buildings
deserves special mention and will be dealt with in more detail
later. But whether a mother was widowed or not, the wearing
toil of bringing up a large family in the Buildings was solely
hers. She could expect little help from her husband.[27]

'My mother was always the first one up. It was considered
the – I can't ever recall my father ever making breakfast
for himself. . . . The women's place was in the home of
course – they did everything.'

Most mothers, by all accounts, were remarkably competent
cooks. The meals they spent their time preparing play a large
part in the memory of a child's day in Rothschild Buildings.
There seems to have been more than one mother like Chaim
Lewis's: 'Nothing pleased her more than to feed us as though
the act of feeding answered every maternal instinct in her.'[28]
Many remember the soups which formed a substantial part of
the mid-day meal during the week. 'I think that our staple diet
was her ability to make a variety of soups from barley, from
broad beans, from farfel, and then there was lockshen',[29] or
potato soup, or borsht; or soups made with 'soup greens',
small bunches of many different vegetables sold in the green-

grocer's at a penny a time; or soups made with chopped meat, perhaps with 'little dough chips – *chipcollach* we used to call them'.[30] These soups could be a main meal in themselves, but[31]

'another day there'd be – I suppose you'd call it Irish stew. It was carrots, onions, potatoes put in there, and bits of meat, you know, Yiddisher meat. . . . We used to have minced meat made into cutlets and they used to be put in the oven; the potatoes and rice were parboiled and then put in with the fat and the onion and the minced meat. . . . In the Lane itself there was one shop which only sold liver there. . . . There was a great big liver used to be in there and he used to cut a piece off, and "Mummy says it's got to be soft" . . . because sometimes the liver wasn't tender enough and used to have to go back with it. . . . And oh, yes! Blooms had their place on the corner of Old Montague Street. And on Monday they'd have the offcuts from the weekend of *vorsht,* all different kinds of *vorsht,* you see, like salami. . . . You'd either fry this *vorsht* or some would have it cold. . . . That was delicious. Oh God, you thought you were so wealthy if you had some of that! And sometimes you'd get the little sausages, like the Viennas – you thought you were the tops when you bought some of those. You'd cook them and the water from that you'd make your gravy; and if you had that with liver and the brown gravy which was nice and thick . . . and you added this to it, and all your vegetables – oh, it was delicious! It was a remarkable thing – out of nothing you could make a meal.'

Food was a strong link with the homeland. In the summer months a family from Austria would sit down to a traditional meal based on yoghurt:[32]

'you had those Jersey potatoes, the very tiny ones; you'd cook those. And you'd have some curd cheese, that sort of thing, and you'd get the radish, cucumber, the whole lot, you know, cut up very small and mixed up with this sour milk stuff. It was gorgeous.'

When puddings were made they would often be butter cakes, honey cakes, biscuits or strudel, but these were delicacies most often reserved for the weekend.

For some mothers the work of running the home was so overwhelming that her children were rarely given the opportunity to sit down and eat their meal with her.[33]

'No, my mother was too busy serving us, and preparing. We never knew when she ate. . . . Her efforts and her energy were directed to make sure that we were fed.'

But this of course was not her only function in the family. Seeing so much of their mother and so little of their father had a large effect on the relationship between parents and children. As well as confidante, provider, manager of the home, she had time to share in play and spontaneous leisure activities – taking the children to Victoria Park on a sunny day in the long holidays, walking arm-in-arm with her daughters in the evenings admiring the naphtha-lit stalls of the Whitechapel Rd and gazing in bright shop windows. And the economic status of her artisan husband rarely made it necessary for her to go out to work; she was always there when the children needed her.[34]

'I can never remember coming home from school at any time but my mother wasn't there.'

But even if mother was always there, children would have to take upon themselves at least some of the burden of running the home. The sheer hard labour that was the mother's lot had to be distributed among her children from an early age to give her as much rest as possible; for if the husband worked a day which began at 8 in the morning and kept him away from home for twelve and a half hours, his wife had to toil a good hour longer either side of that. Only exceptionally would she take on herself all those endless duties of cooking, washing, shopping, mending, cleaning and worrying.[35]

'I really, personally, in my own life, I can't remember doing a lot of chores. My mother really was the what you call the *baleboosta* . . . she was a good housewife.'

Most children, however, coming out of school at 4.30 knew that it was not all play and being waited on at home.[36]

'It was important to come back home. Living on the fourth floor, if my mother needed anything she would expect us to run down and do the shopping.'

Running the whole gamut of errands around the Flower and Dean St neighbourhood has already been explored and was just one of the ways most children were expected to help in the home. In many families the bulk of the heavy housework – cleaning, washing, ironing – would be divided on a rota basis. In other families the labour was divided on more specialised lines. In an Austrian presser's family, for example, where the mother had trouble with her legs,[37]

'We always used to help at home. Ironing was my job. I didn't like scrubbing – my sister would do all the cleaning. My father would like me to iron his shirts.'

Sharing the household chores in this way may appear equable on the surface; but there was one large area of in-equality within the family. The anti-feminism which firmly fixed secondary roles for women in home, religious life and work began very young. In a Lithuanian family of seven children – five boys and two girls – the division of labour was far from fair.[38]

'Well, it was like it happened at that time: if you were a girl *you* did the helping, you felt you had to help. The boys were sort of – weren't expected to help at all, and they didn't.'

Boys, however, were often asked to run errands – a more enjoyable chore than household duties – and this could in-clude one other childhood task dictated by the rhythms of the workshop. During the busy season a man would be expected to stay at his bench – in all departments of the garment industry – until the job was finished. To tide him over till he came home a son or daughter was dispatched with 'a can with a cup that fitted into the top' filled with tea, or soup in a can, with sandwiches. This gave children a first insight into the world of work which was to absorb them so soon. When a boy and girl from the Buildings took their father his supper at a bootmaking factory in Fleur-de-Lys St they were regularly greeted at the door by a man who shouted something back to his fellow-workers in Yiddish: 'And afterwards, when we asked my father what it meant, it meant "Stop swearing!" see, because the children were there.'[39] Late working could generally be anticipated by the family, but very occasionally the exigencies of the tailoring trade demanded that a worker should stick at his machine throughout the night. A trouser-maker from Ekaterinoslav was caught like this in a workshop one night during the First World War and he couldn't let his wife know what was happening.[40]

> 'He was working somewhere in a side turning in Leman Street. I had to go there and find out whether he was all right and take him some food. He sent us a postcard but he got home before the postcard was delivered!'

Children made other contributions to the home economy. Their skills, acquired at home, school or club, could be used to eke out the father's earnings. Girls, in particular, would learn to make their own dresses and blouses, skirts and pinnies. 'My eldest sister used to make all our dresses. . . . She used to make all the clothes.'[41] Occasionally they would make some of their mother's clothes. But this was not a one-way relation-ship. A tailor would make suits for the boys, or a shoe-maker would 'make my boots. Until I was 16 [when she left home] I always had handmade boots.'[42] And a cabinet maker would use his skill and scarce spare time at the workshop to knock up little possessions for his children.[43]

> 'From odd pieces of wood he used to make us toys, my father. My younger sister – I remember he made her a little table, I can see it now. He painted it white – and little stools.'

But in the families of widows – or where the bread winner was sick or unlucky in employment – more and more hardship and responsibility fell on the children, and they had to take upon themselves a large part of the task of keeping the home together. If the struggle for a decent standard of life was waged harder and longer in many of the streets outside Rothschild Buildings, even there, in the families without a mother or father, that struggle could reach heroic proportions. One-parent families were a substantial minority[44] in Rothschild Buildings. They were the poorest members of an unequal society – and those inequalities affected family life at all levels. To see how wide those differences were, even within a superficially homogeneous community like Rothschild Buildings, we must turn to the experiences of one family – the Kaplans.

The Kaplan family

'It's a wonder to me. I never thought I'd live to this age, because I had a terrible life.'[45]

Annie Kaplan was one of the six children (four girls and two boys) in the Kaplan family. Mrs Kaplan was born in Lemberg, Austria, in 1874. She married a tailor and they emigrated to London in 1902, two years after Annie was born. In 1911, Mr Kaplan died from tuberculosis shortly after moving into No. 83 Rothschild Buildings, Thrawl St.

'My mother was a widow at 37. I felt very sorry for my mother. . . . My mother didn't have one penny coming home. My mother come from a comfortable family. And her father used to say a girl mustn't learn a trade because a girl gets married and doesn't need a trade. My mother had no trade at all and we didn't have a penny coming in.'

By shifting from one job to another, by pawning every possession she had brought with her from Austria, by wringing as many pennies as possible from the Jewish Board of Guardians, Mrs Kaplan struggled to keep the home together and feed her children. The Jewish Board of Guardians paid out more than a third of all their fixed weekly and monthly allowances to widows, but these in many cases would pay for little more than the rent. For even this a widow had to sacrifice her self-respect to home visits and prying questions, and in some cases had to sacrifice her children to the West Norwood Orphanage.

> 'My mother went to the Board of Guardians – 12s. a week! Six children! Oh, the Board of Guardians, they were terrible. . . . I remember those days. You had to pay 5s. rent. But then they wanted to take away Becky and Hymie – Morrie was too young – to Norwood. . . . My mother said, "If four'll starve, six'll starve. If I have a piece of bread for four, I'll have a piece of bread for six. . . . No, I'm not giving anybody away. However it'll be", she says, "we're all happy together". . . . So they stopped the money.'

The Board of Guardians' charity was often supplemented by specific organisations which doled out relief in kind, like soup, boots, clothes, 'Bread, Coal and Meat', and some others catered just for this one particular need group, like the Israelite Widows' Society. But unless there were alternative sources of aid widows would have to work not only to preserve their independence but to keep body and soul together. So they took on two jobs – working long hours during the day or into the night for subsistence wages; and catering without help to the needs of young children for every other waking minute they were sent. For the next three years, until Annie and Yetta could leave school and get a job, things were very hard indeed. They never had enough food. In the mornings,

> 'Breakfast? Hard bit of bread and have to take that off to school. We never had a breakfast those days.'

When they came home for dinner:

> 'Nothing when we came home. Cold banana. Cold banana. Our sister always says to me, "If I ever see a banana again I'll

scream!'' My mother used to buy a bunch of bananas. Cold
bananas we had always.'

And after school,

> 'My mother used to put us to bed 5 o'clock. We had nothing
> to eat. We were starving, and that's not a lie. My mother had
> to put us all to bed 'cause we were hungry.'

The Jewish Soup Kitchen, which had moved from 5 Fashion
St[46] to new premises in Butler St★ in 1902, provided relief for
hundreds of families as poor as the Kaplans. It opened for the
coldest weeks of the winter from mid-December. In the dark
winter evenings the queue – 'You never seen such a queue in
your life' – stretched along Butler St and round the corner into
Tenter St. In that queue were 'chiefly women, wan and
hungry-looking under the shawls wrapped over their
heads'.[47] Among them on some evenings were Annie Kaplan
and her friend from Rothschild Buildings, also a widow's
daughter, who used to put her hands over her eyes in shame
because she thought that if she couldn't see anyone, no one
could see her. But someone, perhaps from school or the
Buildings, was always passing, a respectable someone to
whom queueing for charity was an unforgivable crime:

> 'A friend of mine said to me, "*Schnorrer*!" Oh, I cried. "I'm
> not going no more. They called me a *schnorrer*." She lived in
> our flats. I hated her. Always hated her.'

On Fridays, when the distribution of food took place in daylight, attendance at the Soup Kitchen was noticeably lower.[48]
    The 1,000 or so people entitled to relief had to submit to
'careful enquiries' from the investigating officer sent to their
homes by the Soup Kitchen. A successful applicant was given
a numbered kettle to hold the amount of soup for which her
family was entitled. The Kaplans would have been allowed
three quarts of soup and one and a half loaves – 'it was a nice
loaf but the soup was lousy.' Annie, after queueing for a long

---

★ Now Brune St.

time, would hurry home with her kettle and loaves across Commercial St and thankfully up the stairs of Rothschild Buildings.

To help pay the rent of the one-bedroom flat, to buy clothes for her children – 'My mother wouldn't buy no second-hand clothes, never' – to buy a little extra food for Friday night, Mrs Kaplan pawned

> 'Everything! My mother had no wedding ring on her finger. Everything. And my mother came over here, she came with plenty. But talk about before you knew where you was it was all gone.'

Annie would have to queue in the alley behind Hohn's the jeweller's in Whitechapel Rd – the front entrance was for jewellery sales alone – or else to the 'Uncle' at the church end of Fournier St.

> 'My mother had a suit. . . . And that suit went in and out. In on Friday and out on Monday. My father was dead. We always laughed about that suit – he was dead but his suit still went in and out! We can laugh today.'

Like the suit, the candlesticks which decorated the orange-box table on a Friday night were pawned but always redeemed – 'My mother would have never done without candlesticks.' But 'She never got the wedding ring back.'

Yet when all these sacrifices had been made, the standard of life of the Kaplan family was well below that of their neighbours and schoolfriends.

> 'I didn't have no clothes. I used to cry. I remember Fanny and Florrie van Guilder, they went to the Lane to buy lovely dresses, and I wanted a dress, and my mother said she'd got no money. I cried and cried but I never got none. . . . If I wanted ¼d. I used to cry for it and not get it. I remember I went to school – cried myself sick; I wanted to buy – they used to have those peppermints like a walking stick. I

wanted ¼d., and my mother says, "All right, cut my
throat, take ¼d." So I says to her, "I wanna walking stick."
"Well", she says, "you can't have it." '

Mrs Kaplan's irregular work meant that when she did have a
job she worked all the hours she could while it was available.
One of her most regular jobs was as a cook in a kosher catering
concern which specialised in wedding receptions, from which
she could perhaps bring home 15s. plus tips.

'She worked for a woman in Old Montague St; she was a
cook – Mrs Segal. They worked for her. The cook lived in
Old Montague St but they went to the weddings, either the
house or a hall. . . . Very hard work it was. . . . 2 o'clock
in the morning she'd come home. . . . Sometimes she'd
come home and it was as light as this, in the summer. If
they was a long way – I've known her come home 4 or 5 in
the morning. . . . Used to come in, oh, her clothes were
absolutely soaking wet. She had to take everything off and
we used to wait up for her and we used to have everything
ready for her to change. Oh, it was very hard work. But the
money wasn't bad – well, I mean for those days. I mean,
that's the only time we sort of got a bit comfortable. . . .
She'd bring home some food if it was over. . . . They had a
quarter chicken or sometimes they had a drop of milk
over. . . . She used to bring home sometimes cakes – oh,
yeah, we used to wait up all night! . . . My sister and I, we
used to sit and look out the window and wait for her. As she
come up we used to run down to meet her.'

Often she was left little energy for the sort of caring attention other children in Rothschild Buildings would expect from
their mothers.

'My mother never played with us. I never had a lot of love
when I was young. My mother didn't have the time. She
was a very good mother but she never had time for all that.
We never had a party, no birthday, no toys, nothing. No,
my mother didn't even know when was our birthdays.'

As Mrs Kaplan was often at work all day her children had to accept much more of the burden of running the home.

'We all had our work cut out. . . . Like, one of my sisters, she used to make all the clothes . . . and my other sister used to do all the housework. Even my brother used to help with the housework when we was youngsters. . . . I remember our Hymie used to get on the floor and clean it, used to scrub the floor. . . . All the holes she used to fill with me, everything she wanted done she done with me. You know Morrises; the shop? My mother, she owed them money. . . . In those days shops were open till 12, 1 in the morning. . . . I remember my mother kept me up, and when she saw the woman went inside to bed and the husband was in the shop, she told me to go down to get a loaf, otherwise they wouldn't have given it. He didn't realise. . . . I used to look after the money part. . . . Our mother had a card as long as this! Garfinkle used to give us credit. . . . But when I got older and I could see she was being caught I said to her, "I'm gonna give you this lot of money and no more, and if you go in there for credit there'll be murder!" My mother, every time she wanted something she made me stay away from school. If she wanted me to go anywhere, to do anything, if anybody wanted to go to the doctor, I had to go with them. I went to school but I couldn't have had a lot of education those days. . . . You had to stop at home to look after one another when one wasn't well. When we were kids one wasn't well, the other one wasn't well. Yeah, we went to school, but –'

For all its destructive poverty, the Kaplan family remained always united. When one sister married she moved into the flat next door in Rothschild Buildings. When times got better in the 1930s and more of the children were earning, the family were able to take up the Four Per Cent's offer of a brand new flat in Hackney, but even as the children left home they never moved far away. Annie and her mother

'lived here, and my sister upstairs, another one across the road, another one over the other side, my brother still lives

here. We were always a close family. . . . She kept us
together. It was always a warm home.'

Annie and her mother stayed in their Hackney flat until Mrs
Kaplan died there in 1945.

'I was the father in the family. I never got married for that
reason. I could have got married as good as anybody else. I'd
never have left my mother, never, because without me she'd
have been lost. . . . I would never leave my mother. 'Cause
my mother had it hard.'

School days

The congested streets of the Jewish East End were punctuated
at frequent intervals by looming red brick structures whose
black slate roofs dominated even the tallest tenement blocks.
They bore a characteristic resemblance one to another which
made their function immediately apparent, even from a
distance. These were the Board Schools and County Council
Schools which grew up in the wake of the 1870 Education Act.
By the time children were growing up among the immigrant
families of Rothschild Buildings there was no lack of local
schooling for them. There were state schools within ten
minutes' walking distance of the Buildings in Commercial St,
Old Castle St, Old Montague St, Chicksand St, Deal St and
Hanbury St.

Apart from the state-run Board Schools there were important voluntary schools in the vicinity of Rothschild Buildings,
one of which was the famous Jews' Free School (JFS), across
Commercial St in Bell Lane. This school played a formative
part in the early years of generations of East End children and
among the daily roll of 4,300 were many from Rothschild
Buildings. The JFS and the associated Jews' Infant School in
Commercial St, had high status among immigrant parents.
They would try to get their children educated there even if that
meant taking them away from a state school once a place at JFS
became available.[49]

'Well, they'd prefer it. Because it was a Jewish school. . . .
My parents wanted the boys to go to Jewish Free School,
not only my parents, most of them.'

But if the immigrant parents were anxious to send their
children to JFS in an attempt to forestall unwelcome Anglicisation, they were merely playing into the hands of the enemy.

The JFS had a special place in the life of the children of
Rothschild Buildings, as it has for Anglo-Jewry as a whole.
But it is likely that the majority of kids from the Buildings
went to the local state schools, in common with the vast bulk
of East End immigrants.[50] And the state-run institution most
patronised by the children of Rothschild Buildings was
Commercial St School.★

Commercial St School was within five minutes of the
Thrawl St entrance to the Buildings. From under the gate you
turned left, then right down Lolesworth St, crossed Wentworth St, down George Yard† and there you were at one of
the two entrances. Girls and infants had to use this 'most
undesirable'[51] way through narrow and dirty and smelly
George Yard; the boys had their own entrance from Commercial St itself by the side of St Jude's Church.

Commercial St School had originally been a Church of
England school attached to St Jude's Church and Rectory,
from which Canon Barnett had plotted the clearance of the
Rothschild Buildings site in the mid-1870s. It was taken over
by the London School Board in April 1895 as a 'Temporary'
Board School,[52] although it never again reverted to its
denominational status. The old St Jude's School became increasingly inadequate for the number of children it had now to
accommodate and plans were put in hand to build a new
school on some cleared land adjacent to it. Building went on
around the children.[53]

'I remember how we were threatened – if we were naughty
children we wouldn't go to the nice new big school.'

★ Now Canon Barnett School.
† Now Gunthorpe St.

The threats, it appears, were never fulfilled and the staff moved schools in the summer of 1901. Children starting the autumn term were welcomed into the new three- and four-storey building in that distinctive London School Board design. The new school was divided into three departments – Boys', Girls', and Infants'. By 1903 it was accommodating nearly 900 kids – 303 boys, 308 girls and 280 infants.[54]

It was airy and huge. These were the biggest rooms the children of Rothschild Buildings had seen in their lives. The teachers were eager to stress the school's benefits, acquainting the pupils with the luxuries lavished on them by a benevolent society:[55]

'it was a very great thrill. And, you know, there were no fireplaces, and they explained to us that in the winter . . . "You get warm air blown in and it's very healthy for you." The teacher went on about it. "And in the summer you'll have cool air blown in." '

But these things rarely work out as planned and for the next fifteen years the heating and ventilation system gave constant trouble. Classrooms were very cold on winter mornings,[56] for example. But the worst problem was from smoke and sulphurous fumes from the Whitechapel Dust Destructor in George Yard, between Toynbee Hall and College Buildings, sucked in by the fans and blown wholesale into every class-room.[57]

'Very bad smell of smoke and soot in all rooms from 10.35 to 11.10 a.m. It was bad in all three Departments but worst in Boys' Department. . . . One boy was sick and a teacher's nose as well as that of a boy bled as result of smoke.'

The three departments each had their own headmaster or mistress and there was a form teacher for about every forty pupils.[58] These teachers were confronted with special problems shared by few of their London colleagues. In 1896 it was reported that '40% of the boys admitted to the First Standard were ignorant of English'[59] and although this high intake of first-generation immigrants declined after the 1905

Aliens Act began to take effect, over 90 per cent of pupils
would have been Jewish by the turn of the century. One old
pupil thought that 300 of the 304 girls there in one year were
Jewish and that is unlikely to be an exaggeration.[60]

According to the Vice-Chairman of the London School
Board the role of the state schools in the Jewish East End was
'to make all the children good English subjects'.[61] The first
prerequisite of this was, of course, to establish common
grounds of communication. Among first-generation children
of school age or among children born in the East End of
foreign parents, the breakdown of Yiddish as their main
language was the prime task of both state and voluntary
schools alike.

At Commercial St School, teaching English as a second
language was made easier by employing a few Jewish (and
probably Yiddish speaking) teachers,[62] and especially by
getting older pupils to take English classes at times of special
need – during the 1905 pogroms, for instance.[63]

> 'I remember one girl. When I told her to say "and" she
> couldn't, she said "aernd"; and she said "royce" for "rose".
> This used to annoy me, and I did bully the poor girl a little
> bit. One day, in the playground, she was standing in a
> corner crying. I went over to her, and I said in Yiddish,
> "Why are you crying?" And she said, in Yiddish, "Every-
> one's laughing at me – you laugh at me. I can't say like you
> say the word in English, I can't say 'rose', I say 'royce'." I
> said, "But you've just said 'rose'!" After that I became very
> friendly with her.'

If Anglicisation was the avowed aim of the state school
system then it was heartily taken up by established Anglo-
Jewry as a whole. Accordingly, immigrant children were
taken firmly in hand at the JFS, where celebrations for the first
Empire Day in 1904 reached heights of fervour unparalleled by
less insecure sections of the community.[64]

> At 3.40 the song, 'The Flag of Britain', was sung simul-
> taneously throughout the school. Kipling's 'Recessional
> Hymn' was then recited, and lessons on patriotism

followed – 'What the Empire does for us, and what we should do for the Empire'. Finally, at 4.15, the Cadet Corps marched to the Rothschild Hall, where they sang, to the accompaniment of the brass band, 'God Save the King', all the classes joining. The Union Jack was saluted in proper military fashion, and the ceremony concluded with cheers for the King and Country.

But if Anglicisation had problems for the immigrant children of JFS – singing songs whose words meant little and sentiments less – there were probably deeper tensions within the state system. Commercial St School was, for all practical purposes, a Jewish school. But here, at a time of virulent controversy over whether the aliens should be allowed into the country at all there was not the united front that could be maintained at the JFS, and occasionally cracks began to show. Many of the non-Jewish staff were sympathetic to the immigrants, and teachers were won over by the educational aspirations of parents and children.[65] Indeed, probably the majority of staff stayed at Commercial St School throughout our period, presumably satisfied with its environment. But there was a chronic problem of staff shortages and supply teachers were regularly drafted in. Some could be hostile to the new arrivals. Like the remarkable Miss Jackson, employed for a short time just after the Kishenev pogroms:[66]

'She was so patriotic that she wore a Union Jack apron! . . . So she took the class and she said, "Now, all you foreigners who come from Russia – you should all go back to your own country!" And a girl sitting in the front – her name was Yetta Solomons – she was so incensed about that . . . she took out this inkwell and flung it at her, and she smashed her glasses – she wore thick glasses. And all the ink ran down her. I'll always remember that.'

Now whether or not Yetta Solomons's aim was too good to be true, examples of anti-immigrant feeling could not have been very rare. And the smallest spark was sometimes enough to ignite stored up resentment.[67]

'A lot of the children didn't have birth certificates and so when they reached the age of fourteen their parents would have to go and swear an affidavit at the solicitor's to say the child was 14, and the child would have to swear too. At school one day, one of the girls said, "I haven't got a birth certificate, and I've got to swear that I'm 14." So Dinah, this friend of mine, said, "Oh, you don't have to worry. All you have to do is, if you're a Christian you stand up and say, 'I swear by the Lord Jesus Christ', and if you're Jewish you have to swear another way." That's all that she said and she never meant anything derogatory against Jesus Christ. The teacher was out of the room when this happened but there were two Christian girls there. When we went out to play in the playground I could see these two girls walking up and down talking, and pointing at Dinah and our little crowd. When we came back, the teacher of the class called Dinah out to the front. . . . "How dare you stand up and make fun of Our Lord? We don't make fun of your Rabbis or your Gods!" and so on. And Dinah was weeping, with tears falling down her face. "I didn't mean anything", she kept saying, and she didn't, but the teacher wouldn't even let her speak. She was sent out to the headmistress and then she was sent to apologise to all the English staff of the whole school. She was sent to Coventry. The only one who used to speak to her was myself, and I used to meet her outside school. Sent to Coventry with a year's marks taken away from her. Do you think such a thing could happen today?'

It is probably true to say, however, that such incidents were comparatively infrequent and were highlighted against the backcloth of that school routine which was the day-to-day lot of the children of Rothschild Buildings. What was that school day like?

It began around 8.30 with a steady stream of kids clattering down the staircases of the Buildings, their ages from 4 to 14, all dressed differently but in a similar style. There was no uniform at Commercial St School, unlike the JFS whose boys had to wear a jacket and cap with a golden ring – 'That's why we were called the Baigel Boys!'[68] The boys and girls from Rothschild Buildings who went to Commercial St School, however, were dressed in the weekly wear of the children of the respectable working class. For the girls this meant a clean white pinafore, '*always* a pinafore, summer and winter',[69] or a navy gymslip, or a simple blouse and skirt. Hair would be done in a variety of styles, predominantly in braids, and covered on the journey to school by a hat or headscarf. Few wore a topcoat; if a girl was lucky enough to have 'a brown coat with fur round the three capes and fur round the bonnet', she kept it for Shabas. Invariably, the girls wore boots on their feet. The boys went to school in a more standardised dress which approached the sameness of a uniform: 'suits in those years', the turn of the century, 'there was no jerseys. Trousers and a jacket, and a cap – *always* a cap. A Jewish boy had to cover his head. Waistcoat. And boots – *always* boots, never shoes.' Such wardrobes, for boys and girls, would be annually expanded or replenished by the rule kept by many comfortable families – 'something new for Passover, always'. The richer parents bought their children clothes at the time of the Jewish New Year as well, but in less well-off families – 'I don't remember having a new dress for about six or eight years; I had my cousin's cast-offs.'[70]

At 8.50 the school hand-bell was rung by a monitor or 'Teacher Winifred' and already many kids would be milling around the playground; 'invariably we were at school at about 8.30.'[71] Attendance at Commercial St School, like many East End schools attended by the immigrant children,[72] was very good – 93 per cent in the Boy's Department in 1897, for example, although the girls were not as regular.[73] Bribes, probably not needed, were offered for good attendance: 'coloured tickets' and the permission to wear 'bits of coloured ribbon, bows and brooches' for the medallists of the Infants' Department, a tea-party with the headmistress for the older girls, and lantern shows for punctual boys;[74] free clothing was given at the JFS for the best attenders.

For those children who had left home without a breakfast many schools provided something to help them through the day. At JFS you could queue for dry bread and milk (an enamelled cup of milk-and-water as one disgusted recipient remembered it) but you had to be there early and that was difficult if you 'always had something to do' at home. At

Commercial St School hot milk was provided in the coldest periods of the winter for 'children who were weakly but not actually in need of a meal';[75] 'I was supposed to have been delicate so I had hot milk in the morning.'[76] Some parents were so anxious about their children's nutrition that they pushed sandwiches at them through the railings at break time.

Once all these preliminaries had been disposed of, the teachers' whistles assembled the standards in neat ranks and they were marched into the assembly halls to a piano accompaniment – 'Fanny Abrams, she used to play the piano.'[77] These three halls were the showpieces of the school. The girls had theirs decked out with plants, the aspidistra leaves carefully sponged by the monitors, and in pride of place to one side a large aquarium, 'you know, quite a *big* thing, with all the green stuff at the bottom of it'.[78] The boys' hall had flowers and even birds which, according to the government inspector, made 'a beautiful show'.[79] Among all this the children would stand and chant the Lord's Prayer – 'Well, it's our prayer too, the morning prayer, that's the same as ours'[80] – and any announcements would be read by the heads of each department.

For the boys, after 1904, the headmaster was Mr Canby who used to play cricket for Yorkshire, an unpopular man with a reputation for womanising; 'one heard very nasty tales about him.'[81] For the infants there was Miss Davies who was there for many many years. And for the girls Miss Roberts, the governess; in 1901[82] she had 'spent a holiday in Switzerland, and I don't know whether she fell down skiing, broke her leg, and she limped after that. She was medium height, what I can remember of her now, but she was old. Iron grey hair, scraped back. She was very strict. You stood in awe of her.' Miss Roberts, like the other heads, was responsible for pre-meditated corporal punishment with the cane: 'You just went out into the hall and that was that.'[83]

The three departments were segregated as much as possible. The Infants' Department was entered up some external stairs at the side of the school. The normal starting age was 5 years but some children started much younger – especially where mother had to go out to work.[84]

'At the age of 2 years and 8 months I took him [my brother]
to . . . Commercial Street School.'

Such children would wait at the back of their older brothers'
and sisters' classrooms, where lessons finished later, to be
taken home if mother was still out at work.

From 8 years old the children passed into the Girls' or Boys'
Departments – girls in the middle floor, boys at the top. There
they progressed by a system of competitive examination
through the seven standards from 8 to 14 years. If you were
dull, failed to get to school much or had difficulties with the
language you stayed behind in say standard 1, losing your
friends to standard 2. If you were bright,[85]

'I went from the 3rd to the 5th. I was a good scholar. I was
one of those horrible children, you know, really! . . . I
went from the 3rd to the 5th and they all hated me.'

So after morning assembly the older children would march
in standards to their respective classrooms and the lessons of
the day would begin. Each form teacher taught most subjects
so that the day would be dominated by his or her personality.
Take Miss Green, for example, who had the 7th girls'
standard. She had trained as a pupil teacher at the school and
received her certificate in 1898; by 1901 she was 'senior
assistant', experienced enough to take over from Miss Roberts
during the six months' absence following her accident.[86]
Memories of Miss Green, as with those of most teachers, vary
with the favour she showed her pupils. There is common
ground that she had one lung and 'snaggle teeth'. But how do
we reconcile 'She was *very* nice',[87] with, 'Miss Green? I
remember her – old crab!' ?[88] Perhaps because the first was
one of the school's brightest scholars and the second missed a
lot of schooling and had also the misfortune to be left-
handed.[89]

'I used to get it across my knuckles. These days they don't
stop them, years ago they did. I used to see it coming. I used
to change my pen like that and she used to give me one right
over my knuckles.'

Teaching methods at Commercial St School were probably similar to any of the state schools of the period.. They may even have been a little in advance, for the extensive use of blackboards there was radically ahead of the older schools.[90] But the content of lessons was rarely exciting, and perhaps history was worst of all.[91]

> 'Well now, history was something we just went, "William the Whatever-it-was landed in 1066", you know, you repeated the dates. We all had to say, "so-and-so so-and-so 1066", and "came to the throne", and that kind of thing. The history. And then of course in the exams you were given, "What date so-and-so?" and all that sort of thing.'

A whole morning of 'that sort of thing' was perhaps relieved by one of the frequent visitors to the school – usually people of authority, like the middle-class ladies who administered the Whitechapel Children's Care Committee,[92] the attendance officer calling about Joey Finestein again, the officers of the Boot Club, Clothing Club and so on. Worst of all were the LCC nurses, like cleansing nurse Munro whose visits during some spells were weekly and who would, in full view of the school, cart away boys and girls to the cleansing station to be deloused.[93]

The best relief was the liberal dinner-time from 12 till 2, which gave children a reasonable time at home with mother and set the Buildings alive with kids again. Only a tiny minority of children (perhaps forty in the whole school or ½ per cent) were eligible for meals at school. Free school meals were for[94]

> either the children of widows or [those] whose fathers were out of work through ill-health or from some other cause without fault of their own . . . and great care is taken in ascertaining that the right sort of children have the benefit of them.

At a time of controversy over whether school dinners should be given at all, the Commercial St Managers should be commended for marginally setting aside at least one of the diktats of political economy.[95] Any beneficence, however, was kept firmly under an individual's paternalistic control. Because of this the provision of meals was haphazard and only occurred during the winter months, paid for by a manager this year and a 'resident of Toynbee Hall' the next. The place, too, varied from year to year – the Girls' Hall or the Christ Church dining centre', the Sandy's Row premises of the Jewish Children's Penny Dinners Society or the Jewish Soup Kitchen (both ten minutes away across dangerous Commercial St), or in the Parish room 'under the superintendence of the Vicar's wife',[96] for the Gentile kids. Because these meals were for the deserving poor they could be used as a valuable weapon of school discipline, as at the JFS for example.[97]

> 'You'd get a ticket for dinner. . . . If we were bad one day we didn't get it, and I was usually bad. I usually talked a lot, and they stopped me a lot of things for talking.'

Organised charity for specific groups of recipients was just one further tie which was used to bind the spirits and minds of children. For if the state and Anglo-Jewish schools saw their role as the Anglicisation of the immigrant, it was an Anglicis-ation aimed at moulding raw material into model citizens, steeped in the virtues of the middle-class society the schools represented. 'Cleanliness and order' and punctuality and obedience and gratefulness were all 'strenuously promoted'[98] at Commercial St. They were all as much a fact of school life as William the Whatever-it-was and 1066.

Thrift was one more of those unquestionable virtues. The old St Jude's School had run a savings bank which the children had been encouraged to join, but this was 'spoiled' by the introduction of a Boot Club in 1895. Under 10 per cent of children actually paid the 1d. a week which would entitle them to a new pair of boots from 'a firm in Commercial Rd by the name of Solomon'.[99] If you paid so much towards them you were rewarded by the rest being paid from charitable funds supplied by the Ragged Schools Union or the Bare Foot Mission or the School Managers themselves.[100] Alternatively you could sign the Thrift Form which enabled you to receive the boots first and pay off the debt later. There was a Clothing Club, too, which seems to have been less successful.

Although joining the Boot Club was considered respectable by the people of Rothschild Buildings, few would contemplate receiving anything for nothing. The very poorest, of course, had to; the Jewish Schools Boot Fund gave boots regularly to Commercial St School[101] and the Jewish Ladies' Clothing Association handed out 857 articles of clothing there over a three year period.[102] A widow's son at the JFS was glad of the dole of free clothes at Passover time:[103]

'I used to get clothes from Free School – corduroy. I got a jacket and trousers and a pair of boots . . . You could hear somebody walking in them boots a mile away!'

Some resented even this. 'I wore second-hand boots rather than boots for nothing. No, my mother had her pride.'[104] And the independence of a cabinet maker, father of seven children, was common to many families in the Buildings.[105]

'From school I put in for the Thrift Form. . . . I liked the poacher's pockets so I had a corduroy suit and a pair of boots, and I came home so proud of that suit. And in the evening my father came home and saw it. "Where d'you get that from?" "From school", I said. "I signed the Thrift Form." "You can take it back." Charity he wouldn't have. Literally nothing to eat, but charity he wouldn't have.'

That boy would have been among the large majority from Rothschild Buildings who did not have school meals and so would have crowded the cobbles of Wentworth St and George Yard at 1.45 on their way back to school. Whether they went eagerly would depend on what had been arranged for them. For it was not all learning by rote. And within the constraints of the classroom and the East End, teachers tried to give their pupils variety and entertainment.

The best way to relieve the tedium of the normal school day was to give the pupils a holiday. This was more frequently done in Commercial St School than in many others. As the school catered predominantly for Jewish children but had also a minority of Gentiles, the authorities observed both sets of religious holidays from 1899 onwards. In addition, the school ran a 'double session' on Fridays, with lessons from 9 till 2, when the school closed for the start of the Jewish Sabbath. But there were many other excuses for the odd half-day off during the year – a swimming gala, a school football match, Empire Day, prize giving, the Lord Mayor's Show – as well as those one-off events like 'Royal Procession in East End', the Shakespeare Tercentenary, signing the Armistice, and the occasional coal shortage.[106] And for less fortunate reasons certain classes or whole departments would be closed during frequent epidemics: the infants were kept home for a whole month during the measles epidemic of 1911, for example.[107]

The second best alleviation of school routine would consist of visits and trips, games and entertainments. Whitechapel was not conducive to the study of natural history – the 'methylated people' of Itchy Park would have inhibited even a Gilbert White. So a bus ride for the girls to Epping Forest with Miss Roberts to observe the arrival of spring was quite an event. More commonly, a class would go to Victoria Park for nature study, where Mr Harris would 'point out . . . the fauna and that kind of thing'.[108] Nearer school, the opportunity was always taken to absorb any cultural overspill which from time to time reached the East End. Visits to art and other exhibitions at the Whitechapel Gallery were usually arranged by Miss Brian who, if the teachers' attendance register is any guide, was either very susceptible to infections or a hypochondriac of impressive talent. When she did turn up at school she spent much of her time organising parties to the theatre, like the time she escorted, with rare sensitivity, nineteen Jewish boys to sit through *The Merchant of Venice* at the Adelphi in January 1916.[109]

Organised games, like football, cricket, rounders, hockey and running competitions, could not be held at the school through lack of space. Only netball could conveniently take place in the playgrounds, made smaller by the iron railings separating boys from girls. Consequently, the children were bussed to Victoria Park, the playing fields of the East End, once a week in the summer months. The organisation involved in moving fourteen classes of forty or so children backwards and forwards weekly, on a bus ride which necessitated a change at Mile End, must have racked the nerves of even the most experienced staff.

End-of-term entertainments around Christmas (or Chanukah) time were special events prepared for, and looked forward to, for many weeks. The school play, performed for children, parents and the crippled children who were moved into the old St Jude's School building after 1901, was a breeding-ground for the sort of personality clash remembered for over seventy years. Like the time in 1905 that Betsy Schiffenbaum, an upstart favourite of kind Miss Poole the drama specialist, was given the part of the Sleeping Beauty in preference to popular Annie Silverman.[110]

> 'And from then on – you can just imagine – my name was mud! . . . We used to do the plays in Toynbee Hall. And it was a great thrill, it was wonderful. . . .
>
>> Why, what a quaint old-fashioned room,
>> All full of cobwebs, dust and gloom.
>
> I still remember it all!'

Every year the Polish tailors and the Ukrainian cabinet makers, with their wives in their Shabas-best, crowded into Toynbee Hall to see sons and daughters act out strange plays in an incomprehensible language.

The staged excitement of end-of-term entertainments was supplemented from time to time by a real life drama affecting the school – a fire in the hay yard next door,[111] or a child molester caught by the police but only after he had interfered with nine boys.[112] But once in a lifetime came an event which shattered the orderly calm of a school day. In the early years of Rothschild Buildings probably the most dramatic for the parents and children who lived through it was the terrible bombing raid of 13 June 1917, which killed nearly 100 East Enders and wounded 500 more. There had been several harbingers of this traumatic event. From September 1915 onwards the night-time Zeppelin raids had left children exhausted after a night spent sleeping fully dressed, and caused considerable absenteeism.[113] Children had watched wide-eyed the burning Zeppelins brought down near London in

September 1916. And then there was the enormous Silver-
town explosion of 19 January 1917 when the Brunner, Mond
& Co. munitions factory disappeared in a blast which shook
the windows of Rothschild Buildings and which lit up the sky
twenty-five miles away. War had already been brought to the
doorsteps of Londoners but few, if any, air raids had been in
daylight.

But at 11.37 on that June morning – so the school log book
records in a very shaky hand – two German monoplanes
dropped several bombs in the Spitalfields neighbourhood.
One fell in Flower and Dean St, causing damage to some
basement flats in Nathaniel Buildings.[114] At the same time a
bomb fragment broke a window in the Boys' Hall – no one
was hurt. But the news of damage to the school ran quickly
through the bubbling streets of the Flower and Dean St
neighbourhood and was shouted up to figures leaning over the
balconies of Rothschild Buildings and other tenements.
Mothers rushed hatless out of the flats, fathers in their shirt-
sleeves turned out of the sweatshops and they all converged on
Commercial St School. A riot ensued. The 'excited crowd of
parents' scaled the walls surrounding the school and rushed up
to the classrooms. They were held at bay by the headmaster
and another teacher who 'had some difficulty in ejecting them
before children were dismissed at 12.35.' Out of nearly 900
children only 247 were allowed back by their parents in the
afternoon: 'nervous tension of teachers and children
compelled [the] Headmaster to close the school early.'[115]

That day may have been different, but closing the school,
whether at 4.30 on a weekday or 2 o'clock on a Friday, did not
signify the end of schooling for many of the children of
Rothschild Buildings. For one or two weekday evenings, on
Saturday afternoons and Sunday mornings, large numbers
would be expected to attend Hebrew classes. Some would
have to go at all of these times – others only one – but
probably more than one in two attended regularly at some
time.[116] This affected boys more than girls – 'Jewish people
on the whole concentrated more on the boys.'[117]

There were three types of institution where instruction in
Hebrew was given. The simplest was the *cheder*, probably just
a room in the home of the religious teacher or *melammed*. The

chederim were scattered throughout the East End – there were enough for almost one in every street. The teachers were paid a few pence a week and for this the children were expected to spend long hours there, occasionally going before school, during the dinner-break and in the evening.[118] An orthodox cabinet maker would send his two boys to a *cheder* in the evenings,[119] and a presser's wife[120]

'had a private Rabbi for Sammy. Used to live somewhere in Old Montague Street. But my eldest brother went to the Talmud Torah.'

This Talmud Torah was the large religious school in Brick Lane – there were others in the East End but none so convenient for Rothschild Buildings. The Talmud Torahs admitted no girls and the hours at Brick Lane (the largest in London) were Saturdays 12.30 till 2, Sundays 3 till 6, and on four other days 5.30 till 8.30. Classes were as large as 120 children and the youngest were 5 years old. Attendance was sometimes enforced to such an extent that many children fell asleep exhausted over their desks.[121] Perhaps some of this parental enthusiasm was due less to religious zeal than to the doling out of free clothes and boots as a reward for the best attenders.[122]

The Jewish state and voluntary schools themselves ran Hebrew classes for three hours a week and Commercial St was no exception. These Sunday morning classes were run by Mr Harris and his wife. They lived in Muswell Hill where they invited select pupils for tea on Sunday afternoons.[123] Attendance was so high that Sunday morning was almost a normal school day. Girls, as well as the boys, would go to these classes or the Saturday ones held at the JFS or both. They probably served the same purpose for the parents as did Sunday School for their Gentile neighbours, giving them the time alone together they would not otherwise have had.

So some sort of religious education outside school hours was largely unavoidable and in a few cases gave little time for play, except during the holidays. But when you could get it, time out of school was for many the happiest part of school days.

Out of school days

The playground of Rothschild Buildings, like the courts and streets of other working-class districts, was home to the countless games which children pass from generation to generation, games which may vary subtly in tradition but keep the same shape and framework. There were no games unique to Rothschild Buildings,[124] although some had larger significance than others and some were more difficult to play there than elsewhere. None of the games recalled in the oral testimony had a specifically immigrant character, although whether the games Russian children brought with them quickly lost relevance in the London streets or whether they were similar to those of their new environment and so could readily be adapted is not clear.

But whatever the origins of the games they played and the names they called them, there is no doubt that the playground of Rothschild Buildings was put to good use by the 600 or so children who shared it at any one time. After 4.30, when school closed, from 2 o'clock until supper on Fridays, on Saturday and Sunday afternoons and evenings, all day long during the school holidays, the playground would come uproariously alive. Apart from the free play of individuals there would always be groups of boys and girls intent on their own species of enjoyment, each taking place together but separate, in a medley of motion and sound.

There would be the skipping-rope games like Higher and Higher; the throwing a ball against a wall games like Wally; the leap-frog games like Jimmy Jimmy Nanko; the nerve-racking games like Kick Can Hide-and-Seek; the variations on Hop-scotch, especially the one played with orange peel; the games played with clothes like Dark Man's Scenery; the quiet and intent games like Marbles and Gobs; the Ring-a-Ring-a-Roses games where rhymes were sung and where for once girls and boys all joined in; the games of timing and skill like Diabolo and Tibbycat, and the games of strength and speed like Dog-and-the-Bone.[125]

'They used to put a handkerchief in the middle of the play-ground where the drains are. They'd pick sides, say five or six a side. Two of them from opposite sides would walk round the handkerchief and they'd keep an eye on each other all the time. One or the other of them had to pick hold of the handkerchief and run back to his side without being caught by the person that was going round with him. So they was circling and circling and keeping an eye on him and waiting for an opportunity to get hold of it! My brother played it and once he was so excited that he got hold of the handkerchief and run with all his might right into the brick wall of the Buildings! Bang! He knocked himself out and he had a headache for a long time after!'

Then there were the games directed against adults, like variations on Knock down Ginger where flats on opposite sides of a landing had their doors tied together 'and we used to . . . knock on the doors and the people would answer and couldn't open the doors.'[126] Or like

'Another game I'll always remember. Where I lived in E Block is the bottom end of Flowery at the back of Strakers, there was a lamp-post. Just opposite . . . was the big gate which was never opened and we used to tie a cotton across from the lamp-post to the bars of this gate so that anybody's hat used to get caught. Then we ran, ran, ran!'

Then there were the games played at Passover and which leant themselves to that much criticised vice of the Jewish working class – as, indeed, of the London working class as a whole – gambling. Throughout the year 'we used to gamble, there was a helluva lot of gambling',[127] the older boys playing pontoon and pitch-and-toss for pennies, the younger ones playing for nuts, buttons or farthings. Nuts were the favourites at Passover time,[128]

'particularly those little round cobnuts. With them they used to invent their own games, like games of chance, to acquire more nuts. They used to get shoe boxes and make little holes just big enough for the cobnuts to go through and they used to print . . . 2, 4, 6, 8, or whatever over the hole. You used to roll the nut along the floor into the hole and you used to get so many back if you got it in.'

At other times of the year buttons were the favourite token and the son of a Polish tailor found himself in a position of some advantage.

'I was lucky because my father, being in the tailoring, he had access to plenty buttons, of all shapes and sizes! At the time I felt very rich! Mind you, I was also rich at other times because my uncle worked in Spitalfields Market . . . and *he* had access to plenty nuts. We were loaded up with nuts!'

Games like football and cricket were always under threat of interference by the Super or porters, and although it was still possible to play these games and even learn to ride a bicycle there,[129] for the more adventurous the playground held strictly limited attractions, and indeed the street was home to unique and absorbing sights which would draw the most obedient from under the protective portals of Rothschild Buildings.

Street entertainments were of a wonderful variety. As well as the unintended entertainments of the streets where you stood back and enjoyed them, like the fights, the drunks, the markets, the traffic, and the occasional droves of sheep and cattle which blocked Brick Lane from pavement to pavement; as well as calling out names after the street characters like Betsy Bundles or Katy the Horse; as well as being the hunting-ground of the collector of tram tickets or match-boxes or shrapnel during the war; as well as the street-sellers like the coconut man, the toffee-apple man, and Moshe who sold bits of toffee – 'we called it Bugs and Fleas' – for a 'Ha'penny a go'; as well as the daring excitement of the streets, like hitching rides on waggons, dodging the horses and carts which filled up Commercial St, fighting for 'speck' fruit in the Market, fighting your way through streets blocked by kids from another street or another background; as well as the special days and nights of the year which had the streets as their arena, like struggling into Machzikei HaDath during Simchas Torah for your share of the cakes and sweets handed out by the synagogue authorities, or squirting water and throwing confetti over 'the unsuspecting passer-by'[130] on Chometz Bottel night; as well as all of these and more there were the men who made a living by entertaining in the streets, and whose best or only customers were children.

Many of the street entertainers had a wide audience, appealing to the parents and children of Rothschild Buildings alike. Every Monday lunchtime and at most weekends the German band – 'Germans they were' – would play in the streets of Spitalfields. There were four members – husband, wife and two children.[131]

> 'They'd come round – we'd follow them around – they'd come round to Thrawl St and then go walk round to Fashion St or Flower and Dean St and we'd follow the band, we children. . . . My parents would come out in the gate and listen. My father was very fond of music and he had rather a sort of goodish voice, you know, he'd pipe up.'

The buskers, too, were popular among both parents and children; there were the well-remembered men who dressed as women and danced and sang in the street, and there were a couple of men who sang on a Saturday morning: 'Solomon and Levi I think they were referred to. Or they used to sing a song about Solomon Levi.'[132] One sang and the other played a whistle and danced, and they were also great favourites around the workshops. These acts and the hurdy-gurdy players and the other street musicians would pack the landings of Rothschild Buildings, Nathaniel Buildings and the other tenements of the Flower and Dean St neighbourhood. Fathers, mothers and children would peer over and through the railings at the performance below. Some would bring out chairs and orange boxes for more relaxed viewing.[133]

> 'People used to throw ½d. down. As poor as they all were ½d. would come over the balcony. That was the sort of thing that went on all the time. It seemed part and parcel.'

But perhaps the reality was not always so romantic as the memory.[134]

> 'Some of them used to take 1d. and heat it up on the gas and throw it down – that kind of cruel joke.'

It's likely that those street entertainers who relied on children for a living were more gently treated by their audience, and the two most popular among the kids of Rothschild Buildings were the roundabout man and the barrel organ man. The roundabout was drawn by a horse, it had 'half a dozen seats or so', played music when in operation, and would give you a ride if you gave the man old rags, metal or ½d. [135]

But even the roundabout could not compete with Percy the Boots and his barrel organ. Legends arose about this man. His outsize boots gave him his nickname, he was reputedly an epileptic, and, but perhaps this is a modern accretion, he saved up all his money and sent it to relatives in Israel. But his effect on the children, especially the girls, was electrifying. [136]

'He used to come on a Saturday afternoon. And we were young children, and we used to look forward to him, and we all had ½d. clutched in our hand that mother gave us . . . so that he should play the tunes we wanted . . . and the children, the girls, actually danced in the street. [Sometimes they were joined by the lodging house women who danced in their] mauve flouncy dresses to the tune of "Bill Bailey". [But where the children were concerned, at least] it wasn't anything untoward, it was really very lovely. . . . [137] There was one little girl, she was a beautiful dancer, really gorgeous; we used to make a ring round her and clap while she danced.'

Percy the Boots used to push his organ along many of the streets of the East End, well away from the tenement blocks of Spitalfields. The children of Rothschild Buildings, too, would often venture out of the Flower and Dean St neighbourhood to play. The big attraction was Victoria Park. Admittedly there was always Itchy Park and its swings, where unsuspecting Jewish children were inveigled in to watch lantern slides of a Christian complexion arranged by the vicar, but many kids were refused permission to go there because 'they used to sit in there and scratch themselves on the railings.' [138] So to the varied amenities and space of Victoria Park was added the bonus of respectability. Not only would the children be safe to

go there in groups, but it was the sort of place they could take
their parents.

Most children walked to Victoria Park, saving themselves
the tram or bus fares. With pocket money tight, perhaps a
farthing every other day, there was no room for extravagance.
It was about a four mile trek there and back, a journey needing
careful planning among the children who flocked there 'in
their thousands' during the long summer holiday.[139]

> 'I used to collect all the children from the neighbourhood,
> take bottles of water, take their lunch, and we'd all go to
> Victoria Park.'[140]

After a forty-minute walk through the steaming streets of
Bethnal Green you at last had the freedom to indulge in cricket
and football and all the games forbidden within the closeness
of Rothschild Buildings. Other activities like swimming and
the use of a gym, boating and listening to the band, were also
available in the park.

If Victoria Park was a long way from Rothschild Buildings
it was not the furthest afield a child could expect to travel
during his school years. There were several avenues out of the
East End which took a child away for a day, or a week or
longer still.

The first time many children went out of London, even for a
day, was on the annual outing of the JFS to Crystal Palace.
This event was paid for by Lord Rothschild, for whom the JFS
was always a special charity, and again it was a reward for
maintaining certain standards: 'we had to be good for a whole
year, which was very hard.'[141]

> 'And all the boys lined up and the teacher gave you a brand
> new 6d. And the monitor got 1s. 6d. And we marched to
> Aldgate Station.'[142]

Once at Crystal Palace, fun would be organised but none the
less remembered for all that.[143]

> 'See these dogs? [pointing to a pair of colourful china dogs
> wearing large Edwardian ladies' bonnets and seated either

side of the fireplace] I bet you don't believe it. I won them when I was 12 [in 1912] in a race in Crystal Palace. . . . Used to be a good runner once upon a time – good runner and a good skipper.'

Longer spells outside the East End would also be organised by the schools, perhaps with the help of a philanthropic School Manager but more often via the Children's Country Holiday Fund. This was a large body, arranging summer holidays for over 20,000 kids a year. Its Jewish branch arranged for some sixty holidays from Commercial St School every summer. Parents were expected to pay at least some of the expenses, and weekly contributions were begun in February.[144] The CCHF attracted children whose parents could afford the weekly payments and who were not over-concerned about entrusting them to a strange, and perhaps not rigorously kosher, household. But a different group of children could spend some weeks in the summer away from home. These were the sick, especially children who had contracted TB. Convalescence was generally organised by the Jewish Board of Guardians, and children were most frequently sent to Walton-on-the-Naze, where the first of two homes was opened in 1911. A Ukrainian cabinet maker's son was sent there from the Buildings at the end of the First World War, for example.[145] But there were always more patients than places. A 13-year-old Russian girl was due to spend a fortnight in a convalescent home in Brighton – Montpelier Rd; 'how I can remember these things I don't know.' She wasn't told until the last minute that there was no room for her there.[146]

'And my mother took me to Victoria Station, and a nurse or lady came along and read out names, and when she came to my name . . . she said, "You can't go. We've got a letter from the Jewish Board of Guardians. You're to take your daughter home".'

That particular story ended happily, due to the kindness of a working-class family who gave the daughter a holiday by the sea.

But those holidays, like the sunny days spent catching tiddlers in Victoria Park, could not go on for ever.

Young men and women

In those days you were sentenced to school until your fourteenth birthday, a simple enough rule but one with awkward
complications for some children from Rothschild Buildings.
As we have seen, those who were born abroad often lacked
proof of their date of birth so that the daughter of an Austrian
cabinet maker, among others, would find herself in the 'ex-
7th' standard.[147]

> 'I stayed on at school because I didn't have an English birth
> certificate and my mother had to send to Austria to my
> grandfather for my birth certificate. [Once received, it
> would have to be sent away for translation.][148] So I was at
> school – I left school – I was close on 15.'

The large majority of children came away from school
without any educational qualifications whatsoever. A tiny
minority won the annual scholarship to grammar school – the
Central Foundation Schools at Spital Square (for girls) and
Whitechapel Rd (for boys). When a bright girl from the Buildings did so in 1911 only two other girls from Commercial St
passed with her[149] and only one of those could afford to go.
The other had her mother to contend with.[150]

> 'She said, "You can't go because I can't afford the uniform.
> So you'd better stop where you are." '

The more likely reason for refusal was that girls and boys who
went to an elementary school would be out earning money at
14; those, like the girl who passed from Rothschild Buildings,
would not. She left school at 18 and went on to teacher training
college. And the other way of extending education beyond 14
years, by passing the matriculation which involved special
tuition and extra subjects not normally taught (like French),
was reserved for only a handful of favoured pupils each year.

Frustrated of a decent education during school years, many
tried to attend the evening classes which erupted throughout
the East End schools during our period, learning bookkeeping and 'tax-paying'[151] as well as more academic subjects.

But, as we shall see, the world of work and wages into which these 14-year-olds were thrust left little time for serious study and few could pursue their evening lessons with much energy (see Chapter 6, p. 220).

Evening classes were difficult to fit in after a twelve-hour day at the bench, but there was one other institution which had a far greater effect on a large number of adolescents from Rothschild Buildings. This was the youth club. Attendance at a youth club was encouraged at school[152] but it was after that controlling influence was left behind that the club came into its own. It had very specific aims. The Chief Rabbi, calling for the institution of a boys' club in the Commercial Rd area, laid[153]

> great stress on the urgent need for more communal work among such lads after they have left school, and [pointed] out the imminent danger of their lapsing into Hooliganism and crime if some attempt were not made to look after them during the most impressionable period of their lives and so counteract the evil influences of their surroundings.

Girls were open to similar temptations, particularly in the Whitechapel Rd[154]

> in the evening, where may be seen strings of young factory girls, arm in arm, patrolling up and down . . . and thus fostering a 'love of dress' and display, surely greater than can be implanted by a quiet lesson in needlework or cooking at the club.

Concern about juvenile misbehaviour was reflected throughout contemporary middle-class society, and there were 'delinquents' and 'hooligans' among immigrant youth in the East End[155] as among their Gentile neighbours. But in Rothschild Buildings, with the Four Per Cent's careful selection of respectable tenants, troublesome kids formed a very small minority. There were always small incidents – like bundling a young violinist into the dustbins, and his violin with him, setting light to the refuse chutes, petty thieving from stalls and shops[156] – but it would have been almost unthinkable for a youngster from the Buildings to end up in the Jewish Industrial School at Hayes. Equally unthinkable, but not as rare, was the occasional case of a girl who became pregnant while still single. The public shame of such an event in Rothschild Buildings was withering for both girl and parents alike: 'But we never saw her after the birth of the child. The family moved.'[157] The respectability of the Buildings kept such mishaps to a minimum, and amongst the children of Rothschild Buildings the youth clubs would probably have had a large following:[158]

> 'Our life was this: we went to school . . . we rushed home . . . or we went to the Hebrew classes; and then . . . we rushed home again or go to club. . . . The whole of the East End was full of these boys' clubs, which were marvellous.'

For the boys there were indeed a great number of places eager to 'look after them', at the Brady Club (from 1896), the Victoria Club (1901), Hutchison House Club (1905), Oxford and St George's Club (1913) and more. They were funded and organised by the aristocracy of Anglo-Jewry, by the same people who built Rothschild Buildings, who maintained the Jews' Free School, the Jewish Board of Guardians and the whole intricate web of relief for, and controls on, the poor.[159]

> 'When we left school we were called into the Great Hall of the Jewish Free School and we were advised to join the boys' clubs. And either we joined the Jewish Lads' Brigade – I joined Hutchison House . . . and the other boys very often joined the Old Victorians, Stepney Old Boys or Stepney Boys' [motto: The Club for All, and All for the Club].

At Hutchison House, opened by Lionel de Rothschild,[160]

> They hoped to catch the youth of the immediate neighbourhood, and to help them to rise in the world, to help them out of the temptation which they found in the streets, the music-halls and the public-houses. They wanted to instil into the boys ambition, the pride in being Jews and the pride in being Englishmen. (Cheers).

This club, like all the others, concentrated on muscular activities, antiseptic and competitive.[161]

> 'There was a gymnasium: we boxed, played football, cricket, we used to run. Chess. Billiards and snooker. There was ping-pong, handball. . . . We went rambling on Epsom Downs.'

There were also classes in reading, recitation and first-aid, and there was an 'excellent' library. Half the membership subscription was remitted for those studying at evening classes.

The girls of Rothschild Buildings were less well served as far as club facilities were concerned. The only girls' club in Spitalfields was the Butler St Club which rented the premises over the Jewish Soup Kitchen. Formed in 1902, its 200 members were provided with no less than twenty-seven classes including dressmaking, letter-writing, Hebrew, blotter and carpet making, millinery, drill, basket making, drawing and bookkeeping, as well as 'Sunday rambles' and the odd 'invitations to tea at country houses'.[162]

For all their faults, the youth clubs served a purpose, particularly in an area starved of sporting facilities and where some sports, boxing in particular, could provide a spectacular escape-route from poverty. The young men and women of the East End probably accepted what was good in the clubs and rejected the rest. But as well as skilfully exploiting the need for recreation among working-class adolescents, the clubs – like the schools – were vehicles for a conservative ideology. Their effectiveness, however, was limited. The Butler St Club, for example, sought 'to lure girls from the streets, the penny-gaffs and the music-halls',[163] but it succeeded in luring less than 200 girls away from pursuits unacceptable to the middle class. The stronger attractions of that culture of the streets and the music hall and the cinema held greater sway over the youth of Rothschild Buildings than the given culture of the club.

The East End of London, in common with other working-class areas before the end of the First World War, was alive with the music hall. There was Wilton's off Cable St, the Paragon Theatre of Varieties (Mile End Rd), the Cambridge

Theatre (Commercial St), Forester's Music Hall (Cambridge Rd), the Britannia (Hoxton), the London and the Olympia (Shoreditch), the Hackney Empire (Mare St), the Queen's Palace (Poplar), and many more: 'We had plenty; not like now.'[164] At any one of them the respectable youth of Rothschild Buildings crowded into the galleries for 2d., rubbing shoulders with their 'Christian' neighbours. The non-observant would often go on Saturday afternoons, the rest in the evening. The wonderful vitality of the English music hall attracted first- and second-generation immigrants sufficiently Anglicised to understand at least some of the patter; but anyone could go and enjoy the variety acts, the music, the lights and colour.

The music hall had a wide appeal among the young people of Rothschild Buildings, but there were some whose cultural background was more firmly fixed on the homeland. Usually, the Yiddish theatres of the East End would be frequented by the adult workers and their wives, occasionally taking their children to the packed Saturday evening performances. The most popular Yiddish Theatre was the Pavilion, at the corner of Whitechapel Rd and Vallance Rd. The plays had a strong emotional content and always stressed the lost world – and perhaps lost values – of home.[165]

On Saturday night, a melodrama of Jewish life in Austria, entitled 'Father's and Mother's Sorrows', was performed in a packed house, and numbers of people had to be turned away from the doors. The play dealt with a family's sorrow consequent upon the daughter's conversion to Christianity, and with her ultimate repentance and return to the ancestral faith on the Day of Atonement. The audience was exceedingly boisterous in its enthusiasm, and heartily booed the villain who had induced the heroine to leave her home.

But this sort of thing also affected those young immigrants who had perhaps imbibed more of the culture of the homeland than many of their contemporaries. One young trouser-maker who emigrated from the Ukraine in 1913, when she was 14 years old, would never go to an East End music hall. But she and her mother were always at the Pavilion.[166]

'As much as I can possibly go. As long as the theatre was
there and I was in the East End I used to go. . . . Oh, very
good Yiddisher plays. Real, you know, serious plays, not
rubbish. . . . Sometimes, if there was something special
on [like Morris Moskovitch or Jacob Adler, the 'Jewish
Irving'] I'd go on a Monday night, but mostly it was Saturday evening.'

An increasingly important medium of entertainment which
was emerging as the music hall (but not the Yiddish theatre)
declined was the cinema. The first local one had been a seedy
affair in Hanbury St, opened perhaps as early as 1908: 'they had
forms there and they charged you ½d.'[167] But by the beginning of the First World War less spartan places were opening
throughout the East End. The local cinema for Rothschild
Buildings was the Brick Lane Palace, where serials played on
weekday evenings – 'Remember Pearl White?'[168] – and
where peanut shells crunched underfoot, testifying to the
success of Little Hymie, a 'little hump-back fella' who used to
stand outside with 1d. bags of peanuts.

For the more energetic there were dances at local halls where
girls would meet after work on a Saturday afternoon. From a
tailoring workshop in Hunton St, two girls would rush
home – one to Cleveland St (Mile End) and one to Rothschild
Buildings. Freshened up by a meal and a quick rinse at the sink
and changed into their best dresses, they would meet again at
about 5 o'clock. From Cleveland St they made their way to a
hall in Cambridge Rd where they would meet other friends
and dance their boots off till midnight.[169] Alternatively they
would take a 25 bus from Aldgate and venture to the Saturday
afternoon tea dances at the Astoria or the Piccadilly Hotel 'up
West', rendezvous for the boys and girls of the East End.

The place of the matchmaker in forming relationships
among the immigrant young has perhaps been overempha-
sised.[170] Certainly, by the First World War this traditional
method of arranging for Jewish boy to meet Jewish girl had
been almost entirely superseded by the institutions of the East
End working-class environment. Relationships began in the
courtyard of the Buildings – 'there was plenty courting going
on!' – in the workplace, the dance hall, the cinema and the

street. 'Down Whitechapel' was perhaps the most popular place to meet members of the opposite sex. The wide pavements of the Whitechapel Rd were blocked by smart young tailors eyeing smart young milliners, on the Jewish equivalent of the 'Monkey's Parade'.

But if those modern methods of starting a relationship were predominant, there were still archaic leavings from the immigrant background. There were great strictures against marrying non-Jews, and any marriage could be problematic.

Even when the young Jack Brahms had found a Jewish girl and wanted to marry her, his father's old-fashioned attitudes, very strongly held, could sweep all before them, even in the post-Edwardian East End. On Jack's last day at Rothschild Buildings before joining up for the army in 1916, his friends held a party for him at Alf Bernstein's flat in Cephas St, Mile End.[171]

'And a funny thing – there was about six . . . fellas there, and we were one girl short. So Alf says to me, "Well, next door there's about three or four girls, next door." And her name was Mary. And so we invited her in. And as it happened, while I was in the army we used to correspond. Now there's a bit of history with this! Well, when I came out of the army I used to go out with this girl, Mary. As a matter of fact we even got engaged. So one Sunday we were out, and evidently my father went round there and he demanded £100 dowry money! I never knew anything about this! When I went round there one further evening she said, "You can have your ring back!" I says, "Why? Why, what's the trouble?" She says, "Your father wants £100." And that was that.'

And it really was! Mary's father, a master tailor, could not or would not pay; Jack, although 'very upset and disappointed', was so sure that his father would not change his mind that he never discussed it with him or questioned him about it.

'No, I didn't even try and talk him round, no. I just left it at that and finished with her.'

If attitudes like that, which took the romance out of relationships and replaced it with the cash-nexus, were still hanging like a pall over some landings of the Buildings as late as 1920, there was still room for the story-book romance. As on one Saturday evening in the winter of 1909. Betsy Schiffen-baum, ex-star of *Sleeping Beauty* and by then 18 years old, was out walking with a girl friend. They met two boys, one of whom was the girl friend's cousin. 'From that moment he fell in love with me and wouldn't leave me alone.' He would call at the shop where Betsy served behind the counter, pretending he was a customer so that he could snatch a few words. Eventually, he asked Betsy's father if she could walk out with him. Permission was granted, but she had to be home by 11 whenever she went out: 'If I'd come in at 12 o'clock I'd have had my head blown off!' After a six-year courtship they married in 1915.[172]

But courtship and entertainment had to be squeezed into an already packed day. For the end of school days had marked the end of childhood. Work replaced the routine of school life. And a ten- or twelve-hour day at the workshop meant new relationships and new experiences within every sector of a youngster's life in Rothschild Buildings.

Jewish workers and the East End economy

The workers of Rothschild Buildings paid a high price for their 'commodious and healthy' homes. It was exacted not so much in rent but in labour. Society gave tardily and inadequately with one hand and took back rapaciously and efficiently with the other. For twelve hours a day, nearly three-quarters of their waking lives, the tenants repaid that society many times over. Not only did their rents provide the property-owning class with a profit; their labour provided luxury articles which only that class could afford, as well as a profitable return on capital invested in industry. It was this that exposed the 'philanthropy' which provided Rothschild Buildings for the self-interested duplicity it in fact was. Model dwellings were an enlightened means of making workers more productive, one way to create 'a cleanly, orderly and contented proletariat' as the *Daily Telegraph*, in an eloquently unguarded moment,[1] put it.

The not always contented proletariat of Rothschild Buildings formed, as we have seen, a colony of skilled labour. The large majority of bread winners were artisans employed in the East End workshop trades, with a leavening of white-collar workers and small employers of labour. Even this restricted spectrum of skilled workers in commodity production was narrowed yet further, with some 60 per cent being employed in only four industries – clothing, tobacco, boot and shoe, and furniture.

How typical was the class structure of Rothschild Buildings? In that skilled labour was over-represented and the unskilled or labouring class almost entirely excluded, the Buildings were largely typical of model dwellings as a whole, which fended off the casual poor with rents, rules and

TABLE 2

Employment in Rothschild Buildings, 1900

Tailors	63	Labourers	2
Cigar and cigarette makers	23	Leather dressers	2
Cabinet makers	22	Stick makers	2
Bootmakers and kindred trades	18	Baker	1
Cap-makers	12	Bookbinder	1
General dealers	8	Carpenter	1
Teachers	8	Engineer	1
Pensioners	6	Furrier	1
Porters	4	Grocer	1
Travellers	3	Musician	1
Confectioners	2	Various	26
Hairdressers	2		
		TOTAL	210

Source: Four Per Cent Industrial Dwellings Co. Ltd, *Annual Report*, 31 December 1900.

mandatory respectability.[2] But by that very process the Buildings were atypical of the East End – 'the most notorious concentration of casual labour in Victorian London'[3] – and even in Stepney itself, the four trades which employed three out of five workers in Rothschild Buildings accounted for only 27 per cent of the Borough's labour force.[4] In one other respect, however, the Buildings' class structure can again be considered typical and that was in the skills which Jewish immigrants brought with them from Eastern Europe.[5] So that in terms of work and class the population of Rothschild Buildings can be thought of as largely representative of both model dwellings and immigrant Jewry, although such a crude generalisation would hide many and wide variations in earning capacity, poverty and comfort. Everything depended on the market in which people from the Buildings could sell their labour power, a complex weave of relations which affected trades (and individuals within the same trades) in different ways.

   Most Jewish workers in the East End laboured in the workshop trades which had all been established in the area long before their arrival. The major characteristic of the local economy was the small scale of production. It was kept alive, in the face of tendencies towards centralisation and concentration, by several factors. The first of these was the high cost of land in the inner city which made the construction of factories expensive and kept rents for existing floor-space high. Second, the demand structure of the trades most commonly followed – particularly clothing and furniture – required variety in commodity style and quality which worked in favour of small, flexible operations. The extreme subdivision of labour which characterised the manufacture of those commodities also favoured small-scale production: instead of gathering detail workers under one roof a manufacturer could put work out to homeworkers (or subcontracting workshops) who would perform specific operations before returning the article to the manufacturer. In the clothing industry this process was especially aided by the sewing-machine, which became so commonly available during the early years of Rothschild Buildings that many workers had one at home, whether or not they earned the bulk of their wages in the garment industry.

The workshop trades were also characterised by the small amount of capital required to set up in business as either an independent worker or as a small subcontracting employer. In the late 1880s, it had been estimated that a tailor could set up on his own in the East End clothing industry with just £1 capital,[6] and although that would have risen by the early years of this century, a small sum would still have enabled a worker to achieve independence or master status. But often not for long: because the East End workshop trades were notoriously unstable. For the worker, this meant that he or she could be laid off at any time, particularly in those times of the year when work was slack; seasonality of production in the tailoring trade, for instance, was especially marked. And for the employer it meant that lack of orders, combined with high rents and a wage bill commensurate with a labour-intensive industry, would quickly absorb his capital and put him out of business.

Those major East End industries which attracted a large proportion of the Jewish immigrants were tailoring, boot- and shoe-making, cabinet making, cap-making, and tobacco manufacture (mainly cigars and cigarettes). Only one of these trades had moved out of the workshops and into factories to any great extent and that was tobacco manufacture. In the others, the small scale of production was maintained through-out our period, with a high proportion of the workforce being employers of labour or self-employed. A high proportion of workers in the workshop trades also worked at home, either as self-employed artisans or as homeworkers given work by a sub-contractor.

Although the small scale of production remained dominant in the East End throughout our period there were still marked trends away from the workshops and into the factories, as Table 3 reveals. The first of these was towards concentration of the means of production – ownership was being concen-trated in fewer and fewer hands. This produced a rise in that section of the workforce who lived by working for others rather than themselves. Second, production was becoming more centralised; homeworkers (both men and women) were increasingly being driven into the workshops. Both these factors were almost certainly accompanied by a move towards larger factories, which absorbed labour at the expense of both workshops and homeworkers. Lastly, up to the beginning of the First World War, the Jewish industries enjoyed a period of growth, attracting an ever greater proportion of the local labour force. This was with the notable exception of the boot and shoe trade which underwent a spectacular decline in London as a whole from the 1890s,[7] reflected in Stepney where there was a reduction of 37 per cent in the numbers employed in the industry during the decade after 1901.

So that side by side with the dominant mode of produc-tion – the workshop with fewer than fifteen people employed there – existed both factory production and putting-out to homeworkers. Factory production was growing; homework was declining. The workers of Rothschild Buildings laboured in all three of these types of economic enterprise. Some, less typical then than now, stayed all their working lives in a factory employing hundreds of hands. Most went from workshop to workshop, enjoying freer relationships both with other workers and employers than factory discipline

TABLE 3

Characteristics of the Jewish manufacturing industries in Stepney,
1901–11

| | Stepney | | London | | | |
| | | | Ratio employer/ self employed to employee | | Proportion of workforce employed at home | |
Trade	1901	1911	1901	1911	1901	1911
	(numbers)				(%)	
Cabinet makers	2,115	1,897	1:5.9	1:6.2	8.9	7.3
Tailors	21,344	23,128	1:8.6	1:9.1	24.2	22.4
Cloth hat and cap-makers	n.a.	2,058	1:13.1	1:20.9	8.4	6.0
Milliners	449	880	1:8.9	1:11.1	13.3	9.4
Dressmakers	2,008	2,374	1:3.1	1:4.2	34.5	26.4
Boot-, shoe-makers	5,623	3,516	1:4.5	1:4.2	30.9	31.7
Tobacco manufacture	3,380	2,994	1:30.0	1:35.5	2.5	1.9
TOTAL	34,919	36,847[a]				

(a) This represents a 1.5 per cent increase in the Stepney working population employed in these trades in the ten year period (excluding cloth hat and cap-makers). If the boot and shoe trade is excluded the growth is 2.9 per cent.

Source: calculated from 1901 census, vol. 7, pp. 76–92 and 144–5; and 1911 census, vols 9 and 10 (occupations and industries), vol. 9, pp. 34–9 and vol. 10, pp. 155–7.

would allow, but paying for that in bad working conditions and insecurity of employment. Others worked mainly at home, taking work from subcontractors or receiving orders from private customers. Sometimes the same worker moved from workshop to homework or workshop to factory, in and out of the intricacies of the East End clothing industry. And sometimes a worker one year became a master the next, taking advantage of the opportunities for advancement offered in the workshop trades, and in all likelihood succumbing to their pitfalls.

Outside manufacturing, many people in the Buildings, in common with the Jewish East End as a whole, were employed in distribution. In the Buildings lived three types of retailer. The first and most common were street-sellers, retailing either from a market stall in the Lane or elsewhere, or from a barrow which they took round the streets with them. An extension of this, but more rarely pursued, was peddling, where the seller would carry goods from door to door, often far from the East End, for cash sales. And the third form was to sell items on credit on the tallyman (or, more commonly in Rothschild Buildings, tallywoman) system. These types of retailing were of great importance as an alternative to the workshop, and the numbers working in them increased during our period (see Chapter 7). Self-employment in other retail outlets would have been insignificant in Rothschild Buildings, but some were the employees of retailers and other distributors – the shop assistants, who had such a choice of workplaces in both the East End and the West.

Into this intricate world of work were thrust the 14-year-old sons and daughters of Rothschild Buildings, perhaps following paths trodden out by fathers and mothers and relatives before them, perhaps striking out alone. Even with guidance, in almost every case it was a new world. There were new relationships to explore and accept – learning to deal with people who lived by earning wages and people who lived by paying them; new skills to absorb – making fingers think for themselves but only after painful mistakes on the way; new tensions between worker and worker, and worker and governor; new worries about autumn and the fast season, about factory sirens and piece-rates; a new feeling of exhaustion at the end of the day.

Side by side with these unhardened hands worked the men and women of the Buildings – fathers, older brothers, older sisters, widowed mothers – who had gone through all those new experiences of work before, but probably in a different country. And outside the workshops, in the Buildings themselves, mothers, children and sometimes fathers worked at home, either as an alternative to the factory or as an extension of normal working hours.

Inside the workshop or out, the workers of Rothschild Buildings laboured for themselves and their families, and for others. They produced luxury consumer goods for the ruling class; like Mossy Harris who made the riding jackets and skirts which adorned the lady riders of Rotten Row; or Reuben Landsman whose father made a bedroom suite which sold for a price equal to four years' wages for a cabinet maker; or Eva Katchinsky who made hats at 7d. an hour for middle-class women to wear to church on Sundays or synagogue on Saturdays. And they produced capital for the shareholders who could sit back and wait for the dividends to come in; like Minnie Zwart who made army greatcoats for a fraction of the price which helped bloat the profits of war, or Jenny Schlom who made cigarettes for a large city company, swelling the unearned income of the shareholders.

This last case is perhaps the most instructive, for Jenny's was the worst exploited of all the working lives we will examine. Her labour helped make 7 per cent per annum for the shareholders of the Ardath Tobacco Co. In her first year at the factory she could earn up to £2 a week for making 2,000 cigarettes a day; without making a single cigarette, the top shareholders paid themselves forty times as much. During the time when discipline in the factory was being tightened to intolerable levels, profits rose by 91 per cent in four years.[8] The majority of the people who reaped the benefits described themselves as 'Gentleman' or 'Lady', or Physician, Architect, Accountant or other professionals, or Stock Broker or Banker. That was how the shareholders of the Four Per Cent described themselves, too.[9]

This chapter, then, examines individual work experiences, both new and of long standing, both inside and outside the workshop. It is based on personal recollections of working life before the end of the First World War as well as on reminiscences of others' experiences, those of parents or brothers or sisters. These recollections do not pose as a history of East End commodity production from the time of the influx to 1920.[10] Instead they tell of the things which people have remembered from their early years at work, the events, faces and problems which were important to them in their working lives. But in doing so they may give us insights into the wider world of which they were part – the labour market, the relationship between employer and worker, class consciousness; insights into the structure and dynamics of both Edwardian capitalism and the Jewish immigrant proletariat.

1. IN THE WORKSHOPS

Tailors

One in three of all workers in the Buildings at the turn of the century were classified as employed in the garment industry. But that is a simplification which implies a spurious unity. There were many divisions within the industry which, for the workforce, produced compartments from which it was difficult to escape. The major fissures came between bespoke tailoring and ready-made; between ladies' and gents' clothing; and between men's work and women's work. Within each of these, and in some sections more than others, division of labour split up skills and kept them apart. Rather than falling neatly within census classifications, clothing workers would have described themselves as cutters or pressers, or ladies' tailors, or trouser-machinists, or button-hole hands in the gents' tailoring. The sixty-three 'tailors' of Rothschild Buildings in 1900 were divided in this way; and among the men and women living there all sections were represented.

Mossy Harris,* from 142 Rothschild Buildings, left Jews' Free School on his fourteenth birthday, some time in 1908.[11] His widowed mother and her four sons had lived in deep poverty since Mossy's Polish father had died in 1894. For many years they had relied on organised charity to provide them with a standard of living not much higher than the

---

* This is a pseudonym.

Kaplans' – food was so short that the children had 'bread in salt water' for supper many times.

Mossy's earning power, now he had left school, was of crucial importance to the family, but rather than let him go into a dead-end job with good initial earnings but no prospects, Mrs Harris had him apprenticed with the Jewish Board of Guardians. So in 1908, Mossy became one of 244[12] boys apprenticed that year to the Board's Industrial Committee.

It had been for many years the Guardians' policy to widen the scope of employment among the Jewish working class[13] and for this reason Mossy was at first placed with a firm 'in the motor car line'. But this did not work out, and shortly Mossy found himself apprenticed to a firm making ladies' garments for the West End bespoke trade. Although he was eventually to leave the bespoke behind him he remained in ladies' tailoring, never once making on the gents' side, for the rest of his working life. His apprenticeship with this West End master was for five years, 'everything was signed and settled.'

'I was apprenticed in a shop opposite the Lyric Theatre. There was two tailors and a tailoress and a felling hand. I didn't do any part work. I had to make the garment complete. I had to learn to do everything, and eventually I got on very well there, because the guvnor put me under a Frenchman – he was a Jewish Frenchman. And I kept my eyes open and I used to watch this Frenchman like a cat watches a mouse. I watched the way he worked and everything, and after twelve months I went down to the guvnor, and I says, "I've been running about for twelve months", I says, "don't you think I ought to be put on a table?" So he thought to himself it was a bright idea, and so he did, and he put me under this Frenchman.'

Mossy learned the skills of the English journeyman tailor, with work based on 'the old traditional lines of one man one garment',[14] in good class bespoke work. As far as the Jewish side of the garment industry was concerned, this workshop was quite exceptional.[15]

'That work, that was the best class work and every man working in that class of work had to do everything: button-holes, even felling.★ . . . And in six months I made my first suit complete, on my own. . . . So the guvnor says, "Put these on the stand", and he examined it, and examined it. At that time money wasn't what it is now; so he took out 6d. from his pocket and gave it to me as an encouragement! I was about 15. And from that time he put me on regular to make the garment. Later on, when it was about two and a half years already, I thought to myself, "He's supposed to teach me cutting as well." So I went to the Board of Guardians and I explained the matter. . . . So they made a suggestion; they'd send me to the Polytechnic[16] just opposite Selfridge's and take lessons. There was a cutting school there. So I used to go there and learn one day a week; the guvnor used to let me go. One day a week you learnt to do the pattern cutting and then you had to practise on it during the week. The guvnor gave me a length of material to practise on, you see. He was glad because he got out of it, you see, by me taking lessons.'

At the time Mossy was apprenticed, about one in two of the Guardians' apprentices[17] were leaving their indentures before they had been completed. Probably the most important reason for this was that as the apprentice became more skilled he became more exploitable, still being paid apprentices' rates while producing saleable work, although the official reason given at the time was 'unrest in the labour world . . . and growing disregard of the sanctity of contracts'.[18]

'Well, after a time I thought, "This is no good going on like this." And then I started to grumble. So one day I made up my mind to leave my apprenticeship, so I told the guvnor I wanted to leave. So he says, "Well, if you go away I'll tell the Board of Guardians and they'll summons you, because the agreement is between the guvnor and the Board of Guardians." "All right", I says, "you do what you want to do, and so will I." I went back to the Board of Guardians and

★ Felling was delicate hand-stitching which secured the lining to the material along the edges (cuffs, lapels, bottoms and facings, etc.) of the garment.

I explained the whole situation, and they couldn't do nothing. I had to pay £50 premium to learn. That was deducted every week, at the beginning 1s. a week and so on until it came to the amount. The finish was the guvnor had to pay the difference already, to the Board of Guardians. And I went out and looked for a job in the West End.

As it happens I went into a place that was making my guvnor's work outside; he used to take orders – garments – from the guvnor and he used to make it up, like a sub-contractor. When I left I was getting 6s. a week, and I was making garments, so I didn't think he had anything to grumble about – 6 bob a week! And I went into this outside man making the work, and I was getting right away 7s. 6d. a day![19] And then afterwards he hired me, five and a half days a week, half day Sunday.

There was only the guvnor and myself. . . . I remember, it was in an ordinary room, was the workroom, and he used to have, especially in the winter, a fire piled up with coal or coke, I dunno what it was, and you used to sweat sitting in the room only. I used to be afraid there'd be a fire in that room. And was he a worker? He was one of the old Russian men – strong as a horse he was. He used to sit at the table from – whenever I used to come in there he was there. He lived there as well;[20] he had other rooms. We used to work for a shop in Regent St. Used to make riding habits there. . . . There used to be a skirt come sweeping down on one side, and they used to have elastics put in for the feet to hold it in position in case the wind blows it . . . And then the jackets – it had to be cut in, in the front here and a piece put in to allow it to swing round. Some parts were machined, but mostly hand work.'

Sometimes, when a rush was on and orders piled up, the two of them lived together in the workshop. Once,

'it was before a holiday and they were very busy. . . . I worked three days and two nights right off. Only one hour's sleep. I slept in the workshop. I got well paid for it!'

The two of them worked together through the great tailoring strike of 1912 which started in the West End and spread eastwards.[21] Some 10,000 workers struck in the West End alone for a general increase in log prices, but this sub-contractor and his worker were not among them. When Mossy, some years later, was employed as a tailor at a much larger East End wholesale factory, his attitude to unionisation and trade disputes changed for the better.

Mossy Harris worked in the West End until the outbreak of the war. But around 1915 he made a decisive change in his career. He broke with the high class work in the West to labour nearer his home and birthplace in the East End. There were probably two reasons. The first, and more important, concerned his mother's health which was going into a decline that left her barely able to look after herself. If Mossy could find work nearer home he would be away from the Buildings less; he could have his dinners there, for example. Second, good money was being earned in the East End garment industry as a result of increased clothing contracts for the War Office, and wage differentials between the skills of West End bespoke tailors like Mossy and the mass-producing workers of the East were quickly narrowing.[22]

Mossy entered what amounted almost to a different in-dustry. There was a dramatic change in his work routine. At first he reacted against it.

> 'So I did work in a place [off] Commercial St, . . . I worked in a big firm there – Cohen Brothers. Big place. In the West End, garments sort of take two or three days a jacket – best class work – and when I came into this place Cohen's it was a cheaper class of work so they gave me a bundle of four garments in one – four garments together! I thought I'd got two weeks' work nearly! They gave me a couple of lessons, you know, how to get on. But I was there two days at first and I left it. I thought to myself, "I don't like it. I can't put the good work in cheap work." '

But in the end, Mossy was to find his way back to Cohen's after a little more experience of the East End way of working – the natural way for most of the other tailors of Rothschild Buildings. The garment industry in the East End differed particularly from the West in one vital area: the old principle of 'one man one garment' was left behind for 'subdivision of labour'.[23]

At Cohen's, this process had been taken as far as it could.[24] Morris Cohen, one of the brothers, had been among the first to introduce mass-produced ladies' costumes to England.[25] His family's Bishopsgate factory employed 160 workers.[26] Material would come to the tailor from the cutting room, usually several thicknesses being cut at once on a slot-knife. It was then passed to the tailor – like Mossy Harris – who had the 'principal part' in making the garment and was the most skilled and best paid.[27] His job was to prepare the garment for the machinist – basting material, canvas and lining, marking with wax chalk where the machinist should sew the darts, put the pockets and sew the buttonholes. He, or in a place as big as Cohen's then probably a basting-hand or second tailor, would baste and prepare the pocket flaps, cuffs, collars and lapels. Good tailors, according to Morris Cohen,[28] were not easy to come by – although Mossy, with his background in the bespoke, considered that 'in the slop trade they could find men six a penny.' But Mossy *was* a good tailor, and Cohen's were eager to have him back a second time.

After Mossy had prepared the garment he would pass it to the machinist, usually a woman earning 5s. a day to Mossy's 9s. or 10s.[29] After machining, the seams would have to be pressed out by the under-presser, notoriously the most un-skilled and exploited man in the shop. This was the untrained immigrant's way into the garment industry.[30] It was the only way for Mick Mindel's father, also living in Rothschild Build-ings but originally a bookbinder, to find employment in the East End.[31]

'I think you could learn to be an under-presser within a month or so. In those days, I think if you earned 3s. 6d. a week to learn [you were lucky]. . . . Under-pressing in those days was on relatively cheap work, and really meant just openings of seams. In those days, of course, the coats were very long, they were probably 48 inches long – plenty of seams. They had irons then, 14 lb. irons, which were heated by gas; and they used to have a damp cloth, or damp rag as we called it, used to squeeze it through until it was sufficiently damp. You lie the garment down, and you open the seams, put the rag on, and press. So basically it is not a highly technical job – but it's a physical job.'

Mick Mindel's father eventually left the pressing and went back to binding the books he loved so much, but most under-pressers graduated to other jobs in the trade. Long hours – 8 a.m. to 8 p.m. with an hour for lunch and half an hour for tea – and forced work gave a man experience and strength enough to seek employment as a presser. The garment was pressed out after the first stage 'finishing' by women workers who felled the garment by hand. After pressing, it was put on a stand to be 'passed' by the tailor, who marked the position for buttons and other finishings. Trimmings like piping and edging or velvet collars were all sewn on after pressing out, again by low-paid women workers, this time earning 2s. to 2s. 6d. a day.[32]

Mossy, being a skilled worker, was more fortunate than many in that he was less affected by seasonal fluctuations in work. He was kept on during the slack time – particularly September to October – when less useful employees were laid off,[33] making 'samples' to tempt retailers and wholesalers. Not for Mossy were the months of semi-starvation and debt, waiting for the busy season to start, loitering with other workers hundreds strong on the pavement outside Black Lion Yard, hoping for a master to want a tailor or a machinist or a presser and to be the lucky one picked out of the crowd. But if Mossy was not so troubled by the greatest evil of the industry he could not continue to escape the struggle between worker and employer.

The tailoring industry was, like most contemporary East End trades, beset by labour problems throughout our period. The great strike years of 1889 (affecting over 2,000 workers), 1891 (10,000 on strike in the East End alone), 1896 (when over 500 ladies' tailors struck for cotton and silk to be bought by the employer rather than the worker), 1906 (which secured a reduction in the working day and temporary abolition of piece work, concessions forced by 5,000 striking East End workers), and 1912 (when 10,000 East End tailors struck successfully for advances in wages and various concessions), would all have affected the people of Rothschild Buildings. Even when workers did not obey the strike call, like Mossy Harris in 1912, they could not have avoided the increased tensions, even violence, the incessant talk, the worried or hostile expressions of their neighbours.

In the East End, and in a large factory like Cohen's, solidarity was more easily accomplished. In 1907, Morris Cohen dismissed one of his workers and all 160 men and women went on strike to demand his reinstatement.[34] At that time the factory was 'largely unionised' although membership may have declined from then until the war.

'I joined the union[35] when I was at Cohen's. I joined the union but it wasn't unionised. It became a union shop but it wasn't when I was there. So the guvnors used to take liberties now and again. We struck there when there was a whole business about getting higher pay at Cohen's. So they suggested that I speak to the guvnor, you know in every sense of the word; what I say, they said, will be final. There were other places were getting rises, and there was nothing said about it at Cohen's. So I went down to the guvnor and spoke to him. I says, "We want so much", I forget how much increase it was at the time, but it was a good bit, because a lot of places were getting their rises and we were stuck. So the guvnor says he can't do it, and one thing and another, you know, making excuses and one thing and another, as if he could be better off on the dole. So I said that if we can't get the rises "We all leave on Friday."And I went upstairs. Late during the day the guvnor called us down. There was two guvnors there, and they give us the rise.'

Division of labour within the wholesale clothing industry gave rise to a destructive division of interest between worker and worker. Many were paid by the piece, so that machinists depended on tailors who depended on pressers (before passing) who depended on felling hands. A weak link at any point of this chain could affect the take-home pay of everyone concerned.[36] These divisions were reflected in the separate trades unions and associations formed by garment workers in the early years of the century, including the London Clothiers'

Cutters' Trade Union, the Independent Tailors', Machinists' and Pressers' Union, and the Under Pressers', Plain Machinists' and Plain Hands' Union.[37]

The wedge forced between worker and worker by division of labour and payment by the piece was perhaps most noticeable in one particular dimension. That was the inequality between men and women. At the turn of the century, 44 per cent of 'tailors' who lived in Stepney were women. In the clothing industry as a whole (including dressmaking, shirt making, and other dress workers) women comprised some 52 per cent of the labour force.[38] Except during periods of struggle they were divided from men in the work they performed, the wages they earned, and for some years the trade union to which they belonged. And these divisions affected the many women and girls of Rothschild Buildings who laboured in 'the tailoring'.

Tailoresses

Women were employed in most sections of the East End ready-made garment industry. The exclusively male domains of cutter, tailor and presser, already eaten into by division of labour, were further eroded by the First World War.[39] Women pressers and cutters may have been a merely temporary phenomenon created by the shortage of men, but women tailors and under-pressers in the middle-class or slop trade were frequently met with in the early years of the century. But the preponderance of female labour in the garment industry was to be found in those areas traditionally associated with women's work. The women of Rothschild Buildings worked as basting-hands or second tailors, as machinists, felling hands, finishers, buttonhole hands and plain hands; they worked on gents' coats, trousers and ladies' wear. And during the war, most commonly they worked on 'the khaki'.

Minnie Zwart, born at 170 Rothschild Buildings in 1893, left school in 1907 and for the next five years machined the lining into men's caps at a place in Leman St.[40] About 1912, the year of the massive strike which dragged the fast season to a halt, Minnie changed her trade and found a job in the ladies' tailoring. She was taken in by 'a little tiny shop underneath some flats in Shepherd St'* run by a man called Gershon. Compared with Cohen's this was a small affair:

'About a dozen of us really, not many. There was men machiners, there was half a dozen machiners, and the rest were girls working on felling, buttonholes, buttoning, myself' [and one other basting hand].

Mr Gershon took Minnie away from the machine and taught her basting. Minnie was a fast learner and it took her no time to learn the trade, 'because I was a good needle hand and I took it up very quickly. At school I learnt, you know.' Long hours in the workshop – 8 a.m. till 8 p.m. at Gershon's with an hour for dinner, which Minnie took at home, and half an hour for tea – gave plenty of practice which within a matter of weeks turned young girls into experienced hands.

Gershon's workshop made ladies' topcoats – 'Coats that they wore, you know, the long coats and fur collars'. The work came in ready cut.

'I'd baste the linings and foreparts, you know, underneath the coat. There was a forepart, a long piece of cloth. And I'd baste that on ready for the machiner to machine it.'

After machining, pressing, and some finishing the garment would come back to Minnie who put the fur collar on by hand, and then it would be passed by Gershon or his wife who came in to help from time to time. Gershon was

'an all round man himself. But never worked. He managed the place, see that everything was going right. He was always out. Dunno where he got to but next door us was a place where they were backing horses, a shop, and I believe he was in there all day.'

The workshop atmosphere was at most times relaxed; the relationship between Minnie and her employer cordial.

* Now Toynbee St.

'Oh, he was after the girls! . . . Nice looking man. His wife was very jealous of him, I remember. He used to get caught with the girls many a time and she came in, you know.'

Gershon and his wife, both in their thirties when Minnie first met them, befriended this young widow's daughter and often invited her to their home for meals. This example of kindness to young girl workers was not unique. Annie Kaplan met with the same response from her employer at a dress-maker's shop in Greenfield St.★ At Miller's Annie started on the machine at 14, earning[41]

'1s. a week! 1s. a week I earned! My mother used to sit in the gate and wait for the 1s. Friday [so that she could buy some food in the Lane]. You had to wait a long time before you started earning.'

But the Millers were good to Annie, even though they wouldn't pay her more than the normal learner's rate.[42]

'They were very nice to me. She used to sew 2s. 6d. in my coat sleeve; I took my coat off and they sewed 2s. 6d. in it – they knew I was poor. And I always remember. I went to work one dinner time and when I came back it was pouring with rain. She took me opposite to a shop, threw my shoes in the gutter and bought me a new pair of shoes.'

At the beginning of the First World War, Gershon's family business, in common with the whole of the East End tailoring trade, suffered a severe setback. In 1914 the slack season set in early and with a terrible jolt. Thousands of garment workers, Minnie among them, were laid off. Distress in the East End 'could not possibly be more dismal.'[43] The winter of 1914 was a miserable time indeed for the large majority of East End workers, but particularly so for those in the ladies' tailoring. The war contracts which were later to bring unprecedented earnings to men and women in the garment industry – and unprecedented profits to their employers – were a few

★ Now Greenfield Rd.

months away. Steeply rising food prices and higher rents added to the general suffering and hardship. Only in one part of the East End clothing trade were things looking up and that was in the shops making trousers.[44]

Into one of these shops, Harry Temple's in Hunton St, came Sarah Zissman,* a 15-year-old trouser-maker from 189 Rothschild Buildings.[45] She had spent the first thirteen years of her life in Ekaterinoslav before emigrating to South Wales and from there to Spitalfields. Her father, brother and sister were all trouser-makers too, reputedly among the most sweated workers in a section of the industry 'in which the lowest prices and the worst conditions obtain.'[46] But in those early months of 1915 trouser-makers, because of the work stimulated by War Office sub-contracts,[47] were in demand.

'They were begging you to come in and work . . . there were plenty of jobs during the war, and I went round and I saw the ads and I went in and asked if he wanted a machinist and he said yes, and I worked there. We all worked there; my father worked there, [my brother] worked there, we all worked there.'

At Harry Temple's they made 'the breeches that the officers wear, with the leather patches'. The workshop was larger than Gershon's, with ten or twelve machinists, and Temple had invested in expensive buttoning and buttonholing machines. The shop itself

'wasn't bad at all. It was airy. It was a sort of a house, but it was a big room, and he had his office downstairs; if you wanted something we used to go down to the office. It wasn't bad at all as workshops go; I worked in worse ones than that. . . . The place that we had a strike in I worked there when it rained and you had to hold an umbrella on the machine because the rain was coming in.'

Again the relationship between Harry Temple, Sarah and his other workers was genial: 'I got on with him quite well. . . .

---

* This is a pseudonym.

Not with all of them but with *this* – Harry Temple – very good.'

It took only a few months for the rest of the wholesale garment industry to recover from the shock waves which followed the declaration of war. Military work – 'the khaki' – flooded into the East End shops. Supplies, like the supplies of men sent for cannon-fodder to the front, were 'practically illimitable'.[48] Mr Gershon, bowing happily to the inevitable, stopped making ladies' topcoats and made army greatcoats instead.

'The khaki', again ready cut, was delivered by motor van, sent out by the main contractors. Again, Minnie was a basting hand. The material

> 'was too heavy to sit with it on your lap, so you sat on the table and the table took all the weight of it. Very heavy coats they were. . . . I used to do a bit of finishing, put the buttons on sometimes when there wasn't enough basting to do, little odd jobs, you know. Very good at the needle. [Was it hard on the fingers?] Oh yes, sore from the work. Hard work. Get good money but it was hard work.'

Rates of pay on 'the khaki' were certainly good; the gap between women's and men's wages narrowed and average women's wages rose two and a half times over the pre-war level.[49] Sarah Zissman remembered taking home wages as high as £2 5s. – 'I earned a lot because I was very quick.' But profits were even higher. She would probably have been paid 7½d. for trousers while Harry Temple received 10d. from the contractor who in return received 1s. 8¼d. from the War Office. Minnie Zwart's greatcoats produced 2s. 3½d. in wages to the workshop but were sold to the government at 7s. 6d.[50] In addition to increased prices paid to the workers the continuous flow of war work ironed out the seasonality which so bedevilled the garment industry, and although there may have been gaps between sub-contracts these were nothing to the pre-war slack seasons.

But with the increased work, often harder than on the old garments anyway, came longer hours. The pay may have been good and steady, but workers had to do the overtime if it was there.[51] At Gershon's it was

'One continuation of work. . . . P'raps till 10 or 11 o'clock
at night. He had to get a lot out, you know, lot of work out,
and you'd have to work.'

For many families in Rothschild Buildings the war did mean
a rise in living standards. So many children at work earning
steady and good wages meant that families could afford to
spend more money on the home and on small 'luxuries' – lino
for the floor, a sideboard, a dressing table, better clothes – as
we have seen in the chapters on home life and childhood. This
happened not only in Rothschild Buildings but in many large
families lucky enough to share in the 'artificial war prosperity'
which gave 'the opportunity of obtaining a few decent
comforts'.[52]

But better pay was only won at high cost. Food prices in the
East End doubled in under two years from August 1914 to
June 1916.[53] Rents – and evictions – increased until controls
were imposed at the very end of 1915. Wage rates did not, in
many cases, rise without a struggle. In October 1916 500 men
and women struck at Schneider's Whitechapel clothing
factory in protest at the management's demand that workers
buy trimmings and cotton from the firm at prices higher than
were charged elsewhere. The company gave in after a strike
which lasted a week.[54] That same month workers at Lottery's
factory, also in Whitechapel, struck for workers' committees
to arbitrate on dismissals, no reductions in piece-work prices,
no increase in charges for silk and thread, and 'That the fore-
man and passers shall speak properly to the workers and treat
them as human beings.'[55] Labour troubles mounted throughout the East End and London generally, so much so that
government Commissioners could send reports back to
Whitehall which began,[56]

'The unrest is real, widespread and in some directions
extreme, and such as to constitute a national danger unless
dealt with promptly and effectively. We are at this moment
within view of a possible social upheaval.'

Sentiments like those may have sounded unreal in the cosy
family atmosphere of Gershon's or Temple's. But in the larger

factories, where there was a greater and more apparent division between the interests of capital and labour, the struggle could not be hidden behind smiling faces and kind words.

Cabinet makers

By 1911, cabinet makers made up the second largest group of male workers among the Jewish immigrant working class.[57] As such they were well represented in Rothschild Buildings. The fathers and sons of the Buildings helped swell the labour force of the largest furniture manufacturing area of the country. The East End furniture industry was concentrated in the streets to the north of Spitalfields in Shoreditch, Hoxton and Bethnal Green. The nucleus was Curtain Rd – 'The Road' – where almost every address was given over to cabinet makers, upholsterers, French polishers, carvers and a host of small businesses on the periphery of the industry. In and around the East End of 1911 there were some 676 cabinet making workshops; the number of shops and factories allied to the furniture industry as a whole reached 1,021. And Stepney alone was home to 1,883 cabinet makers in that same year.[58]

Reuben Landsman's father was one of those Stepney cabinet makers enumerated in the census of 1911.[59] Isaac Landsman was born about 1877 at Zhitomir in the Volhynia province of Western Russia. He married a Ukrainian woman and already had two sons when they decided to emigrate in 1904. By 1905 they were living at 136 Rothschild Buildings where Reuben was born towards the end of the year.

Isaac Landsman was a good craftsman but a harsh father. He was a religious man and as long as his sons attended Hebrew classes regularly he cared little else about them. It was in his house that discipline was enforced by a cat-o'-nine-tails. And for the few hours that he was home from the workshop or *shul* he rarely talked with any of his seven children.

Reuben's father had brought his skills as a cabinet maker with him from Russia and now exploited them in the workshops of the East End. He changed jobs many times, wheeling his box of tools, his oil-lamp and glue-pot on a hired barrow from shop to shop in an effort to find better conditions or a master he could get on with. Isaac worked for Koor & Cohen in Redchurch St, for Morris in Bethnal Green Rd, for Sidofsky in Hackney Rd, for Isaac Grew in Hoxton Market and others. In 1914 he even went to Salisbury Plain to build huts for the troops, and worked in an aeroplane factory in Chelsea before finally he went into partnership with a man called Goodman in the early years of the First World War. They rented a work-shop at 97 Sclater St, Bethnal Green; before long Isaac was sole master, Mr Goodman having taken a fish and chip shop in Brick Lane.

In those early years Isaac had been a union man, bound up in the struggles of labour in the tumultuous years of the Edwardian crisis. Many East End cabinet makers struck in 1912 and 1913 for increases of $\frac{1}{2}d$. an hour and reductions in hours to $52\frac{1}{2}$ a week.[60] During periods of labour unrest the East End streets often saw tensions between worker and master burst out in violence[61] and few could remain unaffected by the conflict. As a young boy, Reuben would catch snatches of conversation, at card parties on Saturday nights: 'I heard, about unions and strikes. I understand that he had been on strike with the others.'

That struggle for a better standard of life was reflected in Isaac's desire for independence which led him to become a master and in turn an employer of labour – an independence which led him first to 97 Sclater St.[62] Isaac became one of the many small masters in the typical East End mode of produc-tion, 'working with from three to six under him, and with little capital and no machinery.'[63] Isaac made bedroom suites (the Jewish immigrant end of the furniture trade)[64] and side-boards. It was top class work.

'About the first job I saw there was . . . he had a customer for a satinwood bedroom suite. Now at *that* time, about 1915 – £350 that bedroom suite. And he lived at Forest Gate, this . . . customer.'

Most orders came from a large factory in Old St who sub-contracted to Isaac. The finished pieces would end up in Waring & Gillow's, Maples and other expensive London stores. Isaac ordered his timber, usually satinwood, greywood (Italian sycamore), or burr walnut, from any of the local merchants but most often the one on the corner of Commercial St and Wheler St. It was delivered on a horse and cart and unloaded board by board into the cellar where Isaac stood ready to stack it.

'I was a young boy and everything interested me. . . . And I used to be puzzled – people unloading timber and calling out numbers, "five, seven, ten" and I couldn't fathom out and I used to watch. And this used to be going on for quite a while until I realised . . . every board had a number of how many square feet was on it. The unloader . . . would call out and there was somebody there with a book taking tally. . . . And, well, we never done that. And I persuaded my mother – I can't talk to my father. . . . I could never tell anything to him. So I keep pressing her – I worried *her*, she worried *him*, kept worrying until eventually I'm working there, fiddling about, still only a boy, just perhaps two or three months in the workshop. And one day he comes over to me while I'm with the sandpaper, you know, rubbing the mouldings – "Take tally!" And he never gave you time to think, because you had to start doing before he even said anything. . . . "Take tally! What you waiting for?" . . . Anyway I saw a van outside and I must have grasped, so quick, quick, quick, pick up a piece of wood, something small on the floor, get hold of a pencil, get outside and start taking tally. And as they're calling out so I checked. He calls out "seven" . . . so I put it down. And so when they was unloaded so then I could go inside and I reckoned up . . . and where there were about 900 feet and I'd got here about 500 feet I showed it to my father: "That's what *I* make it." My elder brother was there, Jack. My father said, "Here y'are, Jack. Reckon it up!" Jack reckons it; reckons up; reckons again. . . . He can't make it any different. So suddenly it must have clicked in my old father's brain. So he says to the driver, "Send your guvnor round!" Guvnor comes round. . . . "Well, it's too much to go sorting it all out down there. Supposing we [split the difference]?" And after that I always had to take tally! So *Gawd* knows how

many years he'd been working for those bastards! And then
you get people . . . think all Jews stick together like shit to a
blanket!'

The Sclater St workshop relied heavily on the services
provided by the surrounding furniture making area. First
there was the saw-mill just round the corner in Cygnet St
where they would plane and tongue-and-groove wardrobe
ends, doors and tops. For inlay – a common feature of
Edwardian bedroom furniture – Isaac would go to the inlay-
maker who showed him patterns and cut designs ready to be
glued into the veneer. Wood carving was done at the carver's
in Brick Lane who would put thumb-nail mouldings, claw-
and-ball feet and scalloped legs on sideboards. French polishing was done by a friend but 'we didn't have much polishing;
we usually sent it out in the white and whoever we supplied,
they would see to the polishing.' The local carter would
provide the necessary service of hiring himself, his horse and
his cart to the firm when deliveries were made to Old St every
two or three weeks. And in Curtain Rd itself you could be sure
to sell any piece of furniture that was left on your hands, even if
you hawked it at cost price.

At Sclater St, Isaac employed his eldest son Jack and one
other worker. The second son was prevented from going into
the business by his mother, frightened of differences with Isaac
which could have led to blows. But when Reuben left Jews'
Free School in 1919 he 'took it for granted' he would be a
cabinet maker like his father. Characteristically, they had
never discussed it.

'You left school the day you were 14. So I left on a Wednesday. Thursday night my father came home, says, "Why
didn't you come into work?" So I says, "Well, I thought I'd
have a holiday and come in on [Sunday]." So he let that go.'

Reuben started work at 8 o'clock. His father would already
be at the shop, warming up the glue so that the men would
waste no time when they came in. The boy was set to work
doing odd jobs around the workshop:

'going out doing the errands . . . oh buying the sundries,
the bits of mouldings and little bits like that, nails, screws
[from the cabinet ironmongers]; making the tea, sweeping
the floor, take down the shutters . . . get the glue ready,
stand by, perhaps hold something where he needed another
hand. . . . At 7.55 at night I was permitted to put the
shutters up. . . . Now I was following up a serial in the
local pictures. And in those days it was Monday, Tuesday,
Wednesday, and it changed to Thursday, Friday, Saturday
another lot. . . . So come Wednesday night I says to my
father, "I wanna go off early, I wanna go off 7 o'clock."
"Why?" "I'm following up a serial." What the bloody hell
was this! He says, "All right, you can go tonight. But no
more." I had to stay till 8 o'clock. That's when I was just 14.
And all I could *do* was put up the shutters. . . .'

Reuben enrolled at evening classes but the twelve-hour day
would not be varied even for those.

'Evening classes he didn't know – "That's nonsense!" So
after 8 o'clock I'd go to evening classes. Time I got there, of
course, it was late. And by the time I came out about 10
o'clock my belly was down in my boots. And round just
nearby in Fairclough St[65] was the fish and chip shop, so I
could buy some chips and a baigel and come home a bit
easier. This went on a little while and I couldn't take any
more of it. So that was the end of night school.'

Gradually he ceased to be the boy and by his interest and
quickly growing skill entered the ranks of the East End cabinet
makers.

'One day I took a piece of wood laying about . . . and
another piece of wood and I made like a mortice, made a
tenon . . . fitted it in . . . made a nice job and took it to my
father and showed him what I'd done. "Very good." Well,
when I'd made that sample, then after that I began to get bits
of work. And then he began to give me – the first job he
gave me was for a dressing table . . . it was a bit wobbly but
he helped me out with that. And after that I gradually

developed and by the time I was 15½ I was making
wardrobes, double-door wardrobes, with round dummies
on 'em, with marquetry on there. . . . And dressing tables
and wash-stands – I made the whole bedroom suite
complete.'

In the first few months of Reuben Landsman's working life,
distress among demobbed and workless soldiers was widespread:

'[They] would come in and beg to be taught the trade for no
wages. . . . He couldn't afford to pay them and his conscience wouldn't let them be like slaves.'

But Isaac's conscience did not extend to his own family:

'I started off with 2s. In six weeks he increased my wages – I
never asked him for more money – he gave me a 25 per cent
increase; 2s. 6d. a week he was giving me! . . . From 2s. 6d.
it jumped up to 7s. 6d. and then jumped again to 15s. Then I
began to pester my mother that if he paid *me* just like he'd
have to pay anybody else, say 1s. an hour,[66] I'd get about £3
a week and I might be able to give my mother 30s., and
clothe myself. So at least she was sure of getting that 30s.,
where she wasn't sure of getting anything [from the old
man]. So anyway, I pestered her and she pestered him and
he arranged, "All right, 1s. an hour." '

At 15½ years old, Reuben was doing 72½ hours a week in
the workshop at a time when the eight-hour day was becoming increasingly common in industry generally. In the
summer months he started at 6 in the morning and worked
through till 8 or 9 at night. That hard apprenticeship at his
father's workshop in Sclater St made him as skilled a craftsman
as Isaac had been. There his hands became 'so trained you
could feel any slight ripple' in the piece of wood he was
working on. There he earned the cabinet maker's trademark of
knuckles swollen with corns, still there although he had not
been at the bench for more than thirty years: 'I'll take *them* with
me.'

Cap-makers and milliners

The manufacture of ladies' hats and men's cloth caps were two distinct branches of the headwear industry. The workforces were separated by skills, by status, by sex and often by locality. Stepney was the cap-making district of London and by the 1890s the trade was largely 'in the hands' of the Jewish immigrants.[67] The Stepney cap-makers, 2,058 of them in 1911, were evenly divided between men and women, with the large majority of the female labour force being single girls under 25. In 1901, cap-makers formed 10 per cent of wage earners in Rothschild Buildings.

Millinery, on the other hand, was not a trade especially associated with the East End. It was a much larger London industry than cap-making,[68] and it relied almost entirely on female labour. Milliners ranked more highly in the social scale than the majority of women manual workers. Accordingly, in 1911, only 6 per cent of London's milliners lived in Stepney, compared with 73 per cent of cap-makers;[69] the largest numbers were to be found in north and west London. But from the turn of the century the East End millinery industry had slowly expanded.[70] And as a very respectable trade for working girls it should come as no surprise to find young ladies from Rothschild Buildings among the 900 or so Stepney milliners at work around the beginning of the First World War.

Among the cap-makers of Rothschild Buildings was Florrie Edelman★ who moved to C Block with her Austrian father and mother in 1908, when she was 8 years old.[71] The Buildings were to be her home for the next sixty-one years. Florrie left Jews' Free School at Christmas 1914, but, instead of going into the tailoring with her father, was encouraged to take up cap-making by the daughters of the Dutch family on the floor below. These girls worked for Charlie Finegold and his brother at their factory in Middlesex St, and that was where Florrie was taken on in the early months of 1915. This was a larger factory than that customary in the East End,[72] made larger by one floor being given over to the manufacture of ladies' hats.

★ This is a pseudonym.

Florrie was a machinist with Finegold's until some time early in 1916 when the firm moved to bigger and better premises in New North Rd, Hoxton. Fortunately, Florrie then had an offer from a Russian cap-maker, a friend of her father's, to work for him in his workshop at Aldgate Avenue, by St Botolph's Without. That job lasted only a short time because the master suddenly returned to Russia, perhaps along with the many others who welcomed the Revolution of October 1917.[73] Florrie then worked for a time with Marcus, the military cap-makers in Commercial St, where she made NCOs' stripes and put the patent leather bands round officers' caps. But that work was heavy, and in early 1918 she found a place at Joe Soref's factory in White Lion St, Spitalfields.

Joe Soref 'was so big they used to call him Joe the Police-man'. His workshop was over an old stable where, besides horses and a big dog, an elephant was unaccountably installed for some time. The factory was on two floors and arranged to reflect 'the extreme sub-division of work' associated with the cap trade.[74] It was a typical East End shop. Upstairs was the sole cutter who cut the four quarters which were sewn together to form the cap 'tops'. 'We had to go up for 'em. . . . A gross of tops, and that made of quarters. We had to match 'em up. . . .' The cut tops would then go to the girl machinists. Florrie used a power machine for the first time at Soref's; she was instructed to put up her long plaits in case they caught in the power points and gave her a shock. Each girl worked for a male cap-maker who was considered to be the more skilled worker, a point of view reflected in his wage packet.[75] 'We always had to work for men. . . . The girls got ready the tops for the men [by machining the quarters], got all the canvas ready for them.' The four men would put in the peaks, sew in the linings made by a single lining-maker, a skilled female hand, and then the caps would go back to another girl to be finished off – felling the caps, sewing the buttons and press-studs on. The finished caps were then carried back upstairs to be 'blocked off'. 'They had two blockers upstairs' who would press the caps on a wooden head-shaped block with small gas-irons and a damp rag. They would then be packed by a girl who wrapped them in tissue-paper before boxing them up.

When Florrie first worked she earned 5s.; '2s. 6d. I gave my mother, 2s. 6d. she gave me, for spending.' There was no scheme of apprenticeship[76] but even without it employers found ample opportunity to exploit shy school leavers.

'I was a young girl and I was doing work . . . and the girls . . . were getting twice as much as me. Well, I found out and I says to the guvnor, "I'm doing as many grosses of tops as they're doing . . . and I want more money." So he give me more. You know, 2s. 6d. rise.'

But the cap-makers of the East End were better able to protect themselves than many of their fellow workers. The Cap Makers' Union had been formed in 1891, and there were important strikes in 1895 (successful, against rules of employment), and 1896 (unsuccessful, against the dismissal of a man for alleged inefficiency) where there was some violence between masters and pickets.[77] Despite a waning of militancy at the turn of the century leading to the dissolution of the union for a period of nearly two years, East End cap-makers resolved to make May Day 1905 a holiday and struck when their leaders were sacked in revenge, and a lengthy dispute in the summer of 1907 affected the trade in both London and Manchester.[78] By Florrie's time there was no doubting the serious view of the struggle taken by the East End cap-makers.

'Don't talk about strikes! . . . Every Saturday or Sunday there was strikes in the cap trade! I didn't belong to a union, I was a young girl, I didn't bother. [The power machines] had a little head . . . there's no bobbins, it's a chain stitch, very small machine a cap-maker's machine. The head belonged [to the maker] like my husband or all the other men. And they wore little half black aprons. And if they came home with the head [wrapped in the apron] you knew it was a strike.'

A normal working day at Soref's was 8 till 6, although the men worked overtime in the busy months (January to August) to compensate for the slack time during the autumn. Florrie was earning 30s. a week after the end of the war, but Soref's held another consolation for her. She married one of the cap-makers – the one who refused to work with her when she first went there: 'He didn't want me! No. I wasn't good enough.' Their marriage in 1922 marked the end of Florrie Edelman's working life as a cap-maker.

Eva Katchinsky, Florrie's contemporary in Rothschild Buildings, was the daughter of that tailor from Kiev who had emigrated for the second time in 1909.[79] Eva's father had died some three years before she left school in 1914, but he 'always used to say he wouldn't like his daughter to be in a factory, he'd like her to be something great.' So his widow, an independent lady of strong mind, strove hard to force Eva out of the poverty into which the Katchinsky family had been thrust by the premature death of the bread winner. That poverty cut short Eva's opportunity for education in favour of an early start in the labour market.

'Actually, I left school with a lie – I was 13½ – but as I didn't have a certificate my mother had to swear that I was 14 and got me out earlier.'

Eva did housework, and looked after her brothers from Christmas 1913 to June 1914. In the meantime she and her mother looked around for suitable employment and fastened on millinery – 'at least it was ladylike' – perhaps because the daughter of the richest family they knew in the Buildings was manageress of a millinery shop. And so Eva, the young Russian girl just five years in England, became an apprentice at Dinah Barr's ladies' hat shop in Brick Lane on the corner of Heneage St. To Eva, she was Madam Barr.

'She gave me 1s. a week, so there was no premium. She said that if my mother gave her a £50 premium . . . I'd have got 5s. a week.[80] But I don't think my mother knew what £50 looked like at the time.'

To test the worth of her new apprentice Mrs Barr laid little traps for her,

'such as when I swept the shop I'd find 1s. . . . or 6d. And I used to say, "Oo, Mrs Barr, I've found a 6d.!" "Good girl!" . . . I told [my mother], I said, "I find shillings, I find

sixpences, pieces of ribbon". . . . My mother says . . .
"Don't you ever pick anything up!" Not that I would.
"She's trying you out." And after once or twice she said,
"I'm trying you out, Eva, and I think you're good", and she
gave me 4s. a week.'

But in the context of the East End war economy, with rising
wages and faster-rising prices, Eva quickly became dissatisfied. At that time there was ample opportunity for change.
Walking through Fashion St she noticed a board outside Reese
& Bonn's cap factory advertising vacancies for workers in
'HATS'. 'Well, hats were hats', so she went in and made
enquiries. For several months, Eva sewed the linings into
sailors' hats and stitched on the pieces of ribbon, for which she
received 'I think 15s., and because I was under 16 it was, I
think, 6s. war bonus.'

'But I didn't like the work 'cos I wanted to be a milliner, and
my mother wasn't very keen either. She said, "It's as bad as
tailoring! I want you to be a lady." '81

A few months later, the word got around that milliners
were wanted in the City, and from Reese & Bonn, Eva went to
a large millinery factory, employing about fifty hands, at
Gravel Lane. At Supran & Kaufman's, she made proper ladies'
hats, wide picture hats garnished with ribbon, artificial flowers
and even bunches of cherries. To suit the increasingly fashionable demand for simpler hats they made Tam O'Shanters as
well. Some hats, like those on which Eva mainly worked,
were hand-made and destined for respectable middle-class
stores; the machine-made hats adorned the women of the Old
Kent Rd or Poplar High St.

A wire or buckram foundation would be made on a wooden
block and the material – lace, tulle, silk, velvet, georgette,
shantung – would be drawn over it, pleated and stitched by
hand. The milliner would make the hat complete, cutting
material, putting on the trimmings and pressing the pleats
where necessary. On good hats the stitching was fine, but on
the cheap variety large stitches were used and the work
skimped, as at Madam Barr's whose hats 'had a stitch from

here to here'. On machine-made hats, labour was divided between machinist and needle-hand or finisher.

The working day at Supran & Kaufman's lasted from 8.30 till 7 with half a day on Saturday, average hours in the millinery.[82] The regime was not intolerable, and the girls were allowed to buy (and sometimes were given) material to make hats for themselves. Often 'we used to pinch little things like trimmings', which were expensive. Certainly, an improver's weekly wage needed supplementing in every way possible, and even after that wages were only about 35s. a week.[83] When Eva was a 'full-blown milliner', she went on to piece-rates and teamed up with a non-Jewish girl from Forest Gate.

> 'I was quick and she was good. . . . And we became partners and we earned quite nice money. . . . Well, if we took ten hats, she would do the part that she could do better, I would do the part that I could do quicker. And we had a book. Many a time we wished we could put more on, but we couldn't because the hats had numbers. . . . Every week, whatever we finished . . . they put down, they used to say "Eva and Hilda" . . . and added up and we'd share it.'

The partnership broke up shortly before the end of the war when Eva went to work for David Berger, a young workshop owner, at his place in Gun St, Spitalfields. Eva quickly made friends with Berger – 'he came to my wedding, I went to his' – and soon her younger brother joined the firm to learn cutting for the machine-made work. Later the firm expanded and moved to Old St, in about 1921, where Eva was made a forelady. Even though Berger was a good boss and a kind man, he could not resist screwing as much profit as possible from the girls who worked for him.

> 'About 6.50 he would find a few "specials". And those specials took about twenty-five minutes to finish off. But if they worked an hour it was 1s. an hour overtime. And of course, they'd hurry up to botch them off . . . and they used to mumble, "Time we get home – why couldn't he give us an hour overtime?" . . . He'd come the next morn-

ing and say, "Eva! Come here! Look at this!" . . . I said,
"Now look here, Dave. Don't shout at me, I should shout at
you. . . . Now if you gave them an hour, and they knew
they were gonna earn 1s., they would do more, do it well
and be pleased to stay. . . ." "Who are you a forelady for,
me or them?" I said "Both of you. I'm telling you what's
right!" '

Probably David Berger had imbibed some of his father's
attitudes, expressed by the old man on his frequent visits to his
son's Gun St workshop;

'and if he found a piece of ribbon on the floor – we always
laughed at him – he used to say, "Blood! That's blood! Why
don't you pick it up, that's blood!" And I used to say, "Well,
I can't see anybody bleeding!" '

Perhaps if Eva had looked harder she would have seen whose
blood it really was.[84]

2. IN THE FACTORY

Cigarette makers

In 1900, workers in the tobacco industry were the second
largest group of labour represented in Rothschild Buildings.
The branches – tobacco, cigar making and cigarette making –
were entirely separate; more men than women were employed
on cigars and tobacco but from the 1890s onwards the trend
had been to replace skilled male cigarette makers with low-
paid girls and women.[85] From that time also, machines began
to reduce the hand-made trade.[86] In Stepney at the turn of the
century 56 per cent of the 3,380 workers in the industry were
women; ten years later this had increased to 65 per cent. In
1911 74 per cent of women workers were under 25 and only

12.5 per cent of the total were married or widowed.[87] Most of these young single girls were employed on the cigarette side of the trade.

Jenny Schlom left the Gravel Lane County Council School in 1914. At that time she was living in C Block Rothschild Buildings, just across the road from where she had spent her childhood in Nathaniel.[88] She was only to spend about two years in the Buildings, moving to Irene House in 1916 for a short time and then to a house in Heneage St, Spitalfields.

When Jenny left school she worked in a clothing factory in Commercial St, first of all pulling basting stitches and then felling armholes, 'but I didn't like it very much.' She stayed there until the early months of 1915.[89]

> 'And suddenly there was a boom with cigarette making. And around, all the mothers, they were saying, "Oh, it's a very good trade and they can earn lots of money." '

Jenny had seen cigarettes being made by hand before and she knew something of the trade from her mother. Besides, she was anxious to leave tailoring, not caring much for the needle. So she became a cigarette maker, learning the trade at various factories around the East End.

> 'When you go into a factory, a cigarette factory, you don't go as a maker. A 14-year-old starts by cutting the ends off, and she's called the cutter. She goes into the factory and they say "You'll start cutting and we'll show you how to cut." But you graduate from the – being a cutter. And you learn by watching and trying, they let you try here and there, and so you become a maker, you know.'

Jenny spent her longest period as a maker at the Ardath Tobacco Company's[90] enormous factory at 39–51 Worship St. She went there first when she was about 16 years old, some four years after it opened.

> 'It was a very big factory. There were hundreds of girls employed. My number was 242 but there was about 500 or 600 girls.'

Ardath's bought the tobacco still on the stalk;

'They had a stripping room in the basement where the leaves – they used to bring in the tobacco in its raw state – of all different kinds, and the girls used to strip the leaves and throw the stalks away. I remember going down there just to have a look.'

The girls who worked in the stripping room were Gentiles but the makers and cutters were almost exclusively first- or second-generation immigrant Jewish girls.[91] About 200 makers and cutters sat facing each other across rows of wooden tables on each floor of the factory. Each table had three makers and three cutters either side. At the edge of the table was a trough and at the side of each cutter was a raised wooden partition a few inches high running at right angles across the table.

'Now the way they were made was:[92] there was a klonky [made of a material half linen and half parchment]. And they'd cut out a square [about 4 inches wide with two corners rounded off]. They would stick that on [the table] with some starch, onto the edge of the table [so that one half only of the klonky was stuck and one half could be used to roll the cigarette up]. Then they had say a pound or two pound of tobacco in a tin, loose, on the floor, with a lid. Then they would take out tobacco with their hand, maybe about half a pound at a time, and would put that on the table. And as it would be all kind of stuck together they'd go like that [sifting] with their fingers to loosen it. Now, they'd take a fingerful, about the size of a cigarette, and put this along this klonky. Then there was parchment paper that you had to use and a pusher which was like half a knitting needle with a flat top [about 9 inches long]. Had to have a knob. And the top was flat, because it had to push up-wards. . . . Then you would take the parchment which was cut out like a kind of steeple shape [and called a kurtle] and that you would put on the klonky and roll up very tightly, the tobacco, you'd roll it up in the parchment with the pointed like kind of spire [to form a pointed tube]. Now you

had cigarette papers, here [to your left] it was all given to
you by the manufacturers [already rolled] – they called
them cases. Well you took one, and you pushed this
parchment with the point to it through the case. Then you
would take your pusher and push the kurtle up [the pusher
would be stood vertically on the table] and hold your finger
up there [on top of the cigarette]. And that made a cigarette.
And you put that down [in the trough].'

After making, it would be picked up by the young cutter –
usually just out of school – sitting to the maker's right.

'Now they all had edges of tobacco. So you had to cut
those. . . . You had special round kind of scissors, with
round tops, to cut the edges off. They had to be cut *clean*.
Because they had to look good, because they were hand
made and they cost a lot of money. And they had to be
perfect cigarettes. . . . After you cut [one side] you'd hold
about ten in your hand, you'd turn them round, and then
you'd cut them again. And then you had your cigarette.'

The cutter would lay the cigarettes on a tray, and these,

'when there was 2,000 in them, would go out to the forelady. Now there was a forelady sitting – there was about
200 girls in a room – and they had two foreladies, one each
side. When a tray was finished the cutter would take them
out with the maker's [number] on, and she would examine
the cigarettes, and if she saw one had a little tiny hole, or had
a drag of tobacco, she'd just take the cigarette out and throw
it out, and she'd put them in a pile. And she'd call out the
maker's number, not your name, 242 or so forth, and the
cutter would go out and she'd say, "Take these back to the
maker, they've got to be thrown out." So she had to tear
them up, just tear them up and use the tobacco all over
again, mix it up with your own. That would come off the
piece work, because you made them and I mean you would
have to make them over again to make up the number.'

Discipline in the Ardath factory was strict and as the war
went on it became stricter still. There were two reasons for

this. First, there was a general tightening up of industrial discipline which, in some areas of munitions work, for example, took away the workers' rights and almost produced slave labour.[93] Second, the trend towards machine-made cigarettes enabled the tobacco companies to lay off many girls while forcing an increase in productivity on those who remained.

> 'You had to be in by 8 o'clock. And about 7.50 you'd see a stream of girls running as fast as their legs would carry them down Worship St to get there in time, because if you didn't get there on the dot of 8 o'clock the door would be shut in your face. And more than once I got shut out. Only for the morning. In the afternoon you could go in.'

The morning siren heralded the start of five hours' uninterrupted labour.

> 'The conditions were very bad because you had to start work at 8. There was no break whatsoever for tea or for anything, until 1 o'clock. From 8 till 1 you just worked without a break. The only break that you'd have was to go out either to the toilet or wash your hands. I mean you'd get fed up sitting or you'd ache sitting. A stool, a hard stool, no back. A square stool. It was back-breaking.'

A one-hour lunchbreak preceded a further four hours of work, again without a break. The girls were not even allowed to eat sweets at the bench, but would surreptitiously suck them when the foreladies were out of the room.

Cigarette makers were paid by the piece, something like 3s. 6d. for 1,000 cigarettes. Out of that the girls would have to buy their own klonkies, kurtles and pushers, which Jenny would get from a man in Goulston St Buildings. In addition they would have to pay for their own pinafores and laundering – no overalls were provided.

> 'Now there were some girls who could say put their nose to the grindstone, you might say. And sit and roll, and roll and roll. And do nothing else but concentrate on their

work; . . . maybe they were stronger as well, but they could do that. The quickest one could be 3,000 a day. . . . 10s. 6d. a day. . . . £3 a week, that's right. Well I earned about £2 roughly, as I could only do 2,000 a day, roughly, sometimes not even that.[94] I liked to have a chat with my next door neighbour, and I liked to laugh and joke about. It's very monotonous, terribly monotonous work. I mean, you can think of nothing while you're rolling these cigarettes. . . . And the smell of the tobacco gets up your nose and you get terrible catarrh, you know. It's horrible work.'

When the speed-up came even the small pleasures that were available to Jenny in the factory were taken away by the foreladies.

'They were like prison warders! One was a Mrs Murray. . . . She wasn't Jewish, she came from Scotland, and she was very very strict . . . tall and gaunt, I would say, with steely blue eyes, and who frightened the life out of you. I mean, the look of her alone, you know. . . . When the machines came in,[95] afterwards, they just took liberties with the girls and they were very very strict with them. They didn't even allow you to talk. You didn't dare to talk to your next door neighbour. Well when [Mrs Murray] used to go out, immediately there was a noise, you know, like a lot of children when the schoolmaster's out. . . . And then all of a sudden you'd hear a voice booming out, "I've been watching you for the last half hour Number 242. Tomorrow your seat will be changed!" '

The method of paying by the piece combined with the harsh discipline of the factory to set worker against worker.

'Now once the forewoman took out a lot of my cigarettes. And I had this little learner cutter and she was really spoiling my work. . . . If you had a lot of work taken out she'd call you out and you'd stand there; "I can't understand your work, maker." Maker, you were maker, you weren't any name, you were a maker. So I'd say, "Well, I think it's this learner cutter who's spoiling my work." She'd say, "You are not paid to think, maker! We expect you to do good work. It's nothing to do with it." They wouldn't take anything from you at all. And you'd stand like a lemon, but you dare not answer back.'

The symbol of discipline was the manageress.

'She came round and it was like when the Queen came in, you know, there was a hush, silence. And she came sailing in, and she was really – I mean, actually, . . . it was authority. Power. Yes, she was Jewish. Power and authority. [Were the girls frightened of her?] They *were*. We were frightened of everyone, the foreladies as well. Because it was your job. You were terrified in case you were going to be out of work. . . . They could lay you off. They could pick out all the cigarettes that could have been passed in the usual way. You see. But they started to find fault. . . . You were terrified of them. You'd put up with anything.'

The female workers of the cigarette industry were ill-organised to fight against such repression. At a time of unprecedented unionisation among women workers, when twenty times more women in the garment industry belonged to a union in 1917 than three years before, the national female membership of the Cigarette Makers' Union increased from 60 to 180 out of a female workforce of about 20,000. That compared with 32,000 unionised in the clothing trades and 18,000 in the boots and shoes.[96]
Eventually Jenny Schlom could put up with it no longer. Besides the discipline it was unwholesome work anyway; there was the catarrh and the stench of tobacco which never left you so that you'd have to change every article of clothing if you wanted to go to a dance or anywhere after work. But it was the discipline which Jenny reacted against:

'the silence got on my nerves. . . . It's nerve-racking. And I felt ill and I hated it.'

Jenny, a sister and a brother put the money they'd managed to save through the war years into a small dress trimmings business in Lavender Hill, and then left the cigarette trade for ever in the early 1920s. The Ardath Tobacco Company was wound up voluntarily in December 1926. Its assets stood at over £1,630,000 and had multiplied five and a half times since its foundation fourteen years before.

3. IN THE HOME

Homework

In Rothschild Buildings, the largest single category of home-workers was widowed mothers. In Stepney, in 1911, nearly 80 per cent of working widows found work in seven employment sectors: in the garment industry (27 per cent), as charwomen (23 per cent), as domestic indoor servants (12 per cent), as washerwomen or laundresses (6 per cent), in food manufacture or preparation (5 per cent), as midwives and invalid attendants, or in buying and selling (3 per cent).[97] Widows from Rothschild Buildings worked in every one of these sectors except indoor domestic service. Again, this picture of widows' work is more blurred than the neat columns of the census volumes would have us believe. For these women generally entered the most insecure end of an unstable labour market, and if the census enumerators had called more often than once in ten years they would have charted an unsteady course through a succession of jobs, a course followed not out of choice but as necessity and opportunity dictated.

But homework, as well as providing widowed mothers with a major and convenient source of employment, formed an integral part of the East End workshop trades. The same pressures which kept alive the small unit of production also created the demand by employers for homework. And although the trend in the Edwardian period was away from homework a large proportion of the garment industry's labour force still worked at home. Neither was all homework related to the garment industry. Eva Katchinsky's mother, for example, worked in five of the major categories of employment for widows in the seven years between the death of her husband and the end of the First World War.[98] At first she took in washing (a contravention of Rule No. 16, it will be remembered), perhaps the least skilled, worst paid, most laborious and degrading of all occupations. It was often the first resort of widowed mothers, for Mrs Kaplan and Mossy Harris's mother were also both washerwomen for a time: Mrs Kaplan, rather than take washing in went to people's homes, and again neighbours were understanding and supportive.[99]

> 'My mother used to go to Mrs Weitzman and her sister, and her sister-in-law used to get it all together and give my mother 1s. 6d. for the washing. They lived in our flats. She wasn't the only one – my mother could never make a living out of her. She used to go to them and do it in their homes.'

Before the war, Leah Katchinsky had at least two other sources of employment besides taking in washing. She worked as a home help for the Sick Room Helps Society, who employed about 100 women to do housework for invalids, especially confined mothers. During training she would have earned only about 1s. 6d. a week but could get 5d. an hour within a short time.[100] Occasionally, some of her clients would give her washing to do at home and in the spare time that these two jobs left her – as well as running 82 Rothschild Buildings and three children – she took in fur sewing. This was one of the least skilled branches of homework, ranking almost with match-boxes,[101] and sharing with the latter the inconvenience of a noxious trade.

> 'Very cheap furs – just lined them. And we used to have fur hair all over you, blowing about.'

When the war clothing contracts came to the East End in the winter of 1914–15, Leah was able to take in some khaki homework. Again, the work involved was not especially skilled but it was hard and, if standard rates paid to outworkers were anything to go by, earnings were pitifully low. Mrs

Katchinsky, helped by Eva, finished horse blankets by hand; 'very, very hard work'. For similar work it was reported that women were paid 1s. 8d. for 400 eyelet holes on soldiers' kit-bags; one woman earned 5s. 7d. at the work in forty-two hours.[102]

Earnings from homework were not sufficient to drag a family out of poverty but could supplement purchasing power, even at the expense of lost leisure time and physical exhaustion. According to Clara Collett, a Board of Trade investigator into women's working conditions, homework was most often a stop-gap measure to prevent a decline in purchasing power during times of unemployment, or to increase it during normal periods when the earnings of the breadwinner were too low to support the desired living standards. It was thus most often carried out by women who could choose what hours they worked at home as need or inclination dictated – 'there is a large amount of quasi-voluntary employment.'[103]

In Rothschild Buildings, homework was used both as a defence against declining living standards and as a means of improving them. Eva Katchinsky made dresses at home when she was laid off from the millinery at the end of the war, to cushion the blow to the household of her loss of earnings. She had managed to buy a sewing-machine in the war and this now proved a good investment, for not only did she make her own clothes but 'I did blouses for a shop a bit, and now and again a little dress' for Seifert's in Brick Lane.[104] All this was 'quasi-voluntary' in that Eva's home earnings might have meant not having to choose between lino on the floor and new saucepans on the kitchen shelves.

Annie Kaplan used her sister Clara's sewing-machine (a boyfriend had given it her: 'gave her scissors to go with it and everything, and she still wouldn't marry him!') when she came home from a day at the dressmaking shop. Her twelve-hour day ended at 8 p.m. but she would do a couple of hours' machining before bed-time on the 'cut dresses' she brought home with her. This kept her busy on Sunday afternoons as well, taking up nearly all her free time.[105] This was 'quasi-voluntary' in that she was exercising freedom of choice between going hungry and having food in her belly.

Jenny Schlom's mother made cigarettes at home and rolled the paper cigarette cases for 4*d*. – 'four *pence*' – per 1,000. At financially difficult times she got work from her brother, a cigarette maker, and Jenny would take the finished cases and cigarettes to her uncle at Bow. Her mother also helped another Russian cigarette maker who worked at home a lot in his Rothschild Buildings flat: 'if he had an overflow he used to say to my mother, "Would you like to make a couple of hundred?" '[106] Earnings from such homework, monstrous slave labour as it was, could save a visit to the pawnshop or insuperable arrears of rent. And for the Russian cigarette maker it perhaps meant a little extra cash in his pocket for that bottle of brandy which made all the difference to a Saturday night card party.

But there was another class of homeworkers in the Buildings who incidentally had a more important impact on community life. Some men and women worked full-time at home, sharing their time between making up orders for contractors and providing services for their neighbours in the Buildings. Many of the men had retired from the workshop – perhaps through old age or incapacity – and could more easily adapt to working at home. Such a man was Jack Brahms's father.

Mr Brahms was born in Minsk about 1845 and retired from the workshop where he was a tailor when he had reached his mid-sixties.[107] When his wife died in 1911 he retired completely from the workshop, and worked at home as a 'repair tailor'. He repaired and altered men's garments only, sitting at his machine in front of the bedroom window.

> 'Whatever alteration, they'd bring 'em in down to him and he used to do them. All over the Buildings. They all knew him, quite well. . . . He was busy all day and all evening [till] probably 8, 9 o'clock at night. . . . He used to go to synagogue twice a day, morning and evening. That was the only break he had. Course, he never worked on a Saturday, he was that orthodox. And the Sunday he was at it again.'

Mr Brahms was not alone. There was Mr Isaacs who made a

living repairing boots and shoes at his flat in Rothschild Buildings.[108] Many a family would go to him rather than any of the
local *shusters*. And self-employment commonly extended to
dressmaking – a trade with large numbers of women working
for themselves at home.[109]

> 'There was one lady I knew – Klein her name was – who
> lived in Nathaniel Buildings. Earlier on, her husband had
> committed suicide and there she was left with this family of
> four or five children. . . . She was a needlewoman and she
> used to make pinafores and dresses . . . or she would make
> pillowcases for people who wanted them.'

Homework in Rothschild Buildings was rarely carried on
for long periods by men or women sub-contracting from
workshops.[110] Examples of the criminally sweated labouring
women of the East End 'perambulator trade' were not to be
found within the portals of these model dwellings or many
others. In part, at least, homework in the Buildings, with its
stress on self-employment, was an expression of the independence of the workers who lived there, an independence
mirrored in their readiness to move into buying and selling,
often as independent traders.

4. BUYING AND SELLING

Shop assistant

For the enterprising boy – or for the boy forced to be enterprising by home circumstances – there was no shortage of
remunerative employment in the near vicinity of Rothschild
Buildings. He could earn pocket money as a shop boy in the
evenings after school or Hebrew classes, during the holidays
and on Sundays. There were plenty of shops to choose from –
seven grocers' or chandlers' shops in the Flower and Dean St

neighbourhood alone, thirteen more in Brick Lane, up to the railway, and a further thirteen in the Lane itself,[111] apart from those innumerable market stalls. Besides these were the butchers' shops, the dairies, the bakeries, the fishmongers' and fried fish shops, and confectioners' all of which sold food and most of which employed boys for some duty or other. And for Jack Brahms it was only food shops which interested him, and grocers' shops in particular.

Jack Brahms was born in 1897 in a ground floor flat at F Block, Rothschild Buildings.[112] As a boy he was fascinated by the mechanics of the grocery trade, the goods, their names and packages, the rigmarole of weighing out, taking money and giving change. When about 12 years old Jack resolved to enter the other side of that intriguing window, and where else should he go but to Israel Garfinkle's shop, recently opened in Flower and Dean St?

> 'We used to do our little bits of shopping there and I asked Mr Garfinkle if he wanted anybody in the evening. He said, "Yes, you can come and weigh this up or weigh that up and weigh the other." So I went in there every evening. That would have been Monday, Tuesday, Wednesday, and Thursday.'

So after coming out of Jews' Free School, having tea and then rushing off to Hebrew classes at the Great Garden St Talmud Torah, Jack would arrive at Garfinkle's at about 8.15. There he would work until 10 o'clock, going home about an hour before Garfinkle closed for the night. He would open the sacks of flour or sugar and prepare their contents for retail.

This was all that Jack did in his evenings at Garfinkle's, never being involved in selling or dealing with articles sold 'loose', like jam or tea, the latter sold usually 2 oz. at a time, weighed out as the customer asked for it. The financial reward for his help in the shop was not generous, but Garfinkle probably considered he was teaching the boy the mysteries of the grocer's trade. For his eight hours or so a week Jack would be rewarded on a Thursday night with a bag of 'monkey nuts'. It was an arrangement he considered 'very reasonable' at the time.

When Jack left school in 1911 he was happy to continue his career in the trade. Garfinkle did not need the services of a full-time employee. But the infinite number of local shops gave Jack plenty of opportunity, and as he passed Sarah Skylinsky's grocery shop in the Lane around his fourteenth birthday he 'just went in there and asked them' for a job. The Skylinskys took him on.

Jack dealt mainly with Sarah's husband. It was very much a family affair, with Skylinsky's son as the manager, his three daughters working in the shop, and one other assistant. Jack, in his white apron, would be employed to mind the stall outside the shop, where were kept 'cereals, butter beans, haricot beans, rice, barley and all that in hundred-weight sacks'. Again, Jack would just measure the quantities out in pint or half-pint jugs, handling no money at all.

Jack was never very happy there. Skylinsky was a big man, 'very abrupt, very abrupt indeed; I didn't like him at all.' Certainly, the wages he paid were little compensation.

> '5s. a week. Oh, that was from 8 in the morning till 8 at night. And in the winter-time, if you don't mind, I had to go in on Saturday night and clean all the scales up. That was after Shabas went out, and clean the scales up if you don't mind! For the same 5s.'

Eventually, after about six months, Jack Brahms and Skylinsky parted company.

> 'One Sunday morning – 'cos in those days we sold broken biscuits about 4d. a pound. So I managed to just take a little bit of biscuit. And he says, "Go home and tell your father I want him." So I went home – I didn't know what for . . . and told my dad that, "The guvnor wants to see you. I don't know why." And it was because I took a broken biscuit! He said, "Well, if you can take a broken biscuit you can take something else, can't you?" I shall never forget that. That outstands in my life at all times!'

Jack left the shop that Sunday, but the very next day was back in work – again in Wentworth St, but this time not in the

Lane. He was taken on by Asher Dubowski who had a grocer's shop opposite Toynbee Hall, next to Shapiro's bookshop. Dubowski was a tall, thin man who lived with his second wife and several children in Strafford Houses, a few doors along. Jack, another boy, Dubowski and his daughter worked in the shop, the girl mainly running the cereal stall outside on the pavement. At busy times, Thursday nights and Friday mornings, his wife helped out in the shop as well. Besides sweeping up, weighing and putting goods on the shelves from 8 in the morning till 8 at night, Jack was given the job of carrying out Dubowski's sole venture into the wholesale trade.

> 'He used to buy black olives in bulk. And he gave me the job of going round to the shops and selling black olives for him in seven pound [greaseproof] bags. . . . In great big barrels they came in. . . . He weighed them out and he used to give it to me and I took 'em round to the shops [on a barrow], where I sold 'em. In the vicinity. . . . More further out afield in Whitechapel, Fieldgate St and round that way.'

At Dubowski's Jack earned 7s. 6d. a week,[113] all but 6d. of which he handed over to his father. Jack stayed at Dubowski's for about two years. Then the nagging dissatisfactions with life in a small East End grocer's shop close to home revealed themselves in a conversation he had with friends, one evening in 1913.

> 'Myself and the boys from the Buildings there, we gathered round next door Garfinkle's shop; there was a sweet shop there and we used to gather round there and have a chat-chat. When one of the boys said to me, he said, "Why don't you splash out and go somewhere in the West End?" See? So I says to him, I shall never forget this, I says to him, "Such as whereas?" "Oh", he said, "you can go to Selfridge's, or you can go to Whiteley's." And so as a matter of fact I went up to Whiteley's, saw the buyer there and asked him if he had a vacancy for a young man like myself and told him that I'd been in the trade since I left school, which . . . was about two and a half years, and I was taken on there and then.'

Whiteley's was a far different concern than Dubowski's back-street grocer's shop. Here was a major West End provision dealers, supplying the aristocracy of Bayswater and Kensington, employing scores of staff, many of whom earned respectable salaries, and maintaining discipline among them with a rule book of no less than 159 regulations.[114] Jack spent most of his time in the basement warehouse, packing up expensive orders for delivery to the porticoed houses of West London.

At Whiteley's, Jack earned £1 a week, but out of that he had to find his fare on the underground from Liverpool St to Queensway, Bayswater (5d. each way), as well as having to buy lunch and tea at a local café. His leap up and out of the East End probably left him little better off at the end of the week. And those unbending regulations could be exhausting and irksome.

'For a while we started at 8.30 [and finished at 6],[115] but after a while, when I got a year or two older, they had a rota there. That was one of my difficulties. I had to be in there at 6.30 in the morning [till 4]. . . . I had to get up about 4 o'clock in the morning to catch an early morning tram to be down at Bayswater.'

Jack was in no position to argue. Even at Whiteley's, the protection extended to employees was negligible. Shop assistants were almost completely non-unionised.[116]

'I remember that on two or three occasions that these people connected with a trade union tried to persuade 'em but there was nothing doing. . . . They used to have meetings outside the building there, they had meetings occasionally, outside Whiteley's. But nothing happened, really. . . . No, never used to talk about union matters. They just wouldn't join.'

Another of Jack's problems arose from his first encounters at work with non-Jewish people. At Whiteley's, he was isolated: 'I'd go so far as to say that I was about the only one.'

'Oh, they were very anti-Semitic – Yes, oh yes. Specially two or three in the warehouse. . . . But it just went out one ear – I had to keep the job – went in one ear and out the other. Just took no notice of them.'

With the outbreak of war, Jack was approaching 17 years old. At the end of 1915, the government, 'alarmed by the shortage of recruits', began a scheme of voluntary recruitment under the administration of Lord Derby. Under the Derby scheme 'men were asked to attest voluntarily their willingness to serve and to await their call to the colours.'[117] Many Jewish immigrants went to great trouble to avoid military service – Mossy Harris's brother, for example, perjured himself before one of the many tribunals of the time to evade the call up. An exemption certificate from the Russian Embassy was a valuable document indeed. But Jack, perhaps stung by the anti-Semitic taunts of a war-mongering press, which had a greater impact in the basement of Whiteley's than in the East End streets, joined the Derby scheme, donned the armband which announced the fact, and waited for his call-up papers. They came in September 1916. He was to join the 3rd City of London Yeomanry.

'I got my papers to report, I shall never forget it, to a little village called Reefham★ down in Norfolk. Well, they got the date where I had to go and I went on a train from Liverpool St to Norwich, and from Norwich I had to get a sort of side-line to this little village at Reefham and there was quite a batch. . . . The sergeant marched us down to the sort of headquarters and there I started my Army career. It was the Army Cyclists' Corps then . . . They taught me to cycle *their* way . . . pushing one along with you and one on your back! I was there for I should think about six or seven months, and from there I was transferred to the 3rd King's Liverpools down at Liverpool. From there, in 1917 . . . I was sent to France. I was over there and we went to a place called Kemal, and there was a reserve line of trenches there. And unfortunately I got a packet of frost-bite feet, and I got to

★ Reepham.

the nearest dressing station down there. I was back in Aldershot Hospital the same evening. And I was in bed for about ten months with this frostbite. And then from there I went to a place called Fleet in Hampshire, which was convalescence, for quite a while. From there I was sent to Ireland, in County Cork we went, and I was in charge of the baker's shop, issuing out bread to the various people. And then suddenly we heard the church bells going and everything else going and the war had finished.'

Jack's uneventful war – even for an untravelled boy from Rothschild Buildings – ended in demobilisation, soon after Armistice day.

'I came home December 1918. And back at Whiteley's. Back at Whiteley's for the Christmas trade.'[118]

Street-sellers, pedlars and tallymen

There was a significant increase in the number of costermongers, street-sellers and hawkers in London between 1901 and 1911. The increase among men and women of Russian or Polish birth was higher than the average although the numbers involved were still quite small, especially in comparison with those employed in the workshop trades. In 1911 there were 2,229 street-sellers in Stepney; in London as a whole there were just under 900 street-sellers who were born in Russia or Poland, the large majority of whom would have lived in the East End.[119]

The real picture, as usual, is much more complex than any impression left by decennial statistics. Many workers moved in and out of street trading, trying their hand at it when their normal trade was depressed. Some exploited this type of economic enterprise in tandem with other employment which provided the greater part of their income. And the definitions street-seller and hawker mask subtle differences in the method of buying and selling adopted, so that at least three distinct examples of types of street-selling could be found in Rothschild Buildings around the beginning of the First World War.

Jenny Schlom's father, Hyman, was born in Riga on the Baltic and emigrated to England probably in the early 1890s.[120] He worked originally as a bootmaker and his last job was at a workshop in Fleur-de-Lys St. Hyman became one of the 2,107 Stepney bootmakers who left the trade in the ten years after 1901, giving up the boot line around 1910.

With the aid of an interest-free loan from the Jewish Board of Guardians, Hyman scraped together the small amount of capital needed to hire a barrow from a yard in Brick Lane and to stock it with fruit and vegetables from Spitalfields market. He had to get up early to be at the market with his empty barrow by 6 in the morning, and he at first bought potatoes,

'and then he switched over to fruit. It was either pears, and half pears half apples, or strawberries. Whichever fruit was in season he would sell. . . . Yes, nuts as well.'

Hyman would push his barrow round the Spitalfields streets, crying his wares. Being a religious man he left his barrow in the yard on Friday afternoons and Saturdays.

There were some other stall-holders living in Rothschild Buildings, like an ex-walking-stick maker who sold 'hosiery, stockings, handkerchiefs, socks, all drapery of those days' in the Lane.[121] His business, like Mr Schlom's, flourished but just as many failed. Another, younger, walking-stick maker tried to sell books from a stall when he was de-mobbed in 1918 but 'he didn't do good'[122] and gave it up. And an Austrian slipper-maker at No. 159 tried to get out of the boot line before the First World War by 'a bit of buying and selling, you know, like various small items, but he didn't make a go of it.'[123]

A much less typical example of street-selling was that of Joseph Goldring* who had emigrated from Lithuania in the late 1880s.[124] His trade was cap-making but he was a man of radical views, an atheist, who very much resented the surplus value extracted by his employer, whoever he might be.

'No, I think my father was rather unusual, actually. Just as

* This is a pseudonym.

he resented this boss [relationship] and he questioned it – [in
a whisper] I believe he used to lead strikes. I seem to
remember my mother saying that all the women were angry
with *her* because he [was a strike leader].'

In about 1912 he gave up making caps for someone else and
started out on his own – as a pedlar. In London at this time
peddling was a rare calling, although it had declined less in the
provincial Jewish settlements like Manchester, Liverpool and
Glasgow.[125] Joseph bought most of his wares at Rother-
ham's in Shoreditch, mainly 'linen, haberdashery, tablecloths,
towels, socks, sheets perhaps'. He stored these at home,
making shelves in the bedroom and packing things neatly
away. He made a pack, machining it himself – 'just a big bag,
put the things in and flap them over, put a strap on it and carry
it over his shoulder.'

His catchment area was anywhere the early morning workmen's trains from Liverpool St Station would carry him, like
High Wycombe or anywhere within 'perhaps thirty miles'
radius of London'. He would journey out, his heavy pedlar's
pack strapped to his back, about three times a week, favouring
fine days.

'He got on very well with people he went to – this foreign
Jewish man – he got on quite well with them. He liked
them and they liked him.'

Another, much less sophisticated example of almost
spontaneous hawking, but only in the neighbouring streets of
the East End, can be found in the Zwart family.[126] The eldest
daughter, who would have been about 15 or 16 in 1900, was
sent out selling old clothes, given to the family by a rich
relative, in the street markets of the East End. In the same way
her mother would buy a cheap lot of enamelware which the
daughter would carry in a big basket to street markets like the
Lane and Watney St, Commercial Rd. But also,

'sometimes she got my sister to buy envelopes and
. . . writing paper. And she'd go round to different

Buildings and knock at the door and sell packets of envelopes and paper. And get a little profit. Stunning really.'

This type of endeavour was characteristic of the variety of means widows and their families were forced to employ. Just one of the ways in which Leah Katchinsky, for example, earned a living was by entering the tally business.[127] The practice of buying goods on credit from travelling salesmen was common among the London working class by the end of the nineteenth century.[128] Although the tallyman always takes on a masculine gender whenever the phenomenon is mentioned, the trade was not an uncommon one among the widows of Rothschild Buildings; at least one other Russian woman was a tallyman in 'things like drapery' in the early years of the century.[129]

Mrs Katchinsky described herself as a 'Dealer in Hosiery, Drapery, Boots and Shoes, etc.'[130] She was 'rather cute' and did very well in the tally business, starting up during the First World War and running it throughout the inter-war period.

'She borrowed some money from somebody – a few pounds [possibly from the Jewish Board of Guardians]. Things were 1s. a . . . week [a sum which her daughter was often sent out to collect]. But she was a very ambitious woman and she did work hard. . . . And gradually my mother [built it up]. She didn't buy a lot. If you'd ask her for something she'd get an order for those things; if you didn't want it she'd go back and change it.'

Leah Katchinsky bought her goods at discount prices from a City warehouse and sold by samples among the Jewish (and only Yiddish-speaking) housewives of the East End, predominantly around the 'Commercial Road and turnings'. Eventually she regained her independence, working for herself and not slaving at the needle for someone else's profits or, and even worse, relying on charity.

Buying and selling was one way out of poverty which promised both immediate emancipation and a future prize. It had possibilities which the machine often had not: but it needed dedicated labour, luck, flair or cunning to succeed. And there were alternative routes to independence.

7 Conclusions: politics and class

The creation of a Jewish working class

In 1967 a sociologist, questioning commonly held opinions about the class structure of Anglo-Jewry, was led to ask whether a Jewish proletariat was still in existence. He found, contrary to the stereotypes, that there *was* a Jewish proletariat but could give no indication of its size or age structure. That this question, which at 'first sight . . . does seem to be a contradiction in terms', could be asked at all is indicative of the changes wrought by fifty years among the descendants of the immigrant Jews of Rothschild Buildings and their neighbours.[1]

Are the reasons for this rapid disintegration of the working-class community of which the Buildings were one small part discernible within what was probably its golden age? Were the forces which shattered the Jewish proletariat present then or did they arrive later? To answer these questions we must return to the beginning, briefly to sketch the forces which created the Eastern European Jewish working class in the first place.

During the last decades of Eastern European feudalism in the first half of the nineteenth century, the Jewish population of the Pale was displaced on a dramatic scale from its long-established economic and social roles.[2] Under feudalism, the large mass of the Jewish population, nearly 90 per cent in some areas, was engaged in trade of some sort or another, an intermediate class between the landowning aristocracy and the peasantry. Most of the remainder, just one in ten Jews in the Ukraine and Byelorussia in 1818 for example, were independent artisans in the traditional consumer industries of the small Jewish towns – chiefly in the manufacture of clothing.[3]

The growth of capitalism produced the displacement of the Jewish middlemen by creating an indigenous bourgeoisie, prepared to use discriminatory laws in advancing their competitiveness. They crowded the Jewish masses out of their former economic positions in buying and selling.[4] But parallel with this displacement, the emancipation of the peasantry and the capitalisation of agriculture stimulated a large market for consumer goods among the newly created proletariat and the newly enriched peasantry. This resulted in enormous growth in production of the means of consumption long associated with the Jewish artisan – who had produced for the Jewish merchant – clothing, footwear and furniture.

With the destruction of the economic base of Jewish life came a massive concentration of East European Jewry in the great cities of the Pale. It was in the second half of the nineteenth century that Jews became the 'greatest urban people in the world'.[5] According to Abram Leon, out of twenty-one important cities in Poland, Jews were an absolute majority in eleven by the turn of the century.[6] Most were artisans in the traditional trades, manufacturing for the new market opened up by the growth of capitalism. The character of this manufacturing industry was still largely based on the artisan tradition of small workshops and homeworking, and still with a great deal of economic independence.

But with the growth of capitalism came mechanisation and modernisation of industry which relied more and more on low-paid wage labourers needing few of the skills of the all-round artisan. As well as among the Jews, such labour could be procured from the peasants who poured into the towns, displaced by increasing capitalist production in agriculture. The Jewish artisan thus soon found himself competing with workers who had a very low standard of living and were accustomed to hard physical labour. Accordingly, he faced insecurity, unemployment and no opportunity of regaining the living standards he had lost.

All of this happened with the quickness of a lifetime. An unemployed bootmaker who emigrated from Vitebsk in 1900 could have been born to an independent artisan; he, in turn, could have migrated to the city in 1860 from a village where *his* father had run the only tavern as an economically independent trader. That was the sole time of real stability the family could remember. This history had a profound effect on the consciousness of the immigrant. The Jewish immigrants did not attempt merely 'to preserve . . . the social standards and habits of home and communal life in Eastern Europe', as Professor Gartner affirms.[7] *They sought to re-establish the economic independence and security which they and their parents had lost in the Pale.*

Class consciousness in Rothschild buildings

The immigrant worker-artisans who found their way to the Buildings in the 1880s or 1890s found also that the Jewish trades of Eastern Europe were already established in the East End of London. It was in these that they worked. It was here that they and their sons and daughters were to complete the process of proletarianisation which they had begun in the Pale. They would not recapture without a struggle the economic independence which they had lost so suddenly.

That struggle for independence could take two forms. It could be a co-operative struggle for a collective independence. Or it could be a competitive struggle for individual independence. In the early years of Rothschild Buildings both of these opposing tendencies were active within their walls.

The movement for the collective emancipation of the Jewish workers from the tyranny of the workshops in which they now found themselves gathered great strength in the years before the First World War. Its force had three sources. The aspirations of the immigrants took a beating in the grinding labour of the sweatshops. Living standards were little better in London than they had been in the Pale. Second, a minority of Jewish workers brought with them ideas from the most revolutionary proletariat in Europe, new ideas which, after 1905 had behind them the force of action. Third, these ideas landed in fecund soil. For the Jewish workers found themselves caught up in the whirlwind of ideas and action which characterised Britain in the period from the late 1880s to the beginning of the First World War. Socialism and trade union militancy with the East End as a major battleground had an enormous effect on the consciousness of the Jewish immigrant working class. The class struggle between Jewish worker and Jewish master, perhaps ironically intensified by the close personal relationships of the workshop, was frequently brutal. Violent attacks on pickets, masters and even masters' wives were commonplace.[8] In one year, 1906, blacklegs were attacked and threatened by striking tailors; a master boot-maker was hit over the head with a bottle wielded by a striker; and one man died in the extensive riots attending the bakers' strike, which also produced window-breaking, and assaults on masters and blacklegs.[9] Climaxes of industrial action were reached during the great labour disputes of 1889–90, 1906, and 1912–13 in a movement which has been brilliantly described elsewhere.[10]

Rothschild Buildings could not remain unaffected by such momentous social upheaval, and one organisation in particular had strong roots there. This was the socialist-inspired Jewish Workers' Circle or *Der Arbeiter Ring*, formed in the early 1900s.[11] It was to be one of the longest-lived Jewish working–class organisations both in Britain and America.[12]

The Jewish Workers' Circle was a secular and class conscious Friendly Society. Its roots lay within the Judaic tradition of synagogue-based benefit societies which gave financial support by way of death grants and tontines;[13] the *landsmannshaft* organisations of mutual aid for persons from the same town or district in the Pale;[14] and the friendly societies giving aid to further class solidarity which were the international response of artisans to the pressures of capital-isation.[15]

One of its founder members, Morris Mindel, lived at 184 Rothschild Buildings.[16] Back home in Vilna, Lithuania, Morris Mindel had been a member of the Bund – the General Jewish Workers' Union of Lithuania, Poland and Russia – a separatist social-democratic organisation formed in 1897 which is best known for its later quarrels with Lenin and the Bolsheviks. He emigrated at the time of the post-revolutionary troubles in 1905 and lived in Lolesworth Buildings for a time before moving to Rothschild Buildings around 1912. Morris Mindel was a smallish, thickset man with, in his younger years anyway, a dashing black moustache. When first in London he had found work as an under-presser but soon, probably through his contact with Narodiczky, the anarchist printer, set up as a bookbinder in a Fournier St basement.

In his one-bedroom flat, the founder members of Division 1 of the Workers' Circle would gather for their weekly committee meetings. There would be anarchists like Weiner, the General Secretary of the Circle, an associate of Rudolf Rocker and the *Arbeter Frainters*; Weinberg, the radical printer; Morris Myer, the social democrat, Bundist, poet, editor of two Yiddish papers, and opponent of Rocker; and several more. Business was done in Yiddish across the living room table with Mrs Mindel – 'she was a marvellous cook' – handing round home-made strudel to the enthusiastic comrades.

The early aims of the Jewish Workers' Circle were to provide relief from distress outside the 'humiliating' machinery of 'bourgeois societies'; it was 'based on principles of mutual aid, education and enlightenment and the establishment of workers' co-operatives'.[17] At times of struggle, the tiny flat in Rothschild Buildings would be a centre of activity, as Morris Mindel wrote:[18]

> In 1912, during the strike of the tailoring workers, our branch was in a position to give great support to the strikers, and it also sought to turn public opinion in their favour. It helped the bakery workers in their strike [1913] and supported their co-operative, playing an important part in its management.

At other, more normal, times the Workers' Circle performed various functions. Its primary purpose was still that of providing benefits. Contributions were 6d. a week for 'mutual help purposes' and 2d. a week for a benefit fund providing for sickness and burial.[19] But a great deal of work was put into workers' education and 'socialistic propaganda'.

They created their own school to teach the children Yiddish, and to enjoy the works of Mendele, Peretz, and Sholem Aleichem. They established a library and reading room which became a great cultural centre.

Here, first at 136 Brick Lane but after 1924 at Circle House in Alie St, lectures were given by Tom A. Jackson (author of a famous volume on dialectical materialism), A. J. Cook, Selig Brodetzky, Harry Gosling, Harry Pollitt and others. They held concerts, Yiddish theatre productions and art exhibitions.[20]

The Jewish Workers' Circle was eclectic in the organisations it chose to support and the individuals it attracted to it, embracing anarchists, social democrats, Zionists and communists. It attracted its largest membership during the period of anti-fascist struggle between 1934 and 1939,[21] although its cultural and workers' educational impact was certainly larger by far than its peak membership of 3,000 would suggest. It was a fine example of collective independence: class conscious, aware of the Jewish workers' cultural heritage and active in fighting its decay, eager to assume responsibility for their own means of livelihood and destiny. And wanting to do all of these things together.

Individualism

But the struggle for independence was also shaped by forces which tended to foster competitiveness among the immigrant Jewish workers. It is difficult to say how deeply the Jewish artisan class of the Pale of Settlement was imbued with individualism; certainly its previous economic position in trading was likely to have fostered competitiveness rather than collectivism. But once arrived in the East End of London, there were two main forces tending to push the Jewish workers away from mutual help. The first was the structure of the trades in which they found employment. The second was the policy of class control exercised by the Anglo-Jewish bourgeoisie.

We have seen that the structure of East End industry in the

trades traditionally associated with the Jewish artisan was predominantly small scale. The manufacture of the means of consumption on these proportions took little capital; and inevitably the owners of small capital were stimulated to invest it in these spheres of production.[22] In 900 East End Jewish tailoring shops in 1888, 76 per cent employed under ten hands.[23] In 1911, there was one employer in the London boot and shoe trade for every eleven employees, and this does not include those workers who were self-employed. And the large majority of cabinet making workshops were run by a master with from four to eight men under him.[24]

So there was plenty of opportunity and plenty of temptation to escape the wage-slavery of the workshop by trying to become a master rather than indulging in collective struggle. It was seized by many Jewish workers, like Isaac Landsman, who tried to become a master and (as many others) failed several times. And it was fostered by the social pressures of the workshop, which tended against collectivism. It was not only difficult for the workforce dispersed among thousands of tiny workshops to see interests in common and become organised, especially when they were often divided among themselves by piece-rates and sub-contracting: union membership among tailors before 1914 was as low as 2,000 in London, compared with a workforce in Stepney alone of some 14,000.[25] But it was difficult indeed for Mossy Harris to separate his interests from the hard-working Russian who paid his wages, or for Minnie Zwart to strike against a master who was so kind to her, or for Eva Katchinsky to think of herself as exploited by the man who came to her wedding.

There were also alternative avenues to individual independence which did not involve exchanging the position of exploited for that of exploiter. The localised structure of the East End workshop trades allowed many workers to set up as individual contractors, maintaining a semi-proletarian position as an almost independent producer, like Mr Brahms and Mr Isaacs (the *shuster*) in Rothschild Buildings, and Mrs Klein the dressmaker in Nathaniel.

And outside the workshop trades there were archaic modes of distributing goods which allowed individuals with little capital to set up in 'business' on their own – taking the opportunity to return to the economic position of their grandparents in the Pale. Indeed, in the Edwardian period, with its trends towards concentration and centralisation in the East End workshop trades, there was a corresponding growth in the number of people who chose this road to independence. In 1901 there had been 533 Russians and Poles in London described as costermongers, street-sellers and hawkers; by 1911 this had increased to 890.[26] This was the way of escaping proletarianisation chosen by an increasing number like Joseph Goldring, the once-radical cap-maker who took to peddling linen; or Hyman Schlom who once made boots but then made a comfortable living selling bananas; or Leah Katchinsky who exchanged sewing horse-blankets at home for selling drapery on credit round the homes of the East End Jewish immigrants.

Aside from the structure of the economy in which the Jewish workers found themselves, their individualism was fostered by the middle class who tried to take charge of them at work, in school and even in the home.

The Jewish Board of Guardians made interest-free loans to those who wanted to become a master or an independent trader.[27] Between 1900 and 1910, no fewer than 26,479 loans were made at an average of just over £7 each, eloquent testimony to the small capital needed to buy the chance of independence in the Edwardian East End.[28] Probably Isaac Landsman, Leah Katchinsky, Mrs Zwart and Hyman Schlom all took them up at one time or another, repaying the 6d. in the pound a week to the Board's offices in Middlesex St.

And within the Jewish working-class community the hard economic pressures of the East End were compounded by social pressures, at first fostered from without but later exerted from within. Great care was taken by the Anglo-Jewish bourgeoisie to socialise the immigrants immediately on their arrival in this country. Their controls were exercised in the home, at school, in the youth clubs, in the administration of poor relief and in the synagogue – where the Kamenitzer Maggid, loved by the simple faithful as he was, was used by the establishment to counter the atheism of the socialist and anarchist movements, even in his years at Rothschild Buildings.[29] They had the benefit of moulding people whose working-class culture and defences were still in the making;

whose children, eager to learn the ways of their new home, found them defined and limited by both the Jewish voluntary schools and the state schools of the East End.[30]

> I am firmly convinced that the Jewish lads who pass through our schools will grow up to be intelligent, industrious, temperate and law-abiding citizens and, I think, will add to the wealth and stability of the British Empire.

Those controls were designed to produce a new Anglo-Jewry in the image of the old; to assimilate the immigrants not just within English society – but within middle-class English society. It was an assimilation in which Rothschild Buildings themselves were designed to play a part.

Disintegration

The forces of individualism were outweighed by collectivism in these early years of Rothschild Buildings. But there were signs of future trends. They best showed themselves in the drift away from the East End and the Jewish working-class milieu it represented. This geographical mobility had been actively encouraged by middle-class Anglo-Jewry since the turn of the century,[31] and actively aided by the Four Per Cent Industrial Dwellings Co. They had built estates in Camberwell, Stoke Newington and Dalston by 1905. Navarino Mansions in Dalston were opened at the end of 1904 and were, according to Lord Rothschild, 'the best, most modern, and most comfortable of the kind ever erected'. But at that time the pressures towards dispersal were not as great as those towards concentration in the Jewish East End, and the rents of the new dwellings had to be drastically reduced before the many empty flats could be let.[32]

But even in the tightly knit community of Rothschild Buildings, some of these pressures and tensions, showing themselves from time to time in an enforced exclusiveness even among children in the playground, were having an effect in individual cases before the First World War.

One girl, born in the Buildings of Austrian parents, was

among the first of what even by the 1930s had turned into a flood.[33] Perhaps she was more vulnerable to change than many because her mother had died in 1904.[34]

> 'My friends were from other streets. . . . None of them came from the Buildings. I always seemed to find some-body outside who was more or less professional. That sort of thing always appealed to me. . . . I used to go to a poetry-reading at Toynbee Hall. There were quite a crowd of us; we had our own little clique from Commercial Street School . . .'

She left school in 1911 and spent two years looking for work which suited her. Eventually she took up a position as a junior clerk at Bow, and she lived there after leaving home, when about 16. During the First World War she did voluntary social work in the East End and lectured some evenings on literature at the Butler St Girls' Club. Soon she moved away from the East End altogether.

Similarly, Betsy Schiffenbaum began her migration north-wards early – around 1915 when she married an engineer and moved to Stamford Hill.[35]

> 'When I met my husband he came from Burdett Road, and they had a house there. It was quite a posh area. . . . By then I was quite a young lady and I'd begun to realise that there were better places than Rothschild Buildings. People wanted to get out, because it was the Buildings and because it was the East End.'

It took no longer than a generation for these external pressures to become internalised within Rothschild Buildings and the Jewish East End as a whole. The move to North London, from Whitechapel to Hackney, Dalston, Stoke Newington, Clapton and Stamford Hill had begun early and was well established by the 1920s. Perhaps one in three of the East End's Jewish population had left for these richer pastures or, via the north-west passage into Golders Green and Hendon, by 1929.[36]

For the class conscious Jewish workers of Rothschild Buildings and the East End, this movement was ironically paralleled by greater unity and more cohesive political action, particularly during the anti-fascist struggles of the 1930s. Organised anti-Semitism may have provoked a reaction among the masses which bridged class divisions within East End Jewry but there is no doubting the *political* nature of the reaction. Local Communists led the fight against an eviction at the Buildings in 1933 which erected barricades against police and bailiffs, led to the imprisonment of militants and added a new dimension to the type of resistance an eviction had caused twenty years before.[37] Rothschild Buildings was part of the Spitalfields East Ward which elected London's first Communist councillor in 1937.[38] The Buildings bred trade union leaders like Mick Mindel, Morris's son, elected President of the United Ladies' Tailors' Trade Union at the age of 28, and others like Sarah Wesker, who led the East End's trouser-makers in a memorable strike.

But still the social pressures on the individual to escape could not be repressed. They grew stronger as the community grew older. The old routes of independence – street-selling and workshop masters – were superseded by independent positions of bourgeois status – in the professions and in the ownership of house property, factories and marketing outlets. It was eloquently described by Aunt Esther, the 'successful' entrepreneur in Arnold Wesker's *I'm Talking About Jerusalem*.[39]

Flower and Dean Street was a prison with iron railings, you remember? And my one ambition was to break away from that prison.

Having broken out many put everything of the old days behind them.[40]

'The people who lived in Flower and Dean Street – when I used to meet them in later years I always used to be shocked when they used to deny that they ever lived in Flower and Dean Street. You know, telling *me*! I played with them when they were kids, and I would listen to them denying that they lived there!'

The last word can be left with Eva Katchinsky who spent much of her childhood in the Buildings and lived there through the periods of dispersal, not moving away until 1964. In two simple sentences she sums up the life and death of the Jewish working class community in Rothschild Buildings – and in the East End as a whole:[41]

'It was more or less of a little ghetto. Until they started going one higher.'

Notes

Oral sources are referred to in three parts: the first identifies the respondent and should be read in conjunction with the Appendix, which gives brief biographical data; the second identifies the tape, and the third the page number of the transcript. Tapes and transcripts will be lodged at the Tower Hamlets Local History Library, Bancroft Rd, London, E1.

1 Two beginnings

1 Jack London, *People of the Abyss*, 1903 (Journeyman Press edn, 1977), p. 9.
2 Ibid., pp. 113–14.
3 Olive C. Malvery, *The Soul Market*, 1906, p. 217. See also George Sims (ed.), *Living London*, 1902, vol. 2, p. 29, and the same author's *Off the Track in London*, 1911, pp. 12ff.
4 Robert Blatchford, *Julie*, 1900 (?), p. 33.
5 Jack London, op. cit., p. 13.
6 James Greenwood, *In Strange Company*, 1883, p. 158.
7 See *The Seven Curses of London*, 1869, p. 126; *Journeys Through London: or Byways of Modern Babylon*, 1875, p. 87; *Undercurrents of London Life*, 1880, pp. 54f; *Low-Life Deeps: An Account of the Strange Fish to be Found There*, 1881, pp. 193–6. For other accounts of the area in reportage of the time see John Hollingshead, *Ragged London in 1861*, 1861, pp. 44–50; Thomas Archer, *The Pauper, The Thief, and The Convict*, 1865, p. 24, and *The Terrible Sights of London and Labours of Love in the Midst of Them*, 1870, pp. 191f; J. E. Ritchie, *Days and Nights in London, or Studies in Black and Gray*, 1880, p. 142; R. Rowe, *Life in the London Streets*, 1881, pp. 44–9; and G. H. Pike, *Pity for the Perishing*, 1884, pp. 91f and 228f.
8 For full details see London County Council, *Survey of London*, 1957, vol. xxvii, ch. xvii.
9 See Gareth Stedman Jones, *Outcast London*, 1971, passim.
10 Henry Mayhew, *London Labour and the London Poor* (4 vols),

1861, vol. 4, p. 313; James Greenwood, *In Strange Company*, p. 158; S. and H. Barnett, *Practicable Socialism*, 1894 edn, p. 295.

11 James Greenwood, *Undercurrents*, p. 54.

12 Calculated from the manuscript census returns, 1871 census.

13 M. Dorothy George, *London Life in the Eighteenth Century*, 1925, (1966 edn), p. 97.

14 Mayhew, op. cit., vol. 4, pp. 314, 374. Under the Prevention of Crimes Act 1871, it was an offence for lodging house keepers to permit goods to be deposited in the house having reasonable cause for believing them stolen.

15 James Greenwood, *In Strange Company*, p. 158.

16 *Tower Hamlets Independent*, 19 November 1881.

17 *Report of the Commissioner of Police of the Metropolis*, 1870, p. 34.

18 *Tower Hamlets Independent*, 4 February 1882.

19 Mayhew, op. cit., vol. 4, pp. 311–16.

20 Henrietta Barnett, *Canon Barnett: His Life, Work, and Friends*, 1918, vol. 2, pp. 305–6.

21 *Daily Telegraph*, 9 October 1888.

22 Mayhew, op. cit., vol. 4, p. 311.

23 Thomas Beames, *The Rookeries of London: Past, Present, and Prospective*, 1850 (2nd edn, 1852), pp. 149–50.

24 *The Seven Curses of London*, p. 80.

25 162 houses were demolished. See *Report of the Select Committee on Metropolis Improvements*, 1838; *Fourth Report of the Commissioners for Improving the Metropolis*, 1845; and LCC, *Survey of London*, for full story (pp. 256–61).

26 Report of the Dwellings Committee of the Charity Organisation Committee: *The Dwellings of the Poor*, 1873.

27 By the Charity Organisation Society and the Royal College of Physicians. See *Hansard*, 3rd series, vol. CCXXII, col. 98.

28 By Kay-Shuttleworth and Sir Sydney Waterlow on 8 May 1874. *Hansard*, 3rd series, vol. CCXVIII, cols 1944–87.

29 See Charles Gatliff, 'On Improved Dwellings . . . and Suggestions for their Extension', *Journal of the Royal Statistical Society*, vol. XXXVIII (16 February 1875); Octavia Hill, 'Why The Artisans' Dwellings Bill Was Wanted', reprinted in *Homes of the London Poor*, 1875, pp. 76–88.

30 *Hansard*, 3rd series, vol. CCXXII, col. 104, and vol. CCXXIV, col. 452.

31 The Board of Guardians were rigorous enforcers of the Provision of Outdoor Relief Order, issued in 1871. *23rd Annual Report of the Poor Law Board*, PP 1871, XXVII, pp. 90–2.

32 *Whitechapel Board of Guardians*, Minutes, 21 December 1875 and

25 January 1876; *Whitechapel District Board of Works*, Minutes, 10 April 1876.

33 *Report of the Medical Officer of Health for the Whitechapel District* (Whitechapel MOH Report), Quarter Ended 1 April 1876.

34 It was joined with a similar representation for an area west of Commercial St, and the scheme was known as The Metropolis (Goulston St and Flower and Dean St) Improvement Scheme, 1876. See London County Council, *The Housing Question In London, 1855–1900*, 1900, (hereafter LCC (1900)), pp. 118f.

35 Greater London Record Office (GLRO): MBW 1426 (17 October 1877).

36 John Hollingshead, op. cit., pp. 44–50.

37 Estimated from the manuscript returns for the 1871 census.

38 Lloyd P. Gartner, *The Jewish Immigrant in England, 1870–1914*, 1960 (2nd edn, 1973), pp. 38–49.

39 V. D. Lipman, *A Century of Social Service, 1859–1959: The Jewish Board of Guardians*, 1959, pp. 94 and 278–9.

40 Ibid., p. 93, and Gartner, op. cit., p. 42 and 42n.

41 Quoted in William J. Fishman, *East End Jewish Radicals, 1875–1914*, 1975, p. 67.

42 V. D. Lipman, *A Social History of the Jews in England, 1875–1950*, 1954, pp. 76–8.

43 V. D. Lipman, *A Century of Social Service*, pp. 1–3.

44 Records of Jewish Board of Guardians, *Other Committees, 1869–1885*, 14 and 20 May 1884.

45 Gartner, op. cit., p. 21.

46 *26th Annual Report of the Board of Guardians for the Relief of the Jewish Poor*, 1886, pp. 77f.

47 *Jewish Chronicle*, 27 February 1885.

48 Gatliff, op. cit., p. 34.

49 Quoted from a letter by Rothschild (26 March 1886) thanking the Guardians for their sympathy on the death of his mother (Jewish Welfare Board Records).

50 *Jewish Chronicle*, 6 March 1885.

51 Ibid., 13 March 1885.

52 Ibid., 3 July 1885. Four Per Cent Industrial Dwellings Co. Ltd, *First Minute Book* (hereafter *1st Minute Book*), 27 July 1885 and 25 January 1887 (Records in possession of Industrial Dwellings Society (1885) Ltd, 2 Stamford Hill, London N16).

53 Memorandum of Association of the Four Per Cent Industrial Dwellings Co. Ltd, 1885.

54 See COS, *Dwellings of the Poor*, p. 11.

55 *Tower Hamlets Independent*, 19 January 1884.

56 Metropolitan Board of Works, *Minutes*, 8 May 1885.

57 *1st Minute Book*, 11 January 1886.

58 All details from ibid., 10 November 1886 and 2 July 1888 and the *2nd* (1886), *3rd* (1887) and *16th* (1900) *Annual Reports of the Four Per Cent Industrial Dwellings Co. Ltd.* Original plans in possession of Messrs Dowton and Hurst, 10 Portman St, London W1.

59 *1st Minute Book*, p. 23.

60 Four Per Cent Industrial Dwellings Co., *4th Annual Report*, 1888.

61 *Standard*, 2 October 1888.

62 *Morning Post*, 6 October 1888.

63 Tom Cullen, *Autumn of Terror*, 1965, p. 62.

64 *Daily News*, 11 September 1888.

65 *East London Observer*, 15 September 1888.

66 *The Times*, 1 September 1888.

67 Ibid., 4 October 1888.

68 Ibid., 3 and 5 October 1888.

69 *Daily Telegraph*, 13 November 1888.

70 *Pall Mall Gazette*, 1 October 1888.

71 *East London Advertiser*, 6 October 1888.

72 *Saturday Review*, 6 October 1888. See also *Standard*, 10 November 1888, and *St. James's Gazette*, 1 October 1888.

73 *Daily Telegraph*, 22 September 1888. See also *The Times*, 19 September and 18 October 1888.

74 S. and H. Barnett, op. cit., p. 304 (reprinted from the *New Review* and dealing with the Flower and Dean St area).

75 *Daily Telegraph*, 16 November 1888.

76 GLRO: Middlesex Land Registry 1891/19/700.

77 *1st Minute Book*, 28 January 1892.

78 Letter (22 April 1894) from N. S. Joseph to Philip Ornstein, in possession of Industrial Dwellings Society.

79 *Royal Commission on Alien Immigration*, Cd 1742, 1903, Q16, 251.

80 *The Times*, 10 September 1888.

81 *East London Advertiser*, 2 January 1892.

82 *Survey of London*, p. 250.

83 *East London Observer*, 21 April, 30 June and 25 August 1894.

2   Home

1 George Haw, *No Room To Live: The Plaint of Overcrowded London*, 1900, p. 9.

2 See Charles Booth, *Life and Labour of the People in London* (17 vols), 1902, series 3, vol. 2, p. 62.

3 Who wrote of them in glowing terms in a letter to Angela Burdett Coutts (1852) quoted in Millicent Rose, *The East End of London*, 1951, p. 256.

4 See C. Gatliff, 'On Improved Dwellings . . . and Suggestions for their Extension', *Journal of the Royal Statistical Society*, vol. XXXVIII (16 February 1875), pp. 33f; Booth, op. cit., series 1, vol. 3, p. 30.

5 *Report of the Select Committee on Artizans' and Labourers' Dwellings Improvement*, PP 1881, VII, Q538 (Dr Liddle).

6 *Whitechapel MOH Report*, 1897, p. 4: 'That the direct influence of these barrack dwellings upon the health of their occupants – more especially of the children – is adverse, I have not the slightest doubt.'

7 Walter Besant, *East London*, 1899 (1912 edn), pp. 222–3.

8 Robert Williams, *London Rookeries and Colliers' Slums*, 1893, p. 11.

9 George Haw, op. cit., p. 50.

10 Jack London, *People of the Abyss*, 1903, pp. 67–8 and 94.

11 M. Kaufman, *The Housing of the Working Classes and of the Poor*, 1907, p. 28.

12 George Haw, loc. cit.

13 Besant, loc. cit.

14 George Haw, loc. cit.

15 *1st Minute Book*, p. 18.

16 Mrs B, T36, pp. 12–13, for this and following details.

17 Mrs Q, T15, p. 4.

18 Mrs B, T36, pp. 11–12.

19 Miss H, T25, p. 6.

20 Mrs Q, T15, pp. 1 and 4.

21 Mrs B, T36, p. 11.

22 N. S. Joseph marked 'bed-space' in this alcove on the original drawing.

23 Mrs B, T36, p. 10.

24 Ibid., p. 12.

25 Mrs B, T36, pp. 10–15.

26 Mrs J, T18, p. 1.

27 Mrs B, T36, pp. 11, 12 and 14.

28 Mrs J, T18, p. 1.

29 Mrs J, interviewed 16 August 1975 (not recorded).

30 Mrs K, T20, p. 6.

31 Mrs B, T36, pp. 14–15.

32 Mr P's wife, To3, not transcribed.
33 Mr P, To3, p. 3.
34 Opposite p. 245 in the 1903 edn. Reproduced as Plate 1.
35 Mr P, To3, p. 3.
36 This might have been the Metropolitan Gardens Association who in 1907 shared a grand total of £25 among 140 prize-winners. *East London Advertiser*, 1 February 1908. Later, the Four Per Cent ran their own competition for the Company's tenants.
37 Mr P, To3, pp. 3–4.
38 Mr C, T11, p. 5.
39 Mrs B, T36, p. 13.
40 Ibid., pp. 10 and 15.
41 Ibid., p. 10.
42 Mr P, To3, p. 4.
43 See *East London Advertiser*, 1 September 1900: 'During the recent hot weather many of the inhabitants of the [unnamed] buildings brought their beds out into these courts, to escape from the stifling heat within. The place presented a weirdly fantastic spectacle.'
44 Mrs A, To7, p. 2.
45 Miss H, T25, pp. 6–7.
46 Mr C, T11, p. 7.
47 Mrs A, To7, p. 6.
48 *Jewish Chronicle*, 17 December 1909.
49 Miss Z, T17, p. 2.
50 Mrs B, T36, p. 18.
51 Mrs K, T20, p. 2.
52 *1st Minute Book*, p. 127.
53 Ibid., p. 192.
54 Mrs B, T36, p. 18.
55 Mrs A, T13, p. 12.
56 Ibid., T30, p. 18.
57 Mr R, T29, pp. 22–3.
58 Mrs J, T18, p. 7.
59 Mrs B, T36, p. 12.
60 *East London Advertiser,* 14 June 1902.
61 Mrs B, T36, p. 18. These thefts were so common that the local press ran a regular 'Gas Cases' column in their police court reports. And they *did* occur at Rothschild Buildings: Eleazer Levy pleaded guilty to robbing a gas meter of 5d. at No. 138 in 1915. *East London Observer*, 20 February 1915.
62 Mrs B, T36, p. 18, and for much of the following details.

63 Mrs J, T18, p. 7.
64 Mr C, T11, p. 5.
65 Mrs J, T22, p. 15.
66 Mr P, T03, p. 2.
67 Mrs B, T33, p. 9.
68 Mrs N, T10, p. 3.
69 *Tower Hamlets Independent*, 10 August 1878; *East London Observer*, 4 July 1896.
70 Mrs K, T20, p. 5.
71 Four Per Cent Industrial Dwellings Co. Ltd, *16th Annual Report*, 1900.
72 Figures for 1888 and 1900 calculated from the respective *Annual Reports* of the Four Per Cent. For early 1930s see Sir H. Llewellyn Smith, *New Survey of Life and Labour in London*, 1930–5, vol. 4, Map 1.
73 Mrs F, interviewed 1 December 1973, tape destroyed, p. 1.
74 Mr R, T24, p. 8.
75 Miss H, T25, p. 7.
76 Ibid., p. 1.
77 Mr P., T03, p. 2.
78 Miss M, T44, p. 13.
79 Mr U, T06, p. 1.
80 Mrs B, T36, p. 17.
81 Mrs A, T13, p. 13. Cf R. L. Finn, *No Tears in Aldgate*, 1962, pp. 11f.
82 Mrs F, interviewed 1 December 1973, tape destroyed, p. 2.
83 Mr P, interviewed 16 November 1973, not recorded.
84 *1st Minute Book*, p. 23.
85 Report of the Dwellings Committee of the Charity Organisation Society: *The Dwellings of the Poor*, 1873, p. 3.
86 Octavia Hill, *Homes of the London Poor*, 1875 (1883 edn), pp. 10, 25 and 33.
87 *1st Minute Book*, p. 23.
88 Loc. cit.
89 John Garrard, *The English and Immigration, 1880–1910*, 1971, p. 70.
90 *Royal Commission on Alien Immigration*, Cd 1742, 1903, Q9739 (Rev. W. H. Davies).
91 Ibid., Q17,349 (Harry S. Lewis).
92 Ibid., Q9735 (Rev. W. H. Davies).
93 See, for example, Enid Gauldie, *Cruel Habitations: A History of Working-Class Housing, 1780–1918*, 1974, p. 235; and Standish Meacham, *A Life Apart: The English Working Class, 1890–1914*, 1977, pp. 38–9.

94 The rules are in the possession of the Industrial Dwellings Society (1885) Ltd.
95 Miss H, T25, p. 8.
96 Mrs K, T20, pp. 6–7.
97 Mr C, T11, pp. 5 and 7 for this and following details.
98 Mrs B, T36, pp. 13, 14 and 18 for this and following details.
99 *East London Observer*, 26 November 1898.
100 Miss H, T25, p. 5.
101 *1st Minute Book*, p. 126. *Jewish Chronicle*, 17 February 1911.
102 Mrs K, T20, p. 7.
103 *East London Advertiser*, 29 September 1917 and see Miss H, T25, p. 5, and Mrs J, T19, pp. 11 and 12.
104 Council of the United Synagogue, *East End Scheme*, June 1898, p. 39.
105 LCC (1900), p. 89.
106 Council of the United Synagogue, loc. cit.
107 See Booth, op. cit., vol. 17, pp. 10–11.
108 Mrs Q, T15, p. 1.
109 C. Russell and H. S. Lewis, *The Jew in London*, 1900, p. xliii. *Royal Commission*, 1903, QQ4523–4.
110 *East London Observer*, 21 April 1906.
111 *Royal Commission on the Housing of the Working Classes*, PP 1885, XXX, Q4737f.
112 *Royal Commission*, 1903, Q18,366.
113 The housing shortage itself had probably eased by 1908, when a large number of empty houses were noted in Stepney. *East London Advertiser*, 18 January 1908.
114 *Royal Commission*, 1903, Q4519.
115 Mrs K, T20, p. 6.
116 Stepney Borough Council, *Report of Medical Officer of Health*, 1911, p. 76.
117 *Stepney MOH Report*, 1907, p. 56.
118 *Whitechapel MOH Report*, quarter ended 31 March 1883.
119 Ibid., 1894, pp. 16–17.
120 *Royal Commission*, 1903, QQ9739 and 17,349.
121 *Stepney MOH Report*, 1907, p. 56.
122 LCC (1900), pp. 190–213.
123 *1st Minute Book*, 2 July 1888.
124 Mrs A, T09, not transcribed.
125 *Stepney MOH Report*, 1905, pp. 52–3.
126 See the list of Peabody Rules given in *Royal Commission*, 1885, Q11,573.
127 Mrs W, interviewed 30 January 1974, tape destroyed, p. 1.

128 Mrs R, T02, p. 5.
129 Mrs Q, T15, p. 2.
130 Mr P, T03, p. 5.
131 Discussion at Stepney Jewish Clubs and Settlement, 12 August 1975, T16, pp. 1–2.
132 Israel Zangwill, *Children of the Ghetto*, 1892, p. 345.
133 See Anthony Sutcliffe (ed.), *Multi-Storey Living: The British Working-Class Experience*, 1974, passim.

3   Community

1 See Oscar Newman, *Defensible Space*, 1971, passim. Rothschild Buildings complied with the four 'elements of physical design' which contribute to defensible space (pp. 9f).
2 *1st Minute Book*, 10 November 1886.
3 Mr V, T05, p. 1.
4 Miss M, interviewed 15 November 1973, tape destroyed, p. 1.
5 Mrs K, T20, p. 9.
6 Mrs N, T10, p. 2.
7 Mrs K, T20, p. 11.
8 C. Russell and H. S. Lewis, *The Jew in London*, 1900, map of Jewish concentrations in the East End.
9 *Royal Commission on Alien Immigration*, 1903, Cd 1742, Q10,375.
10 In 1914 there were only five non-Jewish names on the electoral register for Rothschild Buildings.
11 The following details come from some autobiographical fragments, recorded on Mrs J, T22, pp. 18–22.
12 Leon Trotsky, *1905*, 1922 (Penguin Books, 1973), p. 100.
13 Ibid., p. 242.
14 Mrs A, T9, p. 10.
15 Mrs J, T18, p. 9.
16 *Royal Commission*, 1903, Q16,502.
17 Miss M, interviewed 15 November 1973, tape destroyed, p. 1.
18 See, for example, Mr R, T24, p. 11, whose uncle emigrated from Lithuania in about 1918 and stayed with the family until finding a home of his own.
19 Mrs A, T07, p. 5.
20 Mrs Y, T35, p. 2.
21 Mr R, T24, p. 15.
22 Mrs J, T18, p. 8 and T19, p. 13.
23 Discussion, etc., T16, p. 3.

24 William Goldman, *A Tent of Blue*, 1946, p. 45.
25 Miss M, T44, p. 15.
26 Mr R, T24, pp. 8–9 and 15. Mummaligge was a dish of sweet-corn, mixed with cheese.
27 Mrs A, T07, p. 6.
28 Mr R, T24, p. 13. See also Rudolf Rocker, *The London Years*, 1956, p. 172.
29 Mrs J, T27, p. 26.
30 Miss M, T44, p. 15.
31 Mrs J, T19, p. 12.
32 Mrs J, T18, p. 8.
33 Mr R, T42, p. 29.
34 Mrs B, T33, p. 7.
35 Mr R, interviewed 7 February 1977, not recorded.
36 *Jewish Chronicle*, 20 January 1911, where it was announced that a full-time Yiddish interpreter was no longer needed at the Thames Police Court. For evidence concerning the breakdown of Yiddish in the third generation of immigrants see Abram Leon, *The Jewish Question: A Marxist Interpretation*, 1946 (New York, 1970), p. 222.
37 Miss M, T44, p. 7.
38 Rocker, op. cit., p. 124.
39 *Jewish Chronicle*, 14 August 1914.
40 Rocker, op. cit., p. 124.
41 See *Report on Alien Enemies in Prohibited Areas*, 1916, Cd 8419.
42 *Jewish Chronicle*, 30 October and 6 November 1914.
43 Mrs A, T07, pp. 2–3.
44 *Jewish Chronicle*, 16 October 1914.
45 Mrs J, T22, p. 15.
46 See Gartner, op. cit., p. 197.
47 Mr U, T06, p. 1.
48 I am grateful for this and other references to the Kamenitzer Maggid to Miss May Maccoby.
49 Mrs N, T10, p. 4.
50 Mrs A, T09, p. 10.
51 *Jewish Chronicle*, 31 May 1957.
52 Mrs B, T33, p. 9.
53 Mrs G, T31, p. 6.
54 *East London Advertiser*, 1 January 1910.
55 Mrs J, T18, p. 6.
56 Mrs K, T20, p. 6.
57 Mrs Q, T15, p. 1.
58 Miss M, T44, p. 11.

59 Mrs N, T10, p. 4.
60 Mr R, T24, p. 13.
61 See Gartner, op. cit., ch. VII.
62 Mrs A, T13, p. 14.
63 There were full-scale riots outside the Machzikei HaDath on many Days of Atonement, notably in 1904. *East London Observer*, 24 September 1904.
64 Cf Chaim Lewis, *A Soho Address*, 1965, p. 41.
65 Mr R, T29, p. 24.
66 Mrs A, T13, pp. 12–13.
67 Mr U, T06, p. 1.
68 Four Per Cent Industrial Dwellings Co. Ltd, *16th Annual Report*, 1900.
69 Mrs K, T20, p. 8.
70 Mrs A, T13, p. 13.
71 Charles Booth, *Life and Labour of the People in London* (17 vols), 1902, series 3, vol. 2, p. 110 described the Buildings' population as 'Poverty and comfort (mixed)' in his Poverty Map of 1898.
72 Mr C, T11, p. 8.
73 Mrs B, T36, pp. 16–17.
74 Mrs N, T10, pp. 3–4.
75 Mrs J, T19, p. 13.
76 Mrs F, interviewed 1 December 1973, tape destroyed, p. 1.
77 Mrs K, T20, p. 9.
78 Miss H, T28, p. 14.
79 Mrs K, T20, p. 8.
80 Mrs A, T07, pp. 1–2.
81 Mrs K, T20, p. 8.
82 Mrs A, T07, p. 3.
83 Mr C, T11, p. 7.
84 Mr D, T43, p. 10.
85 Miss M, T44, p. 14.
86 Mrs J, T18, p. 9.
87 Ibid., T27, p. 26.
88 Mrs K, T20, p. 9.
89 Mr R, T24, pp. 10–11.
90 Mrs Y, T35, pp. 4–5.
91 Mrs N, T10, p. 2.
92 Mr R, T24, p. 16.
93 Miss E, T12, p. 3.
94 Mr R, T24, p. 6.
95 Mr C, T11, p. 6.
96 Miss Z, T17, p. 6.

97 Russell and Lewis, op. cit., map of Jewish concentrations in the East End.
98 Mrs K, T20, p. 12.
99 Details from London Street Directories of that date; approximate dates of arrival of shopkeepers from same source.
100 Miss H, T25, p. 9.
101 Ibid., p. 7.
102 Mrs A, T13, p. 11.
103 Mr C, T11, p. 6.
104 Mrs J, T22, p. 16.
105 Mr C, T11, p. 6. Adulteration of milk was very common in Garfinkle's time. In the year he came to Flower and Dean St, one in seven milk samples taken by the Stepney Sanitary Inspectors was found to be watered. *Stepney MOH Report*, 1910.
106 Mr P, T03, pp. 5 and 8.
107 Mr R, T24, PP 11–12.
108 Mr U, T06, p. 5 and for following quote.
109 A *landsman* of Miss H's mother.
110 Mrs J, T18, p. 4 and for following quote.
111 Mrs K, T21, p. 15.
112 Mr C, T11, p. 6.
113 Mrs J, T18, p. 4. See Chaim Lewis, op. cit., pp. 23–4 for the shopkeeper's view of credit.
114 Miss E, T12, p. 4.
115 Mr R, T24, p. 7.
116 *East London Observer*, 26 November 1898.
117 Miss H, T25, p. 3.
118 Ibid., pp. 3–4.
119 Ibid., p. 9.
120 See complaints about Jewish shopkeepers staying open till midnight or later in *Jewish Chronicle*, 10 December 1910.
121 Mrs N, T10, pp. 2–3.
122 Mr U, T06, p. 5.
123 Miss H, T25, p. 4 for this and following details.
124 Mrs K, T20, p. 4.
125 Mrs F, interviewed 1 December 1973, tape destroyed, p. 2.
126 Mrs L, T37, p. 12.
127 Mrs K, T21, p. 13.
128 Miss H, T25, p. 8.
129 Miss J, T22, p. 16 for this and next quote.
130 *East London Advertiser*, 4 January 1890.
131 Miss E, T12, p. 4.
132 Mrs K, T21, p. 15.

133 Miss H, T25, p. 8.
134 Mrs K, T21, p. 15.
135 *Stepney MOH Report*, 1909, p. 53.
136 Sir H. Llewellyn Smith, *New Survey of Life and Labour in London*, 1930–5, vol. 3, pp. 323–4. The majority of these would only have appeared at the Petticoat Lane market on Sunday mornings.
137 This composite picture is made up of evidence primarily from Miss E, T12, p. 2; Mrs K, T20, pp. 9–10, and T21, pp. 13–14; and Mrs B, T33, p. 8.
138 I. Zangwill, *Children of the Ghetto*, 1892, p. 203.
139 Mr P, T03, p. 3.
140 Ibid., pp. 2–3.

4   Beyond the pale

1 See GLRO: MBW 1549, and *Stepney MOH Report*, 1902, p. 28.
2 Mrs B, T33, pp. 8–9.
3 *Daily Telegraph*, 11 September 1888.
4 *Stepney MOH Report*, 1902, p. 28.
5 Stephen Graham, *London Nights*, 1925 (1929 edn), p. 50.
6 Interview 24 May 1977, T45, not transcribed.
7 Mrs J, T18, p. 8.
8 Miss Z, T17, p. 7 and for next quote.
9 Mr U, T06, p. 2.
10 Mrs J, T18, pp. 7–8.
11 *East London Observer*, 6 August 1898.
12 Ibid., 25 June 1904.
13 *East London Advertiser*, 14 March 1908.
14 Ex-Det. Sergeant B. Leeson, *Lost London: The Memoirs of an East End Detective*, ? 1932, pp. 68–9.
15 *East London Advertiser*, 22 September 1906.
16 Mr R, T24, p. 8.
17 Ibid., p. 14.
18 *1st Minute Book*, 28 February 1887. For the continuing bad reputation of Flower and Dean St among writers, social commentators and the East End press see, for example, Arthur Morrison, *Tales of Mean Streets*, 1903 ('A Confession'); George Sims (ed.) *Living London*, 1902, vol. 2, p. 151 (1902); *East London Advertiser*, 22 September 1906.
19 Mr U, T06, p. 5.
20 Discussion, etc., T16, p. 1.

21   G. H. Pike, *Pity for the Perishing*, 1884, p. 232.
22   *East London Observer*, 23 July 1898; Spitalfields Vestry, *Minutes*, 29 September 1858, 10 and 17 June 1859.
23   *East London Observer*, 15 August 1896.
24   Mrs N, T10, p. 3.
25   Mrs A, T07, p. 4.
26   S. and H. Barnett, *Practicable Socialism*, 1894 edn, p. 306.
27   Booth, op. cit., series 1, vol. 3, p. 80.
28   Ibid., series 3, vol. 2, pp. 61–5. See also *East London Advertiser*, 1 September 1900, containing an article reprinted from the *Daily Mail*.
29   *East London Observer*, 10 December 1898.
30   Ibid., 22 November 1902.
31   Mrs A, T07, p. 3.
32   Mr U, T06, p. 2.
33   Mr P, T03, p. 1.
34   Mr C, T11, pp. 6–7.
35   See *East London Observer*, 5 December 1896 for a particularly bad case of a woman beaten by a man, and ibid., 24 March 1894.
36   *East London Advertiser*, 12 May 1900.
37   See ibid., 26 March 1910 for a case where a Flower and Dean St man, stabbed in the face, refused to prosecute his assailant on the grounds that 'we all have to get our living in the streets and it ain't advisable sometimes to prosecute a member of a gang.'
38   Mr R, T24, p. 8.
39   *East London Advertiser*, 16 August 1902.
40   Mrs K, T20, p. 3 and T21, p. 13.
41   Mr U, T06, p. 2.
42   Mr R, T23, p. 16.
43   Mrs A, T07, p. 4.
44   Mr P, T03, pp. 1 and 7.
45   Leon Trotsky, *1905*, 1922 (Penguin Books, 1973), p. 150.
46   Bernard Gainer, *The Alien Invasion*, 1972, p. 58.
47   *East London Advertiser*, 24 January 1891.
48   Ibid., 13 August 1904.
49   Mrs A, T07, pp. 5–6.
50   Mrs F, interviewed 1 December 1973, tape destroyed, p. 3.
51   Mr P, T03, p. 7. The British Union of Fascists began to take an openly anti-Semitic line from the autumn of 1934. Soon after, the first East End branch of the BUF was formed in Bethnal Green, with another in Shoreditch following immediately after. The first Stepney branch was not formed until July 1936. James Robb, *Working-Class Anti-Semite*, 1954, pp. 92–3, found that

over 25 per cent of working-class adult males in Bethnal Green could be described as 'extreme anti-Semites'.

52 Mrs J, T27, p. 25.
53 William Goldman, *East End My Cradle*, 1940, p. 7.
54 Mrs Q, T15, p. 3.
55 Gartner, op. cit., p. 166.
56 Richard Whiteing, *No. 5 John Street*, 1899 (1902 edn) p. 182.
57 Mrs F, interviewed 1 December 1973, tape destroyed, p. 3.
58 Cf Chaim Lewis, *A Soho Address*, 1965, p. 51.
59 Miss E, T12, p. 3.
60 Mrs K, T20, p. 6.
61 Mrs J, T18, p. 6.
62 *Daily News*, 4 October 1888.
63 *East London Observer*, 24 March 1894.
64 Interviewed 24 May 1977, T45, not transcribed.
65 Mrs B, T36, p. 15.
66 Ibid., pp. 15–16.
67 Mrs A, T07, p. 3.
68 Miss M, T44, p. 5.
69 *Jewish Chronicle*, 18 December 1914.
70 In 1902 there was an outbreak of smallpox (one of the most easily communicated of all infections) at the Brick Lane end of Flower and Dean St. At least twenty-two women in three lodging houses were taken ill and six died. No case occurred in Rothschild Buildings. *Stepney MOH Report*, 1902, p. 28.
71 Miss E, T14, p. 10.
72 Mrs K, T20, p. 5 and cf Dorothy Scannell, *Mother Knew Best: An East End Childhood*, 1974, p. 34.
73 Mrs A, T07, p. 3.
74 Mr P, T03, p. 6.
75 Mr U, T06, p. 5.
76 Mrs Q, T15, p. 3.

5   Growing up

1 See the very informative *Whitechapel MOH Reports*, 1889–99. The *Stepney MOH Reports* are not so helpful.
2 *Whitechapel MOH Report*, 1896, p. 15.
3 Mrs L, T37, p. 1.
4 Miss H, T25, p. 1.
5 Mrs A, T32, pp. 29–30.
6 Formed in 1894 to provide 'women-helps in all cases where

Jewish mothers are unable, owing to poverty, to provide for themselves proper nursing or have no relatives to look after the home during their illness'. The work of the Society was almost entirely devoted to confinements. Payments from the patients were expected to cover a quarter of the costs incurred. *Jewish Chronicle*, 15 November 1901.

7 Mrs A, T32, p. 30.
8 Ibid., p. 32.
9 *Jewish Chronicle*, 16 July 1909, and *Stepney MOH Report*, 1913, p. 69.
10 *Jewish Chronicle*, 15 November 1901, 10 February 1905.
11 Ibid., 15 January 1909.
12 Mrs J, T27, p. 24, and for following details.
13 *Jewish Chronicle*, 21 July 1911.
14 Mr R, T29, p. 23.
15 Mr P, T02, p. 4.
16 Mr R, T29, p. 24.
17 Ibid., p. 25.
18 Mrs Q, T15, p. 2.
19 Mr D, T43, p. 14.
20 Details from ibid., T34, p. 9 and T43, pp. 13–14.
21 Mr P, T39, p. 20.
22 Miss E, T12, p. 6.
23 Mrs A, T30, p. 25.
24 *Stepney MOH Report*, 1907, p. 25: 'Phthisis is more prevalent in this Borough than in the whole of London.'
25 Ibid., 1913, p. 31.
26 Mrs J, T18, p. 1.
27 Mr R, T29, p. 22.
28 Chaim Lewis, *A Soho Address*, 1965, p. 25.
29 Mr R, T29, p. 23.
30 Mrs A, T30, p. 19.
31 Miss Z, T17, p. 5.
32 Miss E, T12, p. 4.
33 Mr R, T29, pp. 24–5.
34 Mrs A, T13, p. 11.
35 Loc. cit.
36 Mr R, T29, p. 23.
37 Mrs K, T20, pp. 3–4.
38 Miss M, T44, p. 5.
39 Mrs L, T37, p. 1.
40 Mrs G, T31, p. 7.
41 Miss H, T25, p. 4 and T28, p. 11.

42 Miss E, T12, p. 1.

43 Mrs A, T09, p. 8.

44 Eight out of sixteen people were the children of widows (six) or widowers (two) before leaving school.

45 Details taken from Miss H, T25 and T28, pp. 1–14.

46 One remarkable feat of memory is displayed by Miss E, T12, p. 4: the soup kitchen must have moved from Fashion St before she was 5 years old, yet: 'There was a soup kitchen in Fashion St, I remember. I was very very young. And I remember a funny old man there with a beard – and looking back now, he'd got a face like a walrus. He was a cleaner or something, one of the helpers.'

47 *East London Observer*, 10 December 1904.

48 *Jewish Chronicle*, 25 December 1903, from which many of the following details are taken.

49 Mrs A, T30, p. 27. There are three documentary sources for Commercial St School, all at the Greater London Record Office. (a) Only one Log Book seems to have survived for this period, that for the Boys' Department for 1913–36; cited as CSS/LB. (b) The printed annual reports of the School Managers; cited as CSS/MR. And (c) the annual reports of Her/His Majesty's Inspectors of Schools; cited as CSS/HMI. (Mrs A is supported by CSS/MR for February 1899, p. 1; February 1900, p. 1, and February 1901, n.p., but contrast Lloyd P. Gartner, *The Jewish Immigrant in England, 1870–1914*, 1960 (2nd edn, 1973), p. 226.)

50 Ibid., p. 228.

51 CSS/MR, February 1905, n.p.

52 Ibid., January 1896, p. 1.

53 Mrs A, T30, p. 22.

54 CSS/MR, February 1903, n.p.

55 Mrs A, T30, p. 22.

56 CSS/LB, p. 13.

57 Ibid., p. 232 (1 January 1914).

58 Ibid., p. 211 (1 January 1915).

59 CSS/HMI, 28 February 1897.

60 See *Jewish Chronicle*, 3 April 1903 which reported that two local Board Schools had 335 and 337 Jewish boys out of a total of 340 in each case.

61 Ibid., 11 October 1901.

62 Three out of seven in the Boys' Department.

63 Mrs A, T07, p. 5.

64 *East London Observer*, 28 May 1904.

65 Gartner, op. cit., pp. 229–31.
66 Mrs A, T13, pp. 14–15.
67 Ibid., T07, pp. 4–5.
68 Mr R, T29, p. 23.
69 Mrs A, T30, pp. 24–5 for these and following details.
70 Mrs L, T37, p. 3. 'Something new for Passover' is reminiscent of the northern working-class custom of buying children clothes at Whitsun.
71 Mrs A, T30, p. 18.
72 *Jewish Chronicle*, 11 January 1901.
73 CSS/MR, February 1897, n.p.
74 Ibid., January 1896, p. 1.
75 CSS/MR, February 1900, p. 1.
76 Miss E, T14, p. 9.
77 Mrs A, T32, p. 34. I am told that the youthful Solomon began his piano career in this way at Commercial St School.
78 Ibid., T30, p. 27.
79 CSS/HMI, 28 February 1903.
80 Mrs A, T32, p. 34.
81 Miss E, T14, p. 10.
82 CSS/MR, February 1902.
83 Miss E, T14, pp. 9–10.
84 Mr R, T29, p. 23.
85 Mrs A, T30, pp. 22–3.
86 See CSS/HMI, 28 February 1898, and CSS/MR, February 1902.
87 Mrs A, T30, p. 28.
88 Miss H, T28, p. 14.
89 Ibid.
90 J. J. Findlay, *Principles of Class Teaching*, 1902 (1907 edn), pp. 392–3.
91 Mrs A, T32, pp. 32–3 for this and following details.
92 Children's Care Committees were formed about 1903 and run by School Managers. They obtained County Council grants for school dinners and individual acts of charity.
93 CSS/LB, pp. 6–7 (April–June 1914).
94 CSS/MR, February 1896, p. 1.
95 See *East London Observer*, 10 December 1904, where the Director of Studies at the School of Sociology argued against school meals in the East End and pointed out that Commercial St School was one of the few providing them. The public meeting at which he spoke had been called by the local branch of the Charity Organisation Society.

96   CSS/MR, February 1900, p. 1.
97   Mrs J, T18, p. 5.
98   CSS/MR, February 1904, n.p.
99   Mrs A, T30, p. 23.
100 CSS/MR, February 1901, n.p.
101 *Jewish Chronicle*, 22 February 1901.
102 Ibid., 6 January 1905.
103 Mr C, T11, p. 5.
104 Mrs J, T18, pp. 9–10.
105 Mr P, T03, p. 4.
106 CSS/LB, pp. 203–5 and 211.
107 *Stepney MOH Reports*, 1911, p. 27; 1912, p. 17; 1913, p. 19.
108 Mrs A, T32, pp. 34–5.
109 CSS/LB, p. 252 (13 January 1916).
110 Mrs A, T30, p. 23 and for following quote.
111 CSS/LB, 16 September 1914.
112 Ibid., p. 233 (11 February 1914).
113 Ibid., p. 210 (14 October 1915) and p. 256 (26 September 1916)ff.
114 Mr P, T03, p. 9.
115 CSS/LB, p. 260 (13 June 1917). A similar incident occurred at the Rutland St County Council School in 1911 during a small fire at the school (*Jewish Chronicle*, 17 November 1911). For details of the air raid see the East End press for 16, 23 and 30 June 1917. Commercial St School was lucky: eighteen children died in a Poplar LCC School.
116 *Jewish Chronicle*, 6 November 1903.
117 Mrs A, T30, p. 20.
118 *Jewish Chronicle*, 6 November 1903.
119 Mrs A, T30, p. 20.
120 Mrs K, T20, p. 9.
121 *Jewish Chronicle*, 6 November 1903.
122 Ibid., 9 April 1909.
123 Mrs A, T30, pp. 20–1.
124 All the games described in the oral testimony and mentioned here are noted in Norman Douglas's marvellous little book *London Street Games*, 1916.
125 Mr V, T05, p. 1.
126 Mr U, T06, pp. 3–4 for this and the following game.
127 Ibid., p. 4.
128 Mr V, T05, p. 2 and for following quote.
129 Mr D, T43, p. 11.
130 *Jewish Chronicle*, 9 April 1909.

131 Mrs A, T13, p. 12.
132 Mr R, T24, p. 10.
133 Miss Z, T17, p. 3.
134 Mr R, T24, p. 10.
135 Miss E, T12, p. 4.
136 Mrs A, T13, pp. 11–12.
137 Cf Jack London, *People of the Abyss*, 1903 (Journeyman Press edn, 1977), p. 110: 'There is one beautiful sight in the East End, and only one, and it is the children dancing in the street when the organ-grinder goes his round.'
138 Mrs F, interviewed 1 December 1973, tape destroyed, p. 1.
139 *Jewish Chronicle*, 30 July 1909.
140 Mrs F, interviewed 1 December 1973, tape destroyed, pp. 2–3.
141 Mrs J, T18, p. 10.
142 Mr P, T03, p. 6.
143 Mrs K, T20, p. 7.
144 CSS/MR, February 1896.
145 Mr P, T03, p. 6.
146 Mrs J, T19, p. 11.
147 Mrs A, T30, p. 26.
148 CSS/LB, pp. 229–30 (25 September 1913 and 22 October 1913).
149 Miss M, T44, p. 8.
150 Mrs L, T37, p. 12.
151 *East London Advertiser,* 27 December 1902.
152 *Jewish Chronicle*, 19 February 1909.
153 Ibid., 1 February 1901.
154 Ibid., 20 March 1903.
155 See J. R. Gillis, 'The Evolution of Juvenile Delinquency in England, 1890–1914', *Past and Present*, 67 (May 1975). For Jewish immigrant delinquency see *East London Observer*, 31 October 1896, 8 January 1898, 29 January 1898, 6 August 1898, 9 April 1904; *East London Advertiser*, 5 May 1900 and 15 February 1902; *Jewish Chronicle*, 20 March 1903.
156 Mrs B, T36, p. 19.
157 Mr R, T29, p. 25.
158 Mr U, T06, p. 3.
159 Mr R, T29, p. 27 and *Jewish Chronicle*, 3 May 1907.
160 *Jewish Chronicle*, 30 June 1905 and 19 February 1909.
161 Mr R, T29, p. 27.
162 *Jewish Chronicle*, 13 and 20 November 1903.
163 Ibid., 19 April 1907.
164 Mrs K, T20, p. 2.
165 *East London Advertiser*, 21 April 1906.

166 Mrs G, T31, p. 5.
167 Mr D, T34, p. 8.
168 Mrs G, T31, p. 5.
169 Ibid., p. 3.
170 Gartner, op. cit., p. 177.
171 Mr D, T43, pp. 11–12 and for following details.
172 Mrs A, interviewed 29 March 1976, not recorded, p. 28.

6 Work

1 *Daily Telegraph*, 22 September 1888.
2 See Gareth Stedman Jones, *Outcast London*, 1971, pp. 184–6.
3 Ibid., p. 98. See also Chapter V and pp. 368–9.
4 Calculated from 1901 census, vol. 7 (County of London report), pp. 144–5.
5 Garment workers 29 per cent (Rothschild Buildings 30 per cent); boot and shoe 11 per cent (9 per cent); carpenters (mostly cabinet makers) 8 per cent (10 per cent); trade and commerce 23 per cent, but in Rothschild Buildings perhaps only 8 per cent. The 12 per cent included within 'various' may contain some who were buying and selling – in 1888 the proportion was 18 per cent. See Lloyd P. Gartner, *The Jewish Immigrant in England, 1870–1914*, 1960 (2nd edn, 1973), pp. 57–8 (his calculations of percentages are inaccurate in two places and have been corrected above).
6 Charles Booth, *Life and Labour of the People in London* (17 vols), 1902, series 1, vol. 4, p. 60.
7 Booth, series 1, vol. 4, p. 69n states that the number of boot makers was rising in the 1880s. It stood, in London as a whole, at 38,989 in 1891, but dropped to 30,259 in 1901, and to 23,269 by 1911, a decrease of 40.3 per cent in twenty years.
8 Public Records Office: BT/31/20466/120215. The figure for nett profits in 1916 was £60,083 8s. 10d.; in 1919 it was £114,755 4s. 8d. In the four years from 1912 to 1916 profits rose by 40 per cent.
9 Ibid. For confirmation of the self-descriptions of the Four Per Cent's shareholders see John Carrier, 'The Four Per Cent Industrial Dwellings Co. Ltd.: The Social Composition of the Shareholders of an East London Dwellings Company at the End of the Nineteenth Century', *East London Papers*, vol. 11, no. 1, pp. 40–6. I am grateful to John Carrier for drawing my attention to this reference.
10 In particular there is one important and obvious gap. I have been

unable to interview a boot maker from Rothschild Buildings – the trade (see note above) employed nine times more men than women; and because women live longer than men, specific male subjects are often harder to find than female.

11 Unless otherwise stated, all oral evidence comes from Mr C, T11, pp. 1–8.

12 V. D. Lipman, *A Century of Social Service*, 1959, pp. 282–3.

13 Ibid., pp. 67–9, and 119–23.

14 Booth, op. cit., series 1, vol. 4, p. 37.

15 Ibid., p. 43. Gartner, op. cit., pp. 86f.

16 The Jewish Board of Guardians were enlightened in their use of technical colleges, paying apprentices' fees there from 1884. Lipman, op. cit., p. 122.

17 Ibid.

18 Quoted in ibid.

19 This was an average rate for a skilled journeyman tailor in the bespoke trade. See *Report of an Enquiry by the Board of Trade into the Earnings and Hours of Labour of Workpeople in the United Kingdom*, 2, Clothing Trades in 1906. PP 1909, Cd 4844, p. 86.

20 As late as 1911, 59 per cent of male employers in the London tailoring trade lived and worked in the same premises.

21 See William J. Fishman, *East End Jewish Radicals, 1875–1914*, 1975, pp. 294–301 for the best account of the dispute.

22 See *Report of the War Cabinet Committee on Women in Industry*, PP 1919, Cd 135, p. 136.

23 Booth, op. cit., series 1, vol. 4, pp. 54–5.

24 *Select Committee of the House of Commons on Home Work*, PP 1908, H of C 246, Q1392.

25 Ibid., QQ1432–3.

26 Ibid., Q1435.

27 Ibid., Q1392.

28 Ibid., Q1497.

29 Ibid., Q1394.

30 *Report from the Select Committee of the House of Commons on Home Work*, PP 1907, VI, H of C, 290, QQ3288, 3346, and 3540.

31 Mr R, T23, p. 1.

32 *Select Committee*, 1908, Q1395.

33 Cf Booth, op. cit., series 1, vol. 4, pp. 53–4.

34 *Select Committee*, 1908, QQ1436–8.

35 Probably the United Garment Workers' Union, formed by the amalgamation of several unions in 1915.

36 *Report of the Committee on Women in Industry*, PP 1919, Cd 167, p. 102.

37 For a full list see *Directory of Industrial Associations in the UK in 1903*, PP 1903, Cd 1707. Separate under-pressers' and pressers' organisations were of particular importance at a time when the under-presser was sometimes hired by the presser himself rather than the master; Rudolf Rocker, *The London Years*, 1956, pp. 166–7.

38 Calculated from the 1901 census, vol. 7, pp. 144–5.

39 PP 1919, Cd 135, pp. 91–2.

40 Unless otherwise stated, all oral evidence comes from Mrs B, T33, pp. 1–9.

41 Miss H, T25, p. 1.

42 *East London Observer*, 2 January 1915 and Miss H, T25, pp. 1–2.

43 *Jewish Chronicle*, 25 August 1914.

44 *East London Observer*, 2 January 1915.

45 Mrs G, T31, pp. 1–4.

46 *Select Committee*, 1907, Q3301.

47 Prior to the war it was illegal to sub-contract War Office work; the Fair Wages Clause was relaxed early in 1915.

48 *East London Advertiser*, 9 June 1917.

49 *Report of the Women's Employment Committee*, PP 1919, Cd 9239, p. 82.

50 *The Woman's Dreadnought*, 21 October 1916.

51 E. Sylvia Pankhurst, *The Home Front*, 1932, p. 91.

52 *East London Advertiser*, 24 February 1917, and Pankhurst, op. cit., pp. 158–9.

53 *The Woman's Dreadnought*, 24 June 1916.

54 Ibid., 21 October 1916.

55 Ibid., 28 October 1916. The military tailors and tailoresses were among the most militant garment workers and there had been a long history of trouble at both Schneider's and Lottery's. See *Jewish Chronicle*, 20 February 1903 and *East London Advertiser*, 25 January 1908.

56 *Commission of Enquiry into Industrial Unrest . . . for the London and South-Eastern Area*, PP 1917, Cd 8666, p. 2.

57 That was so among men born in Russia, Russian Poland, Austria and Rumania and living in London. In 1901, cabinet makers came third to boot makers. Tailors, of course, were by far the largest group in both years.

58 See *East London Papers*, vol. 4, no. 2 (October 1961), p. 89, and 1911 census, vol. 10, pp. 155–7.

59 All oral evidence comes from Mr P, T03, pp. 1–11, and T39, pp. 12–22.

60 *Reports on Strikes and Lock-Outs, and on Conciliation and Arbitra-*

tion Boards in the UK, 1889–1913: in 1912: PP 1913, Cd 7089, pp. 100–10; in 1913: PP 1914, Cd 7658, pp. 148–9.

61 See below, p. 253.

62 Later he had shops in Haig St (Bethnal Green), Curtain Rd and Hoxton. Isaac Landsman died in 1931.

63 Booth, op. cit., series 1, vol. 4, p. 164.

64 Ibid., p. 210.

65 The Fairclough St Evening Classes were the 'largest "Jewish" evening school in London', with over 1,000 pupils in 1911, 99 per cent of whom were said to be Jewish. *Jewish Chronicle*, 3 February 1911.

66 Piece work in the good class trade had been abolished by trade union activity in the earlier years of the century but it still remained in the cheaper work.

67 Booth, op. cit., series 1, vol. 4, p. 293 and series 2, vol. 3, pp. 36–7. See also *East London Observer*, 24 October 1896. But see Gartner, op. cit., p. 94 who wrongly states 'that English girls and women exceeded the number of Jewish male workers. Jewish girls, however, avoided cap making.' Yet in 1911 there were 1,026 Russian, etc., cap makers in London, 27 per cent of whom were women, and this did not include second-generation immigrant girls like Florrie Edelman.

68 13,702 female milliners in 1911 compared with 2,834 male and female cap makers.

69 1911 census, vol. 10, pp. 155–7.

70 437 Stepney girls were employed as milliners in 1901, 846 in 1911.

71 All oral evidence comes from Mrs K, T20, pp. 1–3 and T41, pp. 17–21.

72 Which employed 'not more than twenty persons' according to Booth, op. cit., series 2, vol. 3, p. 36.

73 Fishman, op. cit., pp. 307–8.

74 Booth, op. cit., series 2, vol. 3, p. 37.

75 Ibid.

76 Ibid.

77 *East London Observer*, 24 October 1896, and 8 February 1896. Gartner, op. cit., pp. 120–1. *Reports on Strikes and Lock-Outs . . . 1895*, PP 1896, Cd 8281, pp. 94–5; in 1896: PP 1897, Cd 8643, pp. 118–19.

78 *Jewish Chronicle*, 23 August 1901; 31 July 1903; 19 May, 21 June, 5 July and 16 August 1907.

79 All oral evidence comes from Mrs J, T18, pp. 1–10 and T40, pp. 27–34.

80 The average rate for apprentice milliners and dressmakers was
    4s. 4d. per week. PP 1909, Cd 4844, p. 28.
81 The virtues of millinery as a respectable 'profession', well-paid
    in the 'higher branches', were extolled in 1917 in a women's
    column in the *East London Advertiser* (7 April).
82 PP 1909, Cd 4844, p. 46.
83 Minimum rates for milliners were fixed at 7d. an hour on 7 April
    1919, giving an estimated wage of £1 10s. 7d. a week. PP 1919,
    Cd 135, p. 136.
84 Eva worked as a forelady at Berger's until she married in 1927,
    after which she gave up the millinery.
85 Booth, op. cit., series 1, vol. 4, p. 234.
86 *Jewish Chronicle*, 8 February 1901.
87 1911 census, vol. 10, pp. 155–7, and 1901 census, pp. 144–5.
    The comparable figures for tailoresses were 61 per cent under 25
    and 29 per cent married.
88 All oral evidence comes from Mrs L, T37, pp. 1–13.
89 Demand for cigarettes increased during the war. PP 1919, Cd
    167, p. 115.
90 Their most popular brands were Three Threes and Three Fives.
91 But compare Gartner, op. cit., p. 75: 'by the turn of the
    century . . . the manufacture of both cigars and cigarettes no
    longer employed more than a few hundred Jews.' Yet in 1911
    there were nearly 1,000 Russian, etc., men and women working
    in the trade in London, and this would not have included
    second-generation immigrants like Jenny.
92 I have described the hand-made trade in some detail as its
    processes were almost extinct by 1918 and because I cannot find
    a readily available description elsewhere.
93 Pankhurst, op. cit., pp. 163 and 187–8.
94 These remembered rates may be unrealistically high. Repre-
    sentatives of Messrs Lambert & Butler gave average piece-rates
    as 3s. 7d. to 4s. 4d. per 1,000 but with weekly earnings averaging
    29s. See PP 1919, Cd 167, p. 115.
95 At Messrs Lambert & Butler's, 90–95 per cent of cigarettes were
    made by machine by 1919. Ibid.
96 PP 1919, Cd 9239, pp. 94–106. The estimate of the female
    labour force in cigarette manufacture comes from the 1907
    census of production. PP 1910, Cd 5397, p. 47.
97 1911 census, vol. 10, pp. 155–7.
98 Following oral evidence comes from Mrs J, T18, pp. 1–10.
99 Miss H, T25, p. 1. See also Mr C, T11, pp. 4–5.
100 *East London Observer*, 19 June 1915.

101 Booth, op. cit., series 1, vol. 4, pp. 308–10.
102 Pankhurst, op. cit., p. 93.
103 Booth, op. cit., series 2, vol. 5, p. 112. See also ibid., series 1, vol. 4, pp. 295–311, and *Select Committee*, 1907, Q669.
104 Mrs J, T18, p. 4.
105 Miss H, T25, p. 2 and T28, p. 12.
106 Mrs L, T37, pp. 9–10 and 12.
107 Following oral evidence from Mr D, T34, pp. 7–8.
108 Mrs B, T33, p. 8.
109 In London in 1911, self-employed dressmakers comprised 18 per cent of the total number of women in the trade (compared with 2 per cent of tailoresses and 5 per cent of milliners) and 87 per cent of them (10,596) worked at home. 1911 census, vol. 10, pp. 34–9.
110 This type of outwork was rare among Jewish immigrants, see *Select Committee*, 1907, QQ806–7; *Select Committee*, 1908, QQ1202, 1248, 1256, 1401 and 1442.
111 Figures are from the 1910 street directories and include grocers, chandlers, provision dealers and greengrocers.
112 All oral evidence comes from Mr D, T34, pp. 1–9 and T43, pp. 10–14.
113 These rates would have been considered low twenty years before Jack entered the trade. Booth, op. cit., series 2, vol. 3, p. 217.
114 Wilfred Whitaker, *Victorian and Edwardian Shop Workers*, 1973, p. 20.
115 Hours in 'high-class' West End shops were shorter than in the rest of the trade. Booth, op. cit., series 2, vol. 3, p. 218.
116 Ibid., p. 227.
117 See article on 17th Earl of Derby in the *Dictionary of National Biography* (compact edn), p. 2902, col. 3.
118 Jack Brahms worked at Whiteley's, mainly in the warehouse but also on display stands in the shop, until about 1924 when 'I could see no prospects there' and he became a draper's assistant in the West End until the start of the last war.
119 1901 census, pp. 76–92 and 168; 1911 census, vol. 10, pp. 34–9, and 155–7, and vol. 9, p. 243.
120 Following oral evidence comes from Mrs L, T37, pp. 1–13.
121 Mr U, T06, p. 1.
122 Mrs K, T20, p. 2.
123 Miss E, T12, p. 1.
124 Following oral evidence comes from Miss M, T44, pp. 4–15.
125 See Gartner, op. cit., pp. 58–61.

126 Following oral evidence comes from Mrs B, T33, pp. 6–8.
127 Following oral evidence comes from Mrs J, T18, pp. 1–10.
128 Booth, op. cit., vol. 17, p. 83.
129 Mrs F, interviewed 1 December 1973, tape destroyed, p. 1.
130 I am grateful to Mrs Eva Cohen for letting me see one of her
       mother's tally cards, dating from 1937.

7 Conclusions: politics and class

1 John Carrier, 'A Jewish Proletariat', in M. Mindlin and C.
    Bermant (eds), *Explorations*, 1967, pp. 120–40.
2 For the best analysis see Abram Leon, *The Jewish Question: A
    Marxist Interpretation*, 1946 (New York, 1970), Chapters V–
    VII.
3 Ibid., p. 209n.
4 Ibid., p. 201.
5 Ibid., p. 216.
6 Ibid., p. 203.
7 Lloyd P. Gartner, *The Jewish Immigrant in England, 1870–1914*,
    1960 (2nd edn, 1973), p. 166.
8 For 1908 see, for example, *East London Advertiser*, 25 January, 4
    April and 9 September.
9 Ibid., 3 March (tailors), 20 January (boot makers), and 1, 8 and
    15 September 1906 (bakers).
10 William J. Fishman, *East End Jewish Radicals, 1875–1914*, 1975,
     passim.
11 Ibid., p. 273 gives 1903, but The Workers' Circle Friendly
     Society, *The Circle: Golden Jubilee, 1909–59*, 1959, gives
     variously 1908, 1909 and 1910.
12 Irving Howe, *The Immigrant Jews of New York*, 1976, p. 356.
13 See Gartner, op. cit., pp. 178–80.
14 The Zhitomir Co-op Society joined the Workers' Circle *en bloc*
     in 1911. The Workers' Circle Friendly Society, *Diamond Jubilee,
     1909–1969*, 1969, p. 2.
15 See E. P. Thompson, *The Making of the English Working Class*,
     1963, (Penguin edn, 1968), pp. 289–90.
16 Oral evidence comes from Mr R, T23, p. 1; T26, pp. 17–21, and
     T42, pp. 29–33.
17 Morris Mindel writing in *Golden Jubilee*, p. 7.
18 Ibid.
19 Ibid., p. 8.
20 Ibid., p. 6.

21 Ibid., p. 33.
22 Marx, *Capital*, vol. 1 (Lawrence & Wishart, 1970 edn), p. 587.
23 Charles Booth, *Life and Labour of the People in London* (17 vols), 1902, series 1, vol. 4, p. 47.
24 Ibid., p. 174.
25 Paul Thompson, *Socialists, Liberals and Labour: The Struggle for London, 1885–1914*, 1967, p. 66.
26 The figures for Stepney as a whole are 2,107 (1901) and 2,229 (1911) during a period when the employed population of the borough *decreased* by 5.8 per cent.
27 See V. D. Lipman, *A Century of Social Service, 1859–1959*, 1959, pp. 59–60.
28 Calculated from ibid., pp. 282–5.
29 Fishman, op. cit., p. 213.
30 The headmaster of Deal St School speaking in 1903, quoted in V. D. Lipman, *A Social History of the Jews in England, 1850–1950*, 1954, p. 145.
31 Ibid., pp. 100–1.
32 *Jewish Chronicle*, 17 February 1905.
33 Lipman, *A Social History*, pp. 168–71.
34 Miss E, T12, pp. 6 and 8.
35 Mrs A, T07, p. 4.
36 Lipman, *A Social History*, p. 169.
37 Joe Jacobs, *My Life in the East End: Communism and Fascism 1913–1939*, 1978, pp. 114–15.
38 Phil Piratin, *Our Flag Stays Red*, 1948, pp. 52–4.
39 Arnold Wesker, *I'm Talking About Jerusalem*, 1960, act 3, scene 1.
40 Mr R, T24, p. 14.
41 Mrs J, T18, p. 9.

Name	Date of birth	Where born	Lived in Rothschild Buildings	Parents born	Widowed mother	Widowed father	Nathaniel Buildings	Elsewhere in Flower and Dean St
Mrs A	1891	Galicia (Austria)	1897–1915	Austria				
Mrs B	1893	Rothschild Bldgs	1893–1922	England	X			1922–5
Mr C	1894	East End	1902–52	Poland	X			
Mr D	1897	Rothschild Bldgs	1897–1921	Russia/Austria		X		
Miss E	1897	Rothschild Bldgs	1897–1913	Austria (Galicia)		X		
Mrs F	1898	Rothschild Bldgs	1898–1910	Russia	X			
Mrs G	1899	Ekaterinoslav	1915–39	Ekaterinoslav (S. Russia)				
Miss H	1900	Lemberg (Austria)	1902–35	Austria	X			
Mrs J	1900	Kiev (Russia)	1911–64	Russia	X			
Mrs K	1900	East End	1908–69	Austria				
Mrs L	1900	Nathaniel Bldgs	1914–16	Russia/Poland			1900–14	1917
Miss M	1900	Rothschild Bldgs	1900–45	Lithuania (Russia)	X			
Mrs N	1903	Rothschild Bldgs	1903–28	Russia	X			
Mr P	1905	Rothschild Bldgs	1905–12	Ukraine				
Mrs Q	1909	East End	1913–30	Vilna (Russia)			1912–28	
Mr R	1910	Lolesworth Bldgs	1912–30	Lithuania (Russia)				

Secondary oral sources occasionally used in the text

Name	Date of birth	Where born	Lived in Rothschild Buildings	Parents born	Widowed mother	Widowed father	Nathaniel Buildings	Elsewhere in Flower and Dean St
Mrs S	1903	East End	1932–42	England			1942–7	
Mrs T	1908	East End	1932–70	Austria				
Mr U	1916	Rothschild Bldgs	1916–30	Russia				
Mr V	1928	Rothschild Bldgs	1928–50	Son of Mr C				
Mrs W	1906	East End	1930–1	England				
Mrs Y	1898	East End		Russia				1903–12
Miss Z	1915	Nathaniel Bldgs	1930–7	Poland			1915–30	

GENERAL RULES

For the Family Dwellings of the Four per Cent.
Industrial Dwellings Company, Limited.

1.–All tenants, before taking possession, are required to pay a Deposit according to the tenement chosen. This Deposit is *not* to be considered as Rent, but as security for any damage which may be done to the rooms during the tenancy. Provided no damage is done to the rooms, fittings, or cupboards, and that all windows are left perfect, and all keys given up, the Deposit, or the balance thereof, will be returned to the Tenant. Always further provided that in the event of the Tenant vacating the premises within twelve months from the date of the occupancy thereof, the Deposit shall be forfeited. A receipt for the Deposit will be given by the Superintendent, which must be produced and given up when the Deposit is returned.

2.–The Rents to be paid in advance at the Superintendent's Office every Monday morning. Tenants will not on any account be allowed to be in arrears for Rent, or to take Lodgers.

3.–Notice to give up possession of any Tenement must be given, in *writing*, on or before 12 o'clock noon, on a Monday, to vacate the rooms on the following Monday, otherwise the Tenant is liable for another week's Rent.

4.–Tenants are required to report to the Superintendent any births, deaths, or infectious diseases occurring in their rooms. Any Tenant not complying with this rule will receive Notice to Quit.

5.–The Stairs and Tiled Wall, and passage leading to each set of Apartments to be swept daily, and washed every Friday or Saturday, in rotation, by the Tenants on the respective floors.

6.–All broken windows must be repaired by the Tenants at their own cost; no flower-pots are to be exposed on the outside ledges without sufficient protection (under a penalty of 40s., see Police Act), neither shall any clothes or unsightly objects be exposed to view.

7.–Children are not to play or make a noise on the Stairs, or in the Passages, and are on no account to go on the roof of the Building.

8.–All clothes lines (where permitted) must be taken down unless in actual use, or other persons will be at liberty to use them.

9.–No Carpets, Mats, etc., can be allowed to be beaten or shaken after 10 o'clock in the morning, except on a Friday or Saturday, and in the place set apart for that purpose.

10.–Drunken or Disorderly Tenants will be subject to have their tenancy terminated immediately, and forfeit the Rent paid.

11.–All chimneys in constant use must be swept by the Tenants at least once every three months; in default, the Superintendent may cause the same to be done, and charge 6d. for so doing.

12.–A Tenant wishing to change his apartments for others in the same building, to pay one-half of the expense of the repairs of the rooms he wishes to change to, and half the expense of the repairs necessary to be done to those he leaves.

13.–The Directors or their Agents shall have power, at any reasonable hour during the day, to enter any of the dwellings for the purpose of inspection.

14.–It is strictly forbidden to throw into the dust-shafts or dust-bins, liquids, old bedding, straw, mats, carpets, wicker-work, or anything else likely to create any obstruction, or to throw any refuse into the courtyard. ALL VEGETABLE MATTER MUST BE BURNT.

15.–In order to prevent overcrowding, the Company will exercise the right of deciding what number of persons shall occupy a set of rooms.

16.–Coppers are provided for the use of Tenants for their own washing, but must not be used for the purpose of carrying on the trade of a laundry; nor shall mangling or any other trade be carried on in any Tenement.

17.–Tenants are to report the loss of keys to the Superintendent, who will cause new ones to be fitted at a charge of 1s. each key. Tenants will be responsible for any damage done to the locks or doors through non-compliance with this rule.

P. ORNSTIEN, *Secretary*.

NOTE.–The Gas on the Staircases is turned off at 11 o'clock at night, after which hour such artificial light as may be required must be supplied by the tenants themselves.

Index